Internet Security
Made Easy

Internet Security Made Easy

A Plain-English Guide to Protecting Yourself and Your Company Online

DOUGLAS SCHWEITZER

AMACOM

American Management Association

New York • Atlanta • Brussels • Buenos Aires • Chicago • London • Mexico City
San Francisco • Shanghai • Tokyo • Toronto • Washington, D.C.

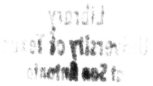

This publication is designed to provide accurate and authoritative information in regard to the subject matter covered. It is sold with the understanding that the publisher is not engaged in rendering legal, accounting, or other professional service. If legal advice or other expert assistance is required, the services of a competent professional person should be sought.

Various names used by companies to distinguish their software and other products can be claimed as trademarks. AMACOM uses such names throughout this book for editorial purposes only, with no intention of trademark violation. All such software or product names are in initial capital letters or ALL CAPITAL letters. Individual companies should be contacted for complete informaiton regarding trademarks and registration.

Chapter 7 includes material from the PKI White Paper, Copyright © RSA Security, Inc. All rights reserved.

Chapter 8 includes material from Microsoft Virtual Private Networking: Using Point-to-Point Tunneling Protocol for Low-Cost, Secure, Remote Access Across the Internet—White Paper, Copyright © Microsoft, Inc. All rights reserved.

Chapter 11 includes material from ''Understanding IPv6'' by David Morton, Copyright © PC Network Advisor, Issue 83, May 1997.

Library of Congress Cataloging-in-Publication Data

Schweitzer, Douglas.
    Internet security made easy : a plain-english guide to protecting yourself and your company online / Douglas Schweitzer.
        p.   cm.
    Includes index.
    ISBN 0-8144-7142-0
    1. Computer networks—Security measures.   2. Internet—Security measures.
    3. Business enterprises—Computer networks—Security measures.   I. Title.

TK5105.59 .S49 2002
005.8—dc21   2001053664

Printing number

10 9 8 7 6 5 4 3 2 1

Contents

A Brief History of the Internet

The Internet is currently the largest network in the world. Actually, the Internet is a globally joined network of networks, or Internetwork. Its roots can be traced to the early 1960s, when the Department of Defense gave engineers the daunting task of creating a wide-area network that could maintain communication links in the event of a nuclear war. The engineers were free to use their own imaginations in determining how this network would be constructed and how it would operate.

It was at this time that engineers at the Massachusetts Institute of Technology (MIT) foresaw a globally interconnected series of computers on which people could access information and exchange data from different locations. In 1965, a computer in Massachusetts was connected with a computer in California using dial-up telephone lines. The results were positive, but the circuit-switched public telephone system proved inadequate for the task, confirming the need for a different type of network. The modern Internet was on its way.

Toward the end of 1966, an engineer at MIT went to the U.S. Defense Advanced Research Projects Agency with the idea of a packet-switched network. Packet switching allows data files to be broken down into chunks, or "packets," which allows them to be randomly transferred to their final destination and then reassembled once they arrive. This system became known as the Advanced Research Projects Agency Network, or ARPAnet. Packet switching proved to be a major advance in the field of computer networking. ARPAnet used many connections to link together four computers—at the Stanford Research Institute, the University of California at Los Angeles, the University of California at Santa Barbara, and the University of Utah. If any one computer were destroyed, information could continue to flow among the others over alternate paths. By the end of 1969, most of the technical details were ironed out and a small four-computer wide-area network called ARPAnet was born.

In 1986, another U.S. government agency, the National Science Foundation (NSF), created a network of five supercomputers called the NSFnet. NSFnet eventually replaced the aging ARPAnet, which was shut down in 1990. NSFnet provided connections around the country, creating small networks by linking universities to their closest neighbors in chains. Those chains, in turn, at some point connected to one of the five supercomputers. Any one computer on any of the chains could eventually communicate with any other computer on any of the chains by forwarding the communication through its neighbor. The modern Internet was here.

Introduction

In February 2001, New York police arrested a thirty-two-year-old high school dropout for allegedly using Web-enabled cell phones, computers at a local library, and virtual voice mail as tools to commit one of the biggest identity theft crimes in history. In March 2001, an FBI investigation revealed that Eastern European hackers had carried out a yearlong crime spree, breaking into dozens of online financial institutions and stealing details on more than a million credit cards. Experts at the FBI's System Administration, Networking, and Security Institute disclosed that Russian and Ukrainian hackers might have relied on a well-known vulnerability that exists in the Windows NT operating system.

Earlier in that same month, the Naked Wife Trojan virus wreaked havoc on thousands of computer systems worldwide, removing critical Windows files and, in its wake, leaving infected computers inoperable. All these attacks underscore the need for improved awareness and better implementation of Internet security practices.

When we use our computers, most of us are task oriented and don't think much about what's actually driving them. We happily surf the Net, send and receive e-mail, conduct business, and access online accounts. We rarely think of the possibility of damage that can be inflicted by lurking predators. Nevertheless, the dangers *are* there. Opportunistic marauders are only too ready to jump at the chance to hack in.

In speaking to PC users, I've come to realize that many home and business consumers lack sufficient knowledge on how to keep their Internet-enabled computers adequately secure. One reason for this is that there is no readily available, easy-to-understand information out there in one concise format. This book aims to teach users at all levels how the Internet works and to show you some tips and tricks you can use to make your PC safer and more secure, while taking advantage of all the Internet has to offer.

Viruses and Internet mail worms wreak havoc on PCs and other computers around the world, seemingly on a regular basis. Not only is *your* computer at risk, but so too is that of anyone with whom you communicate. Once you apply the concepts of this book, you will be protecting yourself and possibly them, in turn.

This book also contains links to some Web sites that offer free anti-virus and Internet security software for personal use. If you have or are thinking of purchasing a high-speed broadband Internet connection, this book is for you. If you want to connect your home or business local area network to the Internet, this book is for you, too.

The information contained herein is the culmination of my experience and activity in the field of Internet security. You will learn the basics of how the Internet works, how to protect your PC from security threats, and where the Internet is headed in the future. This book is not in-tended to cover all aspects of Internet security, but it does cover the most basic, important, and relevant topics relating to Internet security for your PC.

Acknowledgments

It took the skills and effort of many people to bring this venture from just an idea to its completion in the form of this book. I am grateful to my agent Carole McClendon of Waterside Productions, who showed her confidence in me with her guidance while the book was in its nascent stages. I'd like to thank author and friend Tyler G. Hicks for his voice of experience and for giving me the initial impetus to start working on this book.

I also offer thanks to the following people who provided me with accurate descriptions of their products or Web sites: Steve Gibson at Gibson Research Corp.; Elaine Wei at the Wireless Application Protocol Forum Ltd.; Shannon Lehmann at Linksys Group, Inc.; Celina Streeper at Network Ice Corporation; Mark Weil at Ositis Sofware; and Michelle Flippin at Tinysoftware, Inc.

I am grateful to Jacquie Flynn, senior acquisitions editor at AMA-COM, because she was instrumental in my decision to sign on and forge ahead with the book. Her absolute knowledge that I could meet my deadlines allowed me to believe it, as well. I would like to thank Mike Sivilli, associate editor, who helped to shape and hone the details in the book.

To my mother, brothers, in-laws, family, friends, colleagues, and clients: Thanks for being so enthused! I offer heartfelt gratitude to my wife and best friend, Monique, whose encouragement and assistance were most valuable during the writing of this book. The corrections and revisions she suggested were always right on the money. *Wel bedankt!* I must offer thanks to my two sons, Deran and Alex, for bearing with me, understanding when I needed to concentrate, and putting up with playtime being postponed on many an evening :o). My family's love and support are a constant inspiration.

Internet Security
Made Easy

Technical Essentials for Internet Security

A computer network can consist of two computers communicating in a simple local area network (LAN), or it can be as vast and complex as the Internet. Before learning how to protect your PC or network from Internet threats and vandals, you need to have a general understanding of how the Internet works.

The fundamental protocol on which the Internet relies for communication is Transmission Control Protocol/Internet Protocol (TCP/IP). A protocol is a set of rules or principals that governs how a computer communicates across a network. If a wide array of communication protocols were to exist, then the task of connecting them into networks would prove difficult.

In the early 1980s, many computer vendors began to develop their own proprietary networking protocols, and some vendors even developed several different protocols. A set of standards was needed in order to allow different computer platforms to coexist.

It was in 1984 that the International Organization for Standardization (ISO) released the seven-layer Open Systems Interconnect (OSI) reference model to help the multivendor computer systems create networking equipment that would be interoperable. This reference model allows dissimilar operating systems such as Windows, Novell Netware, and Unix to communicate with one another.

Intranets and Extranets

An intranet is a private TCP/IP-based network or microcosm of the Internet, used *within* an organization. You can think of an intranet as a miniature version of the Internet operating within the confines of an organization. Extranets, like intranets, are TCP/IP-based networks but extend the intranet scheme by allowing limited access by outside parties such as customers or vendors.

The OSI Model

The OSI model is a seven-layer conceptual model of how communication across a network (Internet included) should take place. Its purpose is to break down the complexity of networking into seven smaller, more manageable pieces. It determines the various components that may exist on a network and how they should operate. Each of the layers builds upon the previous layer. This layered approach defines not how vendors should implement their products but only how they should conform to the standards and protocols as defined in the OSI model.

The seven layers of the OSI model are:

Physical Layer (**Layer 1**). This is the lowest layer of the OSI model and is concerned with the physical delivery of data from one computer to another. This layer involves the actual physical hardware needed for delivery, such as wires, cables, and switches. Physical components at this layer can be tampered with to cause a security breach.

Data Link Layer (**Layer 2**). This layer is responsible for the movement of data across the physical connection between linked computers.

Network Layer (**Layer 3**). This layer determines the optimal way to move data from one point to another within the network.

Transport Layer (**Layer 4**). This layer segments and reassembles data into a data stream, allowing the transmission of data from sender to receiver.

Session Layer (**Layer 5**). This layer manages and maintains a communication session between data applications.

Presentation Layer (**Layer 6**). This layer works in conjunction with the application layer to provide data representation and formatting, data compression, and data encryption. In summary, it ensures that the data sent are properly presented and readable to the receiving computer.

Application Layer (**Layer 7**). This is the top layer in the OSI model and the one that is closest to the end user. It provides network services to a user program.

The transmission of data through the OSI model is vertical, but data communication takes place horizontally (see Figure 1-1). Each layer passes sent information down to the next layer, until data are received

Figure 1-1. Layered communication in the OSI model.

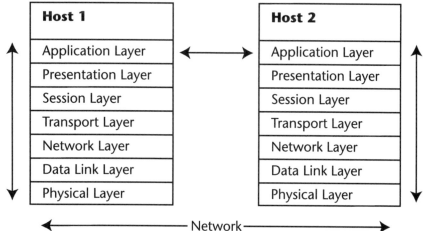

by the receiving computer. The process is then reversed, starting at the Physical layer and working its way up through the model. Communication within these layers takes place horizontally, with each layer communicating with its corresponding peer layer on the other end. For example, the Application layer on the sending end communicates with the Application layer on the receiving end and is not concerned with the fact the data must first travel through the other layers of the model. This model is the framework for Internetworking protocols and applications.

TCP/IP Stack

Entire volumes could be written about the effect that TCP/IP has had on information technology. It is the de facto standard for Internet communications. TCP/IP is not a single set of protocols but actually a collection of protocols (a stack) that allows Internet communications to take place. It was developed so that dissimilar networks could communicate while having the added ability to choose multiple paths to a final destination. Multiple paths are valuable because they allow continued communication on a new path in the event the primary path is severed.

The TCP/IP protocol stack has only four layers that more or less correspond to the seven layers of the OSI model. The difference is that several of the OSI layers have been combined into a single layer on the TCP/IP stack, but it still performs all the functions of the OSI model. As in the OSI model, the TCP/IP model passes data from one layer to the next.

The four TCP/IP layers are:

• *Application.* This layer provides network access to programs and services.

Examples of Application layer protocols are:

—HTTP

—FTP

—SMTP

—SNMP

—Telnet

• *Transport.* This layer provides reliability and flow control so that the data are not transmitted faster than the receiving computer can process them. The two Transport layer protocols are:

—TCP

—UDP

The transport layer uses port numbers as a method for connecting to remote systems across the Internet. Although there are more than 65,000 available ports, the ports #0 through #1,023 are the most frequently used. Each port is an "opening," or portal, through which a specific type of information flows. Each port is necessary when trying to access a particular application. Different applications (e.g., e-mail, WWW, news, chat) have different port numbers. For instance, port #110 allows only e-mail to pass through it. Two computers "work together" by setting up a temporary connection and then use ports to transfer data. If you browse the Web and are downloading a Web page from a remote server, you are likely connecting to port #80 (World Wide Web port) on the server. When you are downloading your e-mail from your Internet service provider's (ISP's) mail server, you are likely connecting to port #110 (Post Office Protocol 3 [POP]) on the mail server. Hackers use port "probes" to scan for open ports as a way to gain entry to your computer when you are connected to the Web (more on ports later in this chapter).

• *Network.* This layer is responsible for routing functions. Path determination and packet switching occur at this layer. The two common Network layer protocols are:

—IP

—ICMP

• *Network Interface.* This layer provides access to the LAN and acts as the interface between the upper layers of the TCP/IP stack and the actual network.

IP Addressing

The "IP" in TCP/IP stands for Internet Protocol. IP provides the structure to link smaller subnetworks into a larger one like the Internet. An IP address is a 32-bit number used to uniquely identify a device or computer on an IP-based network. It is broken down into four 8-bit numbers separated by dotted decimals. An example of an IP address looks something like this:

123.45.67.89

Every computer that connects to the Internet is issued an IP address. One of the biggest problems faced by the Internet today is the lack of IP addresses available. The number of Internet hosts has increased so significantly over the past several years that we are beginning to run out of available IP addresses. The solution is a new IP addressing system known as IPv6, currently under development. It will replace the IPv4 currently in use. It will use a longer 128-bit address scheme, dramatically increasing the number of hosts available for IP addressing. The more numbers you have available, the more "combinations" there are available for Internet hosts.

A temporary solution to the shortage of IP addresses is to issue them on a temporary basis. Many ISPs are obliged to use this scheme because the number of IP addresses issued to them was limited. Every time you use a dial-up connection (modem) to connect to the Internet, you are issued a "temporary" IP address. When you log off, that address is "recycled" and reissued by your ISP to another host computer that wishes to connect. To illustrate this point, next time you are connected to the Internet, try the following:

Step 1. Click on the start menu and go to "Run."

Step 2. In the "Run" dialog box, type in **winipcfg** and click on "OK" or hit the "Enter" key (see Figure 1-2). (Note: This command is for Windows 95/98/ME only; Windows NT users must use **ipconfig**.) A dialog box will appear illustrating your current IP address, issued to you by your ISP, including other important IP parameters (see Figure 1-3). If you were to log off and then log back on, you would find that your IP address had changed. (Note: If you are using cable or digital subscriber line (DSL) to connect to the Internet, this does not happen because your connection is always on, and therefore your IP address remains fixed.)

Dynamic Host Configuration Protocol

IP addresses can be issued on a static (fixed) or dynamic (changing) basis. Dynamic Host Configuration Protocol (DHCP), based on a client/server model, was developed to handle the dynamic issuing of IP addresses. A computer issues a broadcast with the objective of reaching a DHCP server to obtain the needed IP address. Home users connecting to the Internet are often set up to use DHCP by their ISP and, after they connect, receive their IP address and parameters directly from a DHCP server located at their ISP. Years ago, some smaller ISPs would supply this information to the user in written form and instruct the

Figure 1-2. Windows ME "Run" command box.

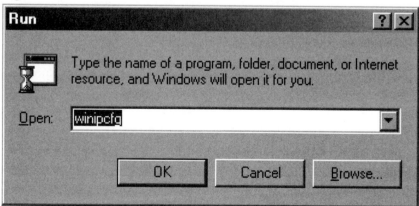

Figure 1-3. Windows ME "IP" configuration box.

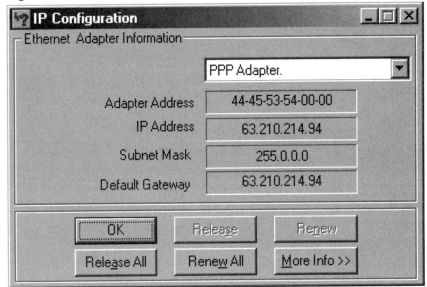

user to enter the data manually. Not only was this time-consuming, but also it left open the possibility of human error. Today, this information is unseen by the user, because it is automatically issued to the requesting computer by the DHCP server.

Address Classes

Any organization that wants to connect its network(s) to the Internet must obtain an IP address from the Internet Network Information Center (InterNIC). Established in 1983, InterNIC is a consortium of the National Science Foundation (NSF); General Atomics; AT&T; and Network Solutions, Inc. In the process of assigning addresses, the InterNIC uses a *class*-based system. This class-based system was developed so that IP addresses could be "given out" to organizations based upon the number of IP addresses they would require.

There are five classes of IP addresses, labeled A through E. Classes A through C are the most commonly used. Classes D and E are used only for special purposes. Here are the IP addresses classes and their usage:

- *Class A.* Class A addresses are used for large networks and allow for up to 16,777,214 hosts per network. A host is any device (i.e., computer, router) connected to a TCP/IP-based network such as the Internet. Many ISPs are issued Class A addresses because of the sheer number of end users they need to connect to the Internet at any given time. (Remember, if you want to connect to the Internet, you need an IP address.)

- *Class B.* Class B addresses are used for midsize networks (like those used by large corporations or universities) and allow for up to 65,534 hosts per network.

- *Class C.* Class C addresses are used for small networks because they allow for only up to 254 hosts per network.

- *Classes D and E.* Class D is used only for multicasting, and Class E is reserved for future use. (Multicasting is the process of sending messages to more than one destination at the same time.)

Public and Private Addresses

Most organizations or individuals are assigned IP addresses from ISPs. The ISPs, in turn, get those addresses from the InterNIC. As mentioned earlier, the number of available IP addresses is dwindling.

The Internet Assigned Numbers Authority (IANA) maintains three blocks of IP addresses, which are reserved for private use. These addresses are not available for connecting to the Internet and are used only in private IP-based networks. In other words, different companies can each use the exact same addresses because they remain within their private networks. Any organization that wishes to use these addresses for private use may do so without any prior coordination with IANA. Since a unique IP address is required for use of the Internet (i.e., *not* solely for use within a private IP network), that address must be assigned to the user by IANA. IANA was the organization that originally handled the assignment of IP addresses, but it now contracts this task out to a not-for-profit organization called the Internet Corporation of Assigned Names and Numbers (ICANN). ICANN is not only responsible for assigning IP addresses but also assigns domain names (e.g., www.anyname.com).

Whenever a private IP network needs to connect to a larger Internetwork, such as the Internet, a default gateway must be specified for all devices to send and receive data outside the private network. To connect a private network to the Internet, a special hardware device called a router is usually used. The router acts as "doorman" in the gateway between the two networks. It allows the passage of information between the two. In essence, when a computer on the private network requests a destination that is not within that private network, such as a Web address on the Internet, that message is immediately forwarded to the router. It is then up to the router to send that request out to the correct place on the Internet. This is known as path determination and packet switching.

Domain Name System

Now that we've introduced IP addressing, an explanation of the domain name system (DNS) follows. As mentioned before, all hosts on IP networks are currently represented by a 32-bit, dotted decimal number. In order to make it easier to remember those Web addresses, the DNS was implemented in 1984. The DNS converts 32-bit numerical IP addresses (e.g., 123.45.67.89) into easier-to-remember domain names such as www.webaddress.com (a worded Web address).

When you type a worded Web address into your browser (e.g., Internet Explorer, Netscape Navigator), your request goes to a special DNS server located at your ISP. The DNS server then checks its database and finds the numerical IP address that corresponds to the domain name you typed. It then forwards that request to its final destination. If you happen to know the 32-bit numerical IP address of a Web site you wish to visit, you can type it into the address field on your browser, and the site will be delivered. By doing this, you "bypass" the DNS system because there *is no need for the conversion.*

Domain Name Structure

As you've noticed, Web addresses end in various letter combinations. Some obvious ones are:

.com—commercial enterprises

.gov—government agencies

.mil—military agencies

.org—organizations

.net—network providers

Most of the domains just listed are in the United States. If an entity is outside the United States, the domain usually ends with an abbreviation of the name of the country hosting that domain. Examples are:

.au—Australia

.be—Belgium

.fr—France

.uk—United Kingdom

The various domains are important because of the vast number of hosts on the Internet. It would not be feasible for any single server to hold all the required address resolutions. To make this task manageable, DNS resolution is spread out among a number of servers using zones. If you type in a foreign country's Web address not stored in the database of the DNS server at your ISP, it is automatically forwarded to a DNS server in the zone that is responsible for handling name resolution for that country.

Another name for a Web address is the uniform resource locator (URL). The format for a URL is:

- Protocol
- Host name
- Port (optional)
- Path
- File name

This is typed "protocol://hostname:port/path/filename.ext." For example, when the URL http://www.comptia.org/certification/index.htm

is typed into the address field of your Web browser, you visit the Web site of CompTIA and find the index of the various Information technology certifications that it offers.

The "protocol" at the beginning of the URL is used to access network resources. The most common protocol is "http," which stands for Hypertext Transfer Protocol. It is used to transfer Web pages across the Internet or any IP network. Another common protocol is "ftp" (File Transfer Protocol), which is used to transfer files across the Internet.

The "host name," also known as the server address, is the DNS name of a host on a TCP/IP network. In our example, the host name is "comptia.org."

The "port" as mentioned before, is the "opening" or portal used for the flow of information in or out of a computer. In our example, the port is "80." Actually, including the port in the middle of a URL is optional. In its absence, the computer will use the default port to transfer data. Most modern Web browsers do not require you to type in "http://" or the port number as part of a Web address because it is known by default. The only time a port must be mentioned in a URL is when it is moved from its default number. Port 80, the default port for HTTP, does not need to be stated unless the remote server moved HTTP to a different port. (In this case, to access HTTP services, you would need to specify the assigned port number.)

The "path and file name" portions of the URL are used to locate specific files on a remote server. The "path" states the "directory" on the remote server where a specific file is located, and the file name specifies the file needed.

Routers

Routers are hardware devices that are generally used to establish pathways between networks of various sizes. One could not write a book about Internet security without mentioning these amazing pieces of equipment. Routers operate at the Network layer (layer 3) of the OSI model and are used to route data packets across networks, including the Internet. Routers have the ability to filter network traffic and are often used as firewalls to filter and control the flow of network data.

When you request a Web site, your ISP forwards that request through several different routers. The job of the router is to forward the data packets to their final destinations. Inside these amazing pieces of hardware run complex software programs, performing many calculations to decide the most efficient path to move data to their final destination. Routers communicate with one another and keep one another "up-to-date" about which routes are available and which ones provide the most efficient path.

If you're curious to see the various routers through which packets cross when you request a Web address, try this simple tracing experiment. While connected to the Internet, do the following:

1. Click on the "Start" button and go to the "Run" menu.

2. In the "Run" dialog box, type the following, exactly: **tracert www.cisco.com** (see Figure 1-4).

3. Now, click on the "OK" button or hit the "Enter" key and observe the list that appears (see Figure 1-5).

This is the entire path and the time in milliseconds it took your request to get you to the server that handles the Cisco Web site. As you can

Figure 1-4. Windows ME "Run" command box.

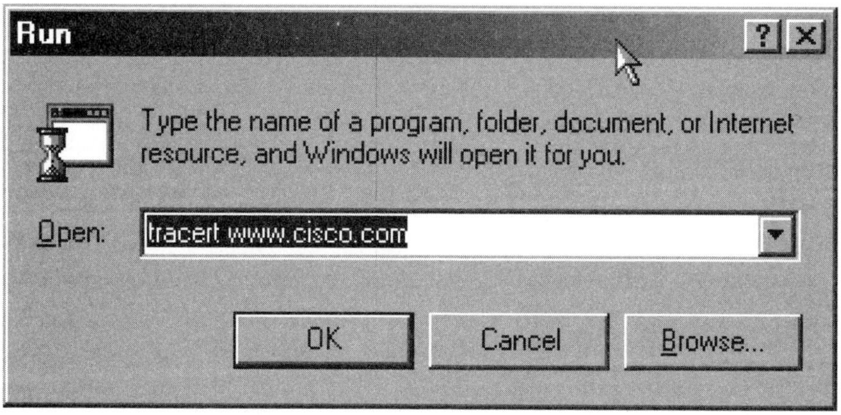

Figure 1-5. MS-DOS prompt running "tracert" command.

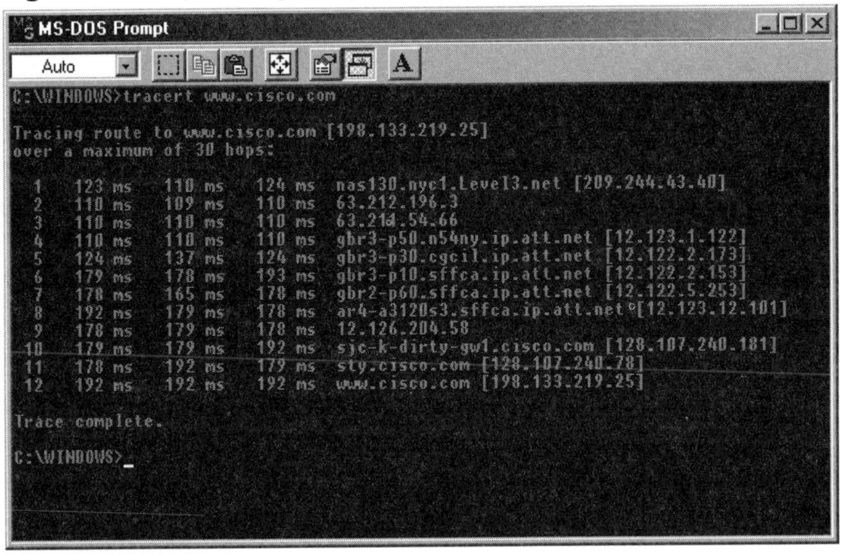

```
C:\WINDOWS>tracert www.cisco.com

Tracing route to www.cisco.com [198.133.219.25]
over a maximum of 30 hops:

  1   123 ms   110 ms   124 ms  nas130.nyc1.Level3.net [209.244.43.40]
  2   110 ms   109 ms   110 ms  63.212.196.3
  3   110 ms   110 ms   110 ms  63.214.54.66
  4   110 ms   110 ms   110 ms  gbr3-p50.n54ny.ip.att.net [12.123.1.122]
  5   124 ms   137 ms   124 ms  gbr3-p30.cgcil.ip.att.net [12.122.2.173]
  6   179 ms   178 ms   193 ms  gbr3-p10.sffca.ip.att.net [12.122.2.153]
  7   178 ms   165 ms   178 ms  gbr2-p60.sffca.ip.att.net [12.122.5.253]
  8   192 ms   179 ms   178 ms  ar4-a3120s3.sffca.ip.att.net [12.123.12.101]
  9   178 ms   179 ms   178 ms  12.126.204.58
 10   179 ms   179 ms   192 ms  sjc-k-dirty-gw1.cisco.com [128.107.240.181]
 11   178 ms   192 ms   179 ms  sty.cisco.com [128.107.240.78]
 12   192 ms   192 ms   192 ms  www.cisco.com [198.133.219.25]

Trace complete.

C:\WINDOWS>_
```

see, your request travels across many different routers to get to its final destination.

Hubs and Switches

Hubs and switches are often used to connect multiple computers to form a network and act as the network's core component. They can be subjected to tampering if they are not housed in a secure location.

Hubs are devices used to build networks in a star topology. A star topology refers to all network devices connected through one central point (a hub). Hubs come in various port densities or sizes. Hubs can have as few as four ports or as many as 24. Hubs act as multiport repeaters. When a hub receives a signal from one of its ports, it simply repeats the signal to all other ports with the exception of the receiving port. Hubs make it easy to build networks by allowing you to quickly add or reconfigure network devices. Hubs require very little configuration and are best suited for small networks.

Switches are devices whose function is similar to that of a hub. Unlike a hub, switches do not act as multiport repeaters. Each port on the switch acts as a hub unto itself. A switch will repeat a signal only to the port on which it, the recipient, is connected. Switches are superior to hubs by virtue of their speed and their ability to connect dissimilar networks. Switches also eliminate the data collision problems that sometimes plague hubs.

Bridges

A bridge is a layer 2 (OSI model) device containing two or more ports. It simply forwards data frames from one LAN to another. Essentially, bridges are used to join only two networks together. They provide a connection but do not offer any security and as a result have been largely supplanted by routers. If more than two networks need to be joined, a more sophisticated device like a router is used. (Note that many inexpensive cable and DSL modems operate as bridges and simply join your computer to the ISP's server.)

Web Browsers and Plug-Ins

The Web browser is the program you run to view Web pages and display them on your computer. The two most common browsers used today are Internet Explorer and Netscape Navigator. Some years ago, Netscape Navigator was the most popular browser used to view Web material. While it still has a loyal following, Internet Explorer is now used more often, largely because Microsoft, the maker of Internet Explorer, integrated its browser directly into the Windows operating system. This bundling of browser and operating system was the subject of much controversy and was one of the reasons the Justice Department took Microsoft to court in a much-publicized antitrust trial.

Web browsers are convenient because they allow users to point and click their way around the Internet. Modern Web browsers now have the added ability to display newer multimedia applications like real-time live video. Most Web browsers allow users to adjust how the browser handles Web material. (Adjusting the browser setting to increase security is covered later in this book.) Many browsers allow users to add browser plug-ins, giving the browser additional functions and capabilities that were not originally included in its design. Be aware that programming flaws present in some browser plug-ins may compromise the built-in security features of your browser. Following is a short list of some of the plug-ins currently available for Internet Explorer or Netscape Navigator:

- Flash—used primarily to display multimedia material that was created using Macromedia's flash authoring software. Flash is used to create Web sites that contain sound and animation and even allow for some user interaction. Flash-based movies look spectacular and add dimension to the Web experience.

- Shockwave—often confused with Flash. Shockwave is used primarily to view Shockwave-enabled Web pages. It provides multimedia interactive Web pages that include animation, graphics, sound, and text. Shockwave-enabled material must be downloaded prior to viewing and does not provide the user with instant playback as Flash does.

- RealPlayer—produced by Real Networks, the RealPlayer plug-in is used to play RealVideo and RealAudio files. It allows for the streaming of audio and video files and even allows a user to listen to online radio broadcasts in real time.

Programming Languages

Hypertext Markup Language

Hypertext Markup Language (HTML) is the programming language used to display Web documents. HTML provides a method for text and graphics to be displayed in various types of Web browsers. When you download and display a Web page from the Internet, you are really downloading the HTML code. That code is then read and interpreted by your Web browser. It's the job of the browser to properly display all the text and images that make up the Web page.

Java

Created by Sun Microsystems, Java was designed to be a multithreaded, object-oriented programming language that could work across many different computer platforms. Java is often used to create small browser programs called applets that can be used in Web pages to provide additional functions not provided by HTML. Java is often used to create animated graphics or for adding special controls to a Web page. Since it is designed to run on different platforms, a Java virtual machine is needed in order for Windows to run Java applets. A Java virtual machine is a special program that runs on a host computer that allows an operating system to run the Java program. Although the Unix, Apple, and Windows operating systems are very different from one another, all can use the same Java applets as long as each of them has a Java virtual machine installed and running. *Because Java programs can directly interact with the operating system (through the Java virtual machine), many hackers use small Java programs or applets as the vector for their mischief.*

eXtensible Markup Language
Designed by the Word Wide Web consortium, eXtensible Markup Language (XML) is used to bolster HTML by adding new functions that were not available when HTML was first developed. For example, XML can display text files created by a word-processing program directly in the browser without the files being in an HTML format.

WEB Caching

WEB caching is the process of retrieving downloaded material from the Web and then storing those data locally. Sometimes a special computer is used to act as the intermediary or proxy to cache Web files between users on a network and the Internet. In this type of setup, the caching computer is called a proxy server. Proxy servers help to eliminate the latency associated with Internet downloads because retrieving Web files locally from the proxy server is much faster than having to retrieve the data directly from the Internet. Proxy servers also act as firewalls and, as such, control access, monitor activity, and protect a network.

Another type of Web caching often used resides right in the Web browser used to view Internet Web pages. Most browsers employ a caching scheme with the purpose of holding frequently viewed Web pages. If a user needs to view Web pages retrieved earlier in a Web session, the browser cache can provide the user with the page without having to go back out to the Internet to retrieve it. This is why pages take longer to download on your initial request. When you go back to view a previously viewed Web page, it pops up almost instantly. Cache settings are found under Internet properties (see Figures 1-6 and 1-7).

Topology

In networking terms, topology refers to the landscape or layout of the network. You may have seen networks referred to as token ring, ethernet, or fiber-distributed data interface (FDDI). Each of these different types of networks has a specific topology inherent in its design. They are often described as star, mesh, ring, or bus. Below are brief explanations of each:

Star—It is called star because all the network devices are connected to a central hub or switch. The hub or switch is the center or focal point of all network connections. When a user sends data to another computer on the network, the hub or switch receives the signal and sends it to the appropriate receiving computer. Because of its uncomplicated design, the star makes it easy to make network changes and can even be combined with other types of network topologies. Star is commonly used in ethernet networks.

Mesh—The Internet is a prime example of a mesh network. In fact, the Internet is the largest mesh network in the world. Mesh networks are distinguished by having multiple paths to the same point. To get an idea of how a mesh network functions, it helps to imagine a net with many crisscrossing segments. Routers are necessary in these mesh networks because of the need for proper routing of data and the complexities of path determination.

Ring—Token ring is the most common type of ring network. In this type of network, a "data token" is passed around the network in a circular fashion. When a computer needs to send data, it "grabs" the

Figure 1-6. Internet Explorer 5.5 Internet properties configuration screen (general tab).

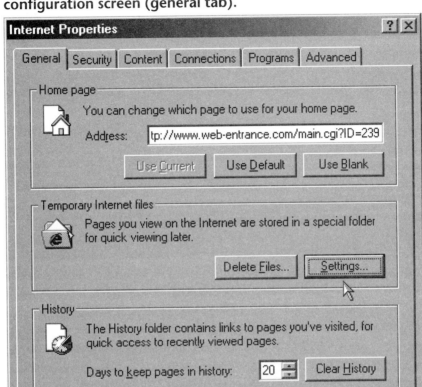

token and places the data packet into it. The token is sent back out to the ring for delivery to its final destination. The reverse is true for receiving data. The token is "grabbed," and the data packet is retrieved from it. Newer technologies such as FDDI use faster fiberoptic technology and two counterrotating token rings to provide added speed and reliability. If one ring collapses, the data are rerouted in the opposite direction through the other ring. In a standard token ring network, if

Figure 1-7. Internet Explorer 5.5 Temporary Internet Files settings screen.

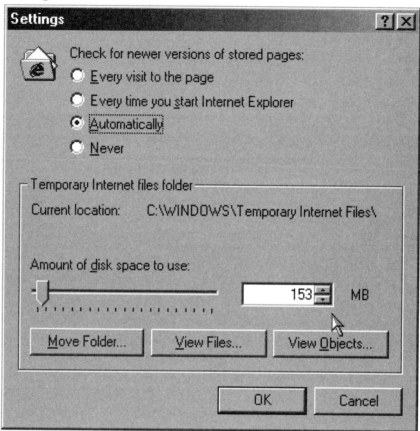

a break occurs in the ring, the entire ring collapses, and all computers on the network are no longer able to communicate with one another.

Internet Service Providers

The majority of computer users access the Internet through an ISP. Usually, these companies provide you with your Internet access for a fee. Some ISPs allow "free" access, but users must put up with a plethora of banner advertisements. Other ISPs finance access by providing marketing research services for client organizations. These subsidize the free access.

Internet access usually comes in two forms. It is charged either by the amount of time used (i.e., hourly basis) or by a flat fee (with unlimited usage). Examples of ISPs are America Online, Compuserve, Earthlink, and Juno.

ISPs get their Internet access through network access points (NAPs), which are part of the "backbone" of the Internet. The ISPs connect to the Internet through the NAPs's high-capacity, high-bandwidth points. NAPs are overseen by the NSF.

Ports

Used to transfer data to the Application layer (layer 1 of the OSI model), ports are used to allow computer systems to track sessions with other computers on a TCP/IP network. Following is a partial list of widely used ports and their respective functions:

Port Number and the Service It Provides

#21	File Transfer Protocol (FTP)
#23	Telnet
#25	Simplemail Transfer Protocol (SMTP)
#53	Domain Name System (DNS)
#69	Trivial File Transfer Protocol (TFTP)
#80	The World Wide Web (HTTP)
#110	Post Office Protocol (POP3)

Important Internet Protocols

Protocols are sets of rules or conventions used between two systems. They determine how information will be exchanged. Two important protocols allow for messaging to take place on the Internet. Each one has a specific function, and it's a good idea to have an understanding of each before getting into issues of security on the Internet.

POP3

Post Office Protocol is used to retrieve messages from an Internet mail server. When you log on to your ISP to retrieve your e-mail, you are connecting to a mail server located at your ISP. POP3 is the most recent version of this protocol and uses port 110 for communication. One feature of POP3 is that when you log on and download your e-mail, all messages currently stored there are downloaded to your computer.

IMAP4

As an alternative to POP3, Internet Message Access Protocol 4 (IMAP4) can be used to retrieve e-mail messages. Although not as popular as POP3, it allows a user to download only specific messages from the e-mail server at the ISP. This provides added security by allowing you to "cherry pick" the messages you want to read while leaving potentially dangerous e-mail on the ISP mail server. (Good for you, bad for the ISP if you fail to download all your messages.)

Other Important TCP/IP

The following protocols provide specialized services that help to augment communications between two computers on a TCP/IP network like the Internet.

ARP

Address Resolution Protocol (ARP) is used to associate a media access control (MAC) address with a TCP/IP address. A MAC address is a unique hardware address that is "burned" into a network interface card (NIC) at the factory by its manufacturer. It is used to identify a specific machine on a computer network.

HTTP

Hypertext Transfer Protocol (HTTP) is used for the transfer of the Web page data that make up much of the World Wide Web. HTTP uses port 80 for communications.

SMTP

Unlike POP3, which is used to retrieve e-mail from a mail server, Simple Mail Transfer Protocol (SMTP) is used to send e-mail to a mail server. Using port 25 to communicate, SMTP is used to send e-mail from your computer to your ISP's mail server, as well as to transport e-mail from your ISP to your recipient's ISP.

FTP

File Transfer Protocol (FTP) is used to transfer files across the Internet. When you log on to a Web site and begin to download a file, an FTP session is initiated. FTP uses port 21 to transfer data from a host to a client computer.

TFTP

Like FTP, Trivial File Transfer Protocol (TFTP) uses port 21 to communicate. The procedure for using TFTP is relatively simple; it is uncomplicated and requires less user interaction than its cousin, FTP. Because it is easy to use, TFTP is often employed to log on to a remotely located router across a TCP/IP network.

SNMP

Simple Network Management Protocol (SNMP) is used for monitoring networks and providing the status of network devices. Hackers often exploit this useful protocol to gain access and to gather information about networks.

Telnet

Telnet is used to provide connectivity between dissimilar systems and is often used in the management of routers. Windows includes a built-in Telnet program as part of its operating system.

TCP

Transmission Control Protocol (TCP) is used in the segmenting and sequencing of data packets. It is a connection-oriented protocol, which means that two computers must establish a reliable working connection before the transmission of data can occur.

UDP

User Datagram Protocol (UDP) is an *unreliable* and connectionless protocol that does not require the establishment of a connection prior to sending data. Because it does not require the acknowledgments, it's faster than TCP in the sending of data.

IP

Internet Protocol (IP) is a connectionless protocol that delivers data to remote hosts in units called datagrams. Its primary function is the delivery of datagrams to their final destination. IP datagrams contain the network source and destination IP addresses. IP does not provide for error checking or flow control. IP is often used in conjunction with TCP to provide these functions.

Agencies of the Internet

Following is a partial list of the agencies that make up the governing body of the Internet:

Internet Assigned Numbers Authority (IANA). Originally, the IANA assigned IP addresses and made sure that unique addresses were issued. As mentioned earlier, IANA now contracts this function out to ICANN.

Internet Corporation of Assigned Names and Numbers (ICANN). A not-for-profit organization that now handles the issuing of IP addresses for IANA.

Internet Engineering Task Force (IETF). This group of people determines how new technologies are to be incorporated into the Internet.

Internet Architecture Board (IAB). This organization oversees the "physical" architecture of the Internet and helps to direct the IETF.

Internet Society (ISOC). This board of overseers has as its primary function focusing on policy issues. ISOC approves the appointments to the IAB, submitted by the IETF.

Requests for Comments

Many of the technologies used on the Internet are included in a collection of official documents called Requests for Comments (RFCs) posted on the Internet. RFCs are official documents. They are sent in as proposals by individuals and organizations wishing to voice their opinions and ideas regarding any issues connected to Internet-related technologies, including security. They are used as a convenient resource for obtaining specific information about Internet-related technologies. These are freely available to all on the Internet. RFCs can be found by going to the IETF Web site at www.ietf.org. Proposed RFCs can be submitted by anyone and are reviewed by the Internet Engineering Steering Group (IESG). The IESG determines whether the comments will obtain an assigned number. The numbers issued to a comment are never reissued to new comments. If a comment needs to be changed, a separate, new comment and number are issued.

Connecting to the World Wide Web

There are numerous ways a home or business consumer can connect to the World Wide Web. The choice depends upon striking a balance between what the consumer requires and the amount the consumer is willing to pay. Some larger, high-speed Internet connections can cost several thousand dollars per month. These are broadband pipes mainly used by larger organizations that need to connect their entire company to the net. These high-speed connections are not within the scope of this book and are not discussed in great detail.

Dial-Up Access

The most common, popular, and inexpensive method of connecting to the Internet is by using standard analog dial-up modems. A modem (a combination of the words *mod*ulate and *dem*odulate) is a device that converts digital information generated by a computer into analog information for transmission over standard telephone lines. Modems are currently one of the slowest means of connecting to the Net. In addition, their speed is greatly influenced by the condition of the telephone line to which they are connected, as well as by the line's distance to the phone company switching station. Many users wonder why they are frequently disconnected from the Net and quickly blame their modem, sometimes even purchasing a new one. However, the culprit is often simply poor telephone line conditions (clicks, pops, or line noise).

Although analog modem technology has changed dramatically over the past twenty years, engineers remain unable to surpass the current 56,000 bits per second (bps) theoretical maximum speed for V.90 analog modems. As a result, newer, different technologies have been developed. The new V.92 modem standard results in a slight increase in dial-up modem upstream speed but still falls short of what's available with broadband-type connections. (Modems use plain old telephone service, which refers to the standard analog phone service that most homes use, to transmit and receive data. Analog refers to information sent in a continuous wave, and digital refers to information sent in pulses.)

Integrated Services Digital Network

The integrated services digital network (ISDN) uses ordinary phone lines to send and receive digital information. It requires two phone lines and can reach speeds of 128,000 bps, twice that of analog modems. It calls for a special modem and an adapter, and it costs more than using a standard analog phone connection.

There are two types of ISDN available for purchase by consumers. The basic rate interface uses two bearer channels (B channels) and one data channel (D channel) for transmitting data. The two B channels carry the data, and the D channel is used for the signal and control of data. Each of the B channels has a potential speed of 64,000 bps, thus allowing speeds of 128,000 bps if both channels are used together.

A nice feature of ISDN is that it offers the ability to switch from two channels to one if one of the B channels is needed to take a phone call while the other is connected to the Internet. Once the phone call is concluded, ISDN automatically switches back to using both channels, once again providing the maximum bps rate.

The second type of ISDN, called primary rate interface, offers twenty-four B channels and boasts a 1,500,000 bps data rate. It is, however, very expensive and best suited for large companies with high-bandwidth requirements. ISDN has been available for some time now and is offered in many municipalities. You need to check with your local phone company for pricing and availability if you are interested.

Digital Subscriber Line

Digital subscriber line (DSL) technology also uses existing telephone lines to send and receive digital information and comes in many varieties, as well. Often, consumers are unsure which "flavor" of DSL is right for them. It's no wonder; DSL is currently offered in roughly eight varieties. It is not accessible everywhere, and availability depends upon how close the consumer is located to a telephone switching station. DSL commonly uses the "three-mile rule" to determine availability. If you are located more than three miles from your telephone switching station, the digital signal rapidly degrades, and DSL no longer becomes feasible.

The two most common types of DSL available to consumers are asymmetric digital subscriber lines (ADSLs) and symmetrical digital subscriber lines (SDSLs). An ADSL uses your existing copper phone line and has a maximum rated speed of up to 1,000,000 bps upstream (sending data) and up to 8,000,000 bps downstream (receiving data). Notice that the downstream data rate is many times faster than the upstream rate. This is where asymmetry comes into play. Most of us are concerned with downloading data at a fast rate and are not overly concerned with upload speeds. This type of DSL is best suited for consumers who need a large download bandwidth.

An SDSL, as the name implies, uses a symmetrical approach. Maximum upstream data rates are around 1,544,000 bps, and the same data rate applies to the downstream rate. This type of connection is best suited for those who need a high-bandwidth connection to both upload and download data.

Other types of DSL connections, such as high-bit-rate digital sub-scriber lines (HDSLs) rate and adaptive digital subscriber lines (RAD-SLs), are more expensive. Table 2-1 illustrates the performance specifications of various DSL options. Unlike standard dial-up access or ISDN, DSL is an always-on connection to the Net and, as such, has inherent security risks associated with it. (These are addressed in Chapter 4.)

If you're unsure what type of DSL is appropriate for you, several Web sites are available to make the choice a little easier. A favorite Web site concerning DSL, http://www.2wire.com (see Figure 2-1), offers comprehensive coverage of DSL technology. At this Web site you will find tools and information that can help you determine what type of DSL connections are available in your area, as well as the prices DSL providers are currently charging. Another Web site that provides information about this emerging technology is www.dslreports.com (see Figure 2-2). It also offers reviews and opinions and can help you make sense out of DSL technology.

Cable Modem Technology

Of all the broadband technologies available, this connection is a personal favorite. Cable modems use a technology called Data Over Cable Service Interface Specification (DOCSIS™). This technology sends and

Table 2-1. Performance specifications of DSL options.

Service	Downstream Speed	Upstream Speed
ADSL	8 Mbps	1 Mbps
HDSL	1.5 Mbps	1.5 Mbps
IDSL	128 Kbps	128 Kbps
RADSL	610 Kbps	90 Kbps
SDSL	1.5 Mbps	1.5 Mbps
VDSL	13 Mbps	1.5 Mbps

Note: All values are approximate and assume you are within three miles of your telephone switching station.
Mbps = millions of bits per second (8 bits = 1 byte of data).
Kbps = thousands of bits per second.

Figure 2-1. Screen shot of 2wire.com Web site.

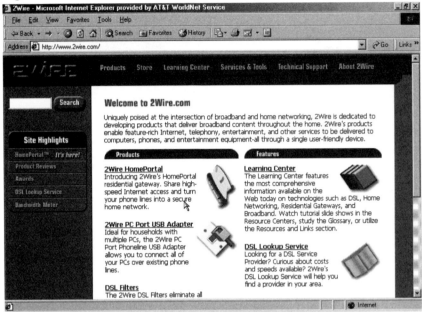

receives data using the coaxial cable TV connections many of us already have and typically costs less than comparable DSL.

Because many of us already have cable TV in our homes, providing cable broadband has been the top priority for most U.S. cable companies. The main advantage of this technology is the speed at which the data are moved and the fact that, because it uses amplifiers, it doesn't have the distance problem associated with DSL. The main disadvantage is that cable technology uses a shared bandwidth scheme; the amount of available bandwidth is shared among all users. As more users jump on the cable "bandwagon," download speeds become slower.

Cable infrastructure was originally designed only for downstream data travel. To accommodate the upstream data requests made by today's cable modem users, many cable companies were forced to upgrade their cable lines. Cable modem technology boasts download speeds of up to 27,000,000 bps, but users often find they actually achieve data rates that are substantially slower (2,000,000 bps or less).

Figure 2-2. Screen shot of dslreports.com Web site.

Keep in mind that, since data packets travel down your street along the cable line, there is the slight risk that a well-informed hacker could intercept your data as they travel downstream. To combat this, some cable providers have resorted to various types of data encryption to help protect end users. Like DSL, this is an always-on connection to the Internet. Check with your local cable provider for pricing and availability.

Satellite Broadband

For those who live in rural or very remote areas, satellite Internet access may be the only choice for high-speed Internet access. Using small satellite dishes, these broadband connections have faster data transfer rates than either dial-up or ISDN but fall short of the speeds achieved by cable or DSL.

One type of satellite technology uses your telephone modem to send out data requests to the Internet. The response (requested data) is then returned to you via the satellite. Downstream data rates are in the 400,000 bps range for this type of satellite connection, considerably faster than dial-up connections. The main drawback is that you still need your telephone modem to send out data requests.

A new type of satellite-based Internet connection by StarBand Communications allows users to send and receive data entirely through the satellite dish. This type of broadband connection has download speeds of up to 500,000 bps and upload speeds of 150,000 bps. In order to use this type of connection, you need to point the dish toward a clear, unobstructed view of the southern sky. The advantage of this connection is that it's available to almost everybody who can meet this requirement. The disadvantages of satellite Internet access are the cost of the equipment and the monthly access charges, which tend to exceed those of cable and most DSL. You can visit the StarBand Communications Web site at www.starband.com for more details and current pricing.

Other wireless technologies now exist that use radio waves to connect to the Internet. These technologies are still in the developmental stages and are best suited to handheld wireless devices for mobile Internet users or for building-to-building connections, where running cables is not feasible.

T1 and T3 Connections

T1 connections are dedicated lines that use twenty-four data channels and reach speeds of up to 1,544,000 bps. A T-1 line actually consists of twenty-four individual channels, each of which supports 64,000 bps. Each one of these channels can be configured to carry voice or data traffic. This type of connection, provided by the local telephone carrier, can cost upward of $1,500 per month. Many telephone companies allow you to purchase just a few of these channels (Fractional T-1) if you require less bandwidth. Because of their high cost, even fractional T-1 connections are not usually economical. A T-3 line is nothing more than twenty-eight T1 lines aggregated together to form

672 channels. A T-3 line can achieve speeds of up to 43,000,000 bps. Very few private networks require this amount of bandwidth. T-3 lines are used largely by Internet service providers to connect to the Internet backbone and are even a component of the backbone itself.

Frame Relay

Frame relay is a packet-switched protocol that is used to connect devices on a wide area network (WAN). Designed around newer fiberoptic networks, the frame relay networks available in the United States support data transfer rates of 1,544,000 bps (T-1 speed) and 45,000,000 bps (T-3 speed). Frame relay assumes a much more reliable network infrastructure and, as a result, requires more error checking than X.25. Many telephone carriers can provide frame relay service to their customers who require connections at 56,000 bps up to 1,544,000 bps or T-1 speeds. Frame relay is implemented as a public network and, as such, is regarded as a WAN protocol. Consumers purchase access to a frame relay service by the specific amount of bandwidth they require. Because of the higher cost involved, this type of connection is not practical for the single home or small business. It is better suited for larger organizations.

Asynchronous Transfer Mode

Asynchronous transfer mode (ATM) is a technology for transmitting data in the form of cells or packets that are a fixed size of 53 bytes. An advantage to using small fixed cells is that it allows many different types of media (e.g., audio, video) to be transmitted without allowing any single type of media to monopolize and bog down the line.

Currently, ATM supports data transfer rates ranging from 25,000,000 to 622,000,000 bps. Many engineers feel that ATM is the solution to the Internet bandwidth dilemma. Others disagree. ATM creates a fixed channel between two nodes when data transfer is required. This is very different from Transmission Control Protocol/Internet Protocol, which divides messages into packets, then allows each data packet to take a different route from the source to the destination.

ATM is considered an excellent way to combine voice, data, and video transmission on the same high-bandwidth network.

X.25

X.25 is a broadly used standard for WANs. Popular in Europe, it was first developed in 1974 by the International Telegraph and Telephone Consultative Committee, or CCITT. Its purpose was to provide networks with the option of providing permanent or switched virtual circuits. By the nature of its design, X.25 provides reliable connections and end-to-end data flow control. Since each device on an X.25 can control more than one virtual circuit, X.25 must provide each circuit with error and data flow control. Because of the overhead required for intense error checking and data flow control, X.25 tends to operate much more slowly than other WAN standards, such as ATM or frame relay.

Summary

Since connecting to the World Wide Web can be accomplished by many means, remember the following before deciding which method is best suited to your needs:

- ✓ Dial-up access uses analog technology and ordinary telephone lines and is one of the least expensive, but also one of the slowest, means of connecting to the Web.

- ✓ ISDN, like dial-up, is a type of digital connection. ISDN uses a pair of ordinary phone lines and is more expensive, but twice as fast as dial-up access. It is available in most parts of the United States.

- ✓ DSL uses existing telephone lines for the digital transmission of data and comes in a variety of speeds and prices. It is faster and usually less expensive than ISDN. The main drawback to this always-on connection is that it requires that the user be located within three miles of a telephone switching station.

✓ Coaxial cable uses the cable TV coaxial cable for transmitting data. This type of broadband connection is one of the fastest available to consumers. Priced similar to the cost of DSL, this technology uses a shared bandwidth scheme. With shared bandwidth, the connection can slow down if too many users in the same geographical area are using the same cable line.

✓ Satellite is best suited for those in very remote or rural areas. This type of connection is both slower and more expensive than DSL or cable broadband connections.

✓ T1 and T3 are both big on bandwidth and big on cost, leaving these broadband pipes best suited for larger organizations.

First Steps Toward Internet Security

The first step to securing your Internet connection is to understand the mind-set of the typical hacker. The expression "know your enemy" applies here. If you learn to think like a hacker, you'll be better able to understand where your computer is vulnerable and how to protect it. Without providing an advanced course in forensic computing, this chapter illustrates the most common vulnerable points on your Internet-enabled Windows computer and how hackers try to exploit them. (If you wish to learn more about cybercrime and other Internet security issues, visit the U.S. Justice Department's Web site concerning cybercrime at http://www.cybercrime.gov. Cybercrime is covered in Chapter 10.)

Hackers and Internet opportunists exploit weak points, which often appear in the form of security holes on your computer. The more seasoned and experienced hackers at the head of the pack are hard to combat. Fortunately, they are few. More prevalent on the Net are rookie or apprentice Internet marauders who wish to show off their newfound technical prowess by causing harm to innocent victims. Known as "Script-kiddies," they often have had little formal training and study. Because of their lack of experience, they have not developed the traits that once went hand in hand with the qualities of more seasoned and experienced hackers. Your chance of being affected by this type of Internet menace is much greater.

One of the first steps you can take is to make sure your operating system and Internet browser are up to date. We often hear or read about some Internet mail worm that has quickly spread around the world, inflicting millions of dollars in damage. This usually happens because the software engineers who wrote the program overlooked a security flaw in e-mail software. After a worm strikes the public, it is usually followed by an announcement from the targeted software's manufacturer stating that the manufacturer will make public the availability of a "patch" to repair the problem. The patch is supplied free (at the manufacturer's Web site) to authorized users of the software. Those not affected by the worm often neglect to download the patch, which leaves them open to future attacks.

The easiest way to keep your operating system and browser up to date is to use the built-in "Windows Update" program. Windows Update is usually found at the top of your "Start" menu in later versions of Windows. The update is done while you're connected to the Internet. Specific instructions guide you through the process. Alternately, you can visit http://www.microsoft.com to find updates. This is important if you use an earlier version of Windows, which doesn't have the automatic update feature. Keeping your operating system and browser up to date is critical to Internet security.

Buffer overflow attacks are very common on the Internet. These types of attacks cause a large amount of data to flood part of your computer's buffer memory, causing it to overflow and spill over beyond a certain memory region. This type of attack can crash a system and even allow a hacker to break into your computer. Operating systems and browsers have been known to contain flaws that leave them vulnerable to this type of attack. By keeping their software up to date, users can prevent these types of attacks, as well.

Secure Browsing

The more bits used for encryption, the higher the security level becomes. Standard versions of Internet Explorer or Netscape Navigator use only up to 56-bit encryption for secure Internet connections. Strong encryption actually appears on the U.S. munitions list because it is considered a potential threat to national security. This type of technology is banned for export to foreign countries. In fact, when seeking to download such software technology, the user must first verify that he is located in the United States. The highest level of encryption legally allowed is 128-bit, many times stronger than 56-bit. Both Internet Explorer and Navigator are available in 128-bit versions. Using 128-bit encryption is highly recommended if you need to perform any secure transactions online. You can determine that you are connected to a secure Web site if the Web address starts with "https://" (the "s" meaning "secure") and a small padlock appears at the bottom of the browser (see Figure 3-1).

If you are unsure of the level of encryption supported by your browser, while your Internet Explorer browser is open, select "Help," then "About Internet Explorer." The Cipher Strength (see Figure 3-2)

Figure 3-1. Screen shot of Verisign Web site.

Figure 3-2. About Internet Explorer information screen.

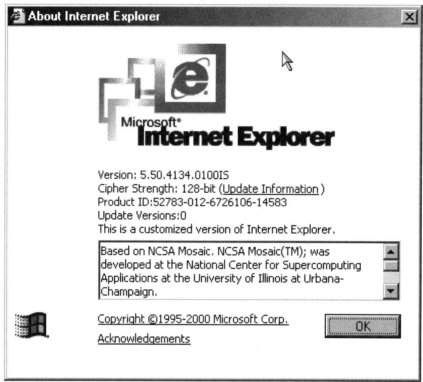

shows your browser's current encryption level. If you use Navigator, while online, select "Help," then choose "Software Updates." This will take you to Netscape's home page. Once there, use the "Your Installed Software" link to determine your browser's level of encryption. Here you will find explanations and links for upgrading your browser to a higher encryption level.

Note that for Internet Explorer there are no upgrade patches for increasing your browser's encryption level. You'll need to download and install the full version of the browser to achieve 128-bit security.

Configuring the Browser

All contemporary browsers allow for adjustment in the level of security they provide. By adjusting the Web browser settings, you can increase security well above the default level. To view your current setting and to make adjustments, follow these steps.

For Internet Explorer users, there are two ways to access the controls. One way is to open up the browser and select "Tools," then "Internet Options," then "Security." A faster way is to right click on the Internet Explorer icon on your desktop and open the "Properties" menu. You now have access to all the controls for your Internet Explorer Web browser. Click on the "Security" tab to modify the default browser settings (see Figure 3-3).

If you are using Netscape Navigator™, with the browser open, select "Edit" from the menu bar at the top, then click "Preferences," then "Advanced." Here you will be able to make changes to the default browser settings.

When you first select "Internet Options," you will be in the "General" settings tab (see Figure 3-4). In this tab, you will see controls for both the "Temporary Internet" file and the "History" folder. It is a good idea to periodically purge (delete) your temporary Internet files and to clear your History. In so doing, you free up valuable disk space and prevent others from monitoring your browsing habits.

A Quick Note About Cookies

Those who surf the Web have heard the term "cookie" used in one way or another. These are tiny, innocuous text files used to identify users and their interests. When you visit a Web site, that site's Web server may store cookies on your computer in a special directory. When you return to that site at a later time, the cookie is sent back to the visited Web server to provide information about you. This is done to personalize your visit. A client revisiting a Web site may be greeted by name and offered specially tailored information. A music retailer, for example, might inform you of the newly released CD by your favorite recording artist. Or, you might be informed about your local weather and traffic conditions. While some people like this personalized "service," others find it to be intrusive. The bottom line is these files are relatively harmless in terms of security and are not cause for alarm.

Internet Security Made Easy

Figure 3-3. Internet Explorer 5.5 Internet Properties configuration screen (security tab).

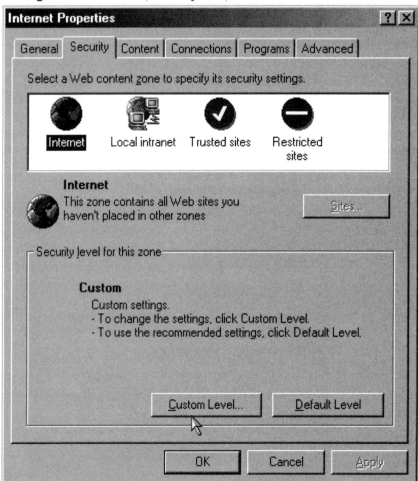

Cookie Monitoring/Removal

As innocuous as cookies are, you may wish to have Internet Explorer prompt you before you accept a cookie. By doing this, you will be notified by a pop-up dialog box before a cookie is deposited on your hard drive. To find your cookie controls under Internet Explorer, access the security settings as explained in the section on configuring the

Figure 3-4. Internet Explorer 5.5 Internet Properties configuration screen (general tab).

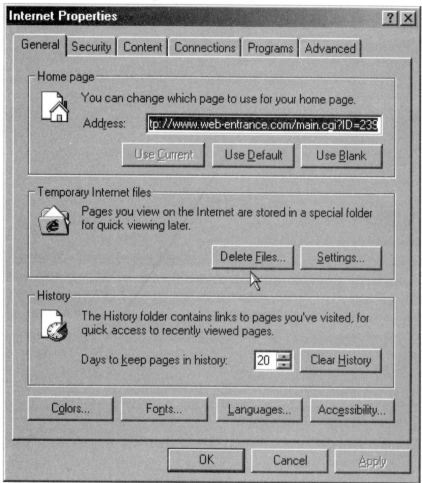

browser. Cookie settings are found by accessing the "Custom Level" button under the "Internet Zone" (see Figure 3-5). The three choices available are "Disable," "Enable," or "Prompt" (see Figure 3-6). Many Web sites will not allow you access unless your browser is configured to accept cookies. Cookies are relatively harmless, but keep in mind that they do allow someone to monitor your browsing habits.

Figure 3-5. Internet Explorer 5.5 Internet Properties configuration screen (security tab).

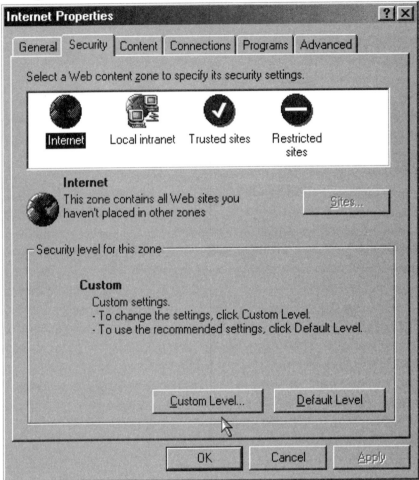

Even though some sites require you to accept a cookie before you may enter, that doesn't mean it must remain on your hard drive. Numerous third-party software vendors have programs that can eliminate cookies from your computer. These are mainly shareware programs that you download and try free. If you decide to keep the program, you're asked to pay a small fee. This short list includes the Web addresses where you can download some of these shareware utilities.

Figure 3-6. Internet Explorer 5.5 Internet Properties Configuration Screen (security settings).

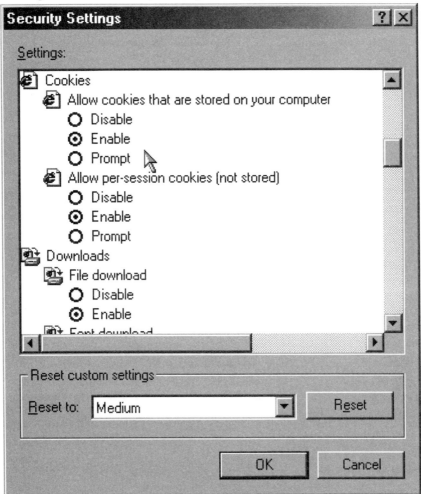

- *Cookie Cutter PC* from AyeCore Software (http://www.ayecore. com) offers a simple interface. With this utility you can easily delete all or a select list of cookies.

- *Cookie Pal* from Kookaburra Software (http://www.kburra.com) is one of the easiest to configure and includes an activity log to view cookie sessions.

- *Cookie Terminator* from 4Developers LLC (http://www.4devel opers.com) is an easy-to-use, single-screen interface that allows you to delete one, several, or all cookies either automatically or manually.

Many Internet security software programs contain cookie-monitoring and removal tools in addition to other Internet security utilities. These are addressed later in this book.

Internet Viruses

Having seen many Internet users "bitten" by Internet-borne viruses in the past, I cannot emphasize enough the importance of antivirus software. Like their biological counterparts, viruses reproduce by passing from one host to the next. Computer viruses are programs that must be executed (or run) in order to affect the host machine. A virus is a software program that has been intentionally created to affect a computer, usually in an adverse way. Viruses can be categorized three ways:

Nondestructive. These types of viruses are like malicious practical jokes. Aside from messages that pop up periodically to alert you of their presence, they usually cause no physical harm to your computer programs.

Destructive. These are the most dangerous viruses and the type that cause the most harm to the host computer. They affect the hard drive of the host computer by causing irretrievable data loss or by completely erasing all hard drive data.

Nuisance. These types of viruses are more annoying than destructive. They usually cause intermittent problems and cause your computer to behave in an unusual or odd fashion. A typical symptom of this type of virus is your computer "locking up," forcing you to reboot in order to continue using your application.

Within these three categories, there are different classes of viruses. They are grouped according to which part of the computer's system they infect. Following is a list of the types of computer viruses as summarized by the TruSecure Corporation (http://www.trusecure.com), formerly known as the National Computer Security Association.

Master Partition Boot Sector Viruses. This type of virus attaches itself to the master boot sector of your hard drive. The master boot sector is located at the very beginning of your hard disk and contains a small amount of computer code (512 bytes) necessary for your computer to "boot up," or load, your operating system shortly after you turn it on. This type of virus runs every time you boot up your computer, allowing it to complete its mission without any interaction on your part. Many computer users don't realize they have been affected by this type of virus until it is too late. Damage by this type of virus is usually extensive. Most modern computers can be set up to automatically determine whether any modifications have been made to the master boot sector before the operating system is executed and loaded. If a modification is detected, the boot-up process is halted and an audible and/or visual alert is provided, allowing you to shut down the computer immediately. It can then be rebooted using a removable media disk such as a floppy, thereby bypassing the contaminated hard drive. The benefit of this method is that it allows you to run antivirus software stored on the removable media disk, which can eliminate the boot sector virus that is infecting your hard drive. To see whether your computer has the built-in boot sector virus alert, check the user manual that came with your computer.

Executable File Viruses. This type of virus attaches itself to executable files. These file names end with the extension ".exe" or ".com" (e.g., "explorer.exe" or "command.com"). When executed, the virus code copies itself into the computer's main memory and then affects other executable programs when they are launched on the computer.

Multipartite, Parasitic, Stealth, and Polymorphic. These types of viruses are the most difficult to detect and defend against. They often display characteristics of several different types of viruses, including the boot sector and the executable varieties. The difference is that they go a step further by hiding or continually altering themselves to avoid detection.

Conventional Macro Viruses. These viruses are also known as Meta viruses. They can work on multiple platforms (e.g., Windows, Linux) and affect the macros typically used in Word and Excel. A macro is a series of Word or Excel commands and instructions that group together as a single command to accomplish a task automatically. Instead of manually performing a series of time-consuming, repetitive actions in Word or Excel, you can create and run a single macro— basically, a custom command—to accomplish the task for you. One such virus, known as "The Concept," alters the global template used in Word or Excel and affects all the files that subsequently use that template.

Active Communication-Enabled Viruses, Trojans, and Worms (e.g., Happy99, Melissa, and Love Letter Vandal). These are the most prevalent type of viruses on the Internet. They typically arrive disguised as the attachment portion of an e-mail. They usually have an intriguing, catchy phrase, tempting an unsuspecting recipient to open and execute the attachment. Once executed, the program begins to cause its damage to its new host—your computer. These miniature programs or scripts often replicate by sending a copy of themselves to several (or all) of the people in your e-mail address book. In this way, these types of viruses are able to quickly spread across the Internet and create so many casualties in a short time.

The Trojan Horse

There are a wide variety of Trojan horses. They each have distinctly different characteristics, which carry out specific and unique functions. Following is an example of three common types:

✓ *Remote Access Trojan Horse.* This type of Trojan horse allows a hacker to have control over your computer from a remote location.

✓ *Password Stealing.* This type of Trojan horse searches a computer looking for unencrypted passwords with the intent of stealing them.

✓ *SubSeven.* This Trojan horse is very popular and very dangerous. Hackers often perform SubSeven port scans on your computer to see whether you have this Trojan horse installed on your computer. The SubSeven Trojan horse can be acquired in numerous ways, including via Internet Relay Chat (IRC), I-Seek-You (ICQ), opening comprised e-mail attachments, and reading electronic greeting cards. A SubSeven Trojan horse can be activated from a remote location. It is dangerous because it can commandeer your computer, causing it to perform, along with other similarly compromised computers, a distributed denial of service attack on a targeted Web site.

Virus Protection

Anyone who uses the Internet is at risk of being affected by a virus. High-quality, up-to-date antivirus software should not be considered "optional" if you regularly use the Internet. Many different companies provide software for this purpose. Some of the Internet security software suites discussed later in this book have antivirus software components built in as part of their package. Here is a short list of some of the most commonly used stand-alone antivirus programs:

Norton Anti-Virus™ from Symantec Corp. (http://www.symantec.com) is one of the leading antivirus software products. Available for all consumer versions of the Windows operating system, it automatically updates itself while the user is connected to the Internet. It automatically scans all e-mail attachments (those that use the Post Office Protocol 3 (POP3) e-mail standard) for viruses and mail worms. It is designed to work with all of the popular e-mail software programs. Pop-up windows alert the user if a virus is found; then repair wizards help eliminate the virus.

McAfee VirusScan™ from Network Associates (http://www.nai.com) not only protects you from virus threats but also goes a step further by backing up critical files. By creating a backup of the most recent version of your documents in a protected area of your hard drive, it enables you to easily recover files if the originals become corrupted due to a virus. These files are then secured in a special partition that is created when the program is initially installed. As with most antivirus software, users are able to update the software via the Internet. This product has the ability to catch viruses in an attachment and can alert you of a virus before e-mail is opened. As with Norton Anti-Virus™, this product works with the most popular e-mail programs. VirusScan is fast, easy to use, and effective for saving files from virus damage.

PC-cillin™ by Trend Micro (http://www.antivirus.com) is an effective antivirus program that is able to catch infected e-mail as you receive it. This means that viruses are eliminated before they are even opened. Utilizing an incremental update procedure to download only the changes in the virus pattern file, PC-cillin™ reduces the time and bandwidth needed to stay up to date. Recent versions of the program can even prevent children from browsing inappropriate Web sites by controlling which Web sites they may visit. Trend Micro also allows users to sign up for its weekly newsletter. It alerts users to new and dangerous Internet viruses or mail worms. This is a useful feature for those who "forget" to regularly update their antivirus software. Trend Micro also offers HouseCall, a free online virus-scanning program. By connecting to the Trend Micro Web site using Internet Explorer, you can scan your hard drive for viruses via the Internet and then eradicate them. Configuration options are limited with this online scanner but, in a pinch, it can give your computer a quick check and eliminate any viruses that may be present.

Inoculate-IT Personal Edition™ by Computer Associates (www.cai. com) is a full-featured antivirus software available free to home computer users. It works with all consumer versions of Windows and provides free updates and free online help. It contains many of the same features found in the other products mentioned, including automatic updates. Since many antivirus software products cost $20 to $50, for those on a budget, or for anyone wanting free, high-quality antivirus protection, this product is appealing.

Many computer users have antivirus software, yet fail to regularly update the virus definitions. Regular updates are *crucial* to Internet security and protection. Virus updates should be performed at least on a monthly basis or even more often, if any new viruses are publicized. Most antivirus programs allow the user to create an emergency floppy or zip boot disk during installation. This boot disk is vital and should always be created and then stored in a safe place. In the event a virus does prevent your computer from booting up, the disk can be used to allow the user to boot from it and run a virus scan and repair directly from the floppy or zip drive. Windows also contains a utility for creating a boot disk, but, since it does not contain a virus-scanning program, it may not be sufficient in the event of a virus attack.

E-Mail Attachments and Spam

E-mail has become so popular that it's a wonder the U.S. Postal Service can still compete. E-mail has revolutionized how information is exchanged. Chapter 7 examines how to send and receive *secure* e-mail by using digital certificates and signatures. For now, here is a review of the basics of e-mail.

As wonderful and popular as e-mail is, it poses many security threats to its users. Because of its widespread use, e-mail is one of the fastest and easiest ways to circulate viruses, worms, and Trojan horses. Open an e-mail attachment only when you're sure of the identity of the person who sent it and what the content is. You can determine the content prior to opening the attachment by using antivirus software. Many e-mail viruses are designed to appear as though they were sent from someone you know. Internet mail worms can send copies of themselves to everyone listed in your e-mail address book. The unlucky recipient will receive the e-mail, think it came from you, open it, and execute the attachment, thereby activating the virus, which will then send itself to everyone in *that person's* address book. This is how e-mail viruses are able to spread so quickly and cause such severe and costly damage. The need for antivirus software is critical. Even if an attachment appears legitimate, it should be scanned with up-to-date antivirus software before you open it.

The Rules of Safe E-Mail

It's important to protect yourself as best as you can from infected e-mail. Follow these guidelines to keep a virus from infecting your computer and wreaking havoc:

- ✓ Do not download any files from unknown people or organizations. Sometimes e-mail is made to appear as if it came from a relative or someone you know. If you have reason to doubt the origin of an e-mailed message, a quick confirmation that the sender is someone you trust will add an extra margin of safety.

- ✓ Do not open any file attached to an e-mail message unless you know what it is, since some viruses duplicate themselves and multiply through the attachments in e-mail messages.

- ✓ Do not open any files attached to an e-mail message from an unknown or suspicious source.

- ✓ Do not open any file attached to an e-mail message if it contains an uncertain subject line.

- ✓ Delete junk e-mail and chain letter–style e-mails. I suggest that you do not respond to them in any manner. These types of e-mail are regarded as spam, unsolicited, invasive e-mail that congests your e-mail box.

- ✓ Exercise caution when downloading files from the Internet. Ensure that the source is a legitimate and reputable one. Verify that an antivirus program checks the files at the download site. If you're uncertain, don't download the file at all, or download the file to a floppy and test it with your own antivirus software.

- ✓ Update your antivirus software on a regular basis. Hundreds of new viruses are discovered each month. Periodically check with your software vendors for updates.

✓ Back up your files on a regular basis. If a virus destroys your data files, you will be able to replace them with your backup copy. I advise you to store your backup data files in a location separate from your work files, one preferably not on your computer.

✓ When attachments seem questionable, it is best to be very cautious. Do not open, download, or execute any files or e-mail attachments in such circumstances. Not executing is the most important of these caveats.

Stopping Spam

Unsolicited, junk e-mail, or spam, as it is commonly known, has become a growing problem on the Internet. Although it is not a security issue, many people want to know how to cut down or eliminate the amount of spam they receive. If spam has become a nuisance on your computer, there are a few ways to eliminate it.

✓ *Never reply to spam*. Sending a response to spam often results in an increase in the spam you receive.

✓ *Notify your Internet service provider (ISP)*. In order to better serve their customers, many ISPs have some type of spam filter incorporated into their e-mail server system. Some ISPs have even gone so far as to take legal action against spammers.

✓ *Determine the point of origin*. Many spammers use fake e-mail addresses; however, with a little detective work you may be able to ascertain a domain name or an e-mail address by examining the e-mail message header. If you receive any clues as to the spammer's identity, you can then visit http://www.network solutions.com (see Figure 3-7) and perform a domain name look-up using the "who is" box/function to obtain some details and maybe even a postal address of the originating domain.

✓ *Use your own spam filter software*. By using your own software, you will not be subject to repeat spam e-mail. There are several easy-to-use spam-filtering software programs available. *Mailmoa* by Moazon, Inc. (free at http://www.moazon.com/english)

Figure 3-7. Screen shot of Network Solutions Web site.

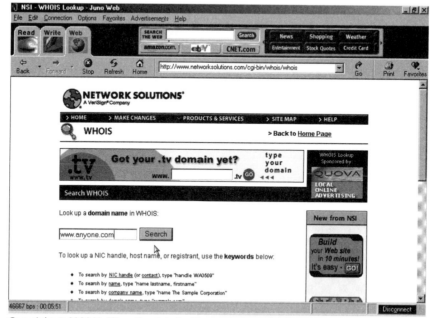

supports unlimited e-mail accounts (POP3 and even many Web-based e-mail accounts such as Hotmail.com, Lycos.com, and Mail.com) and can quickly show the content of all e-mail accounts. It uses a preprogrammed set of spam filters and allows you to add to the list of unsolicited e-mail addresses. It allows you to remove unwanted e-mail from your POP3 e-mail account prior to downloading it to your e-mail program. You can even password protect your e-mail from unwanted viewing. *Spam-Eater* by High Mountain Software (free; standard version at http://www.hms.com) is an advanced spam-filtering tool that boasts a 90 percent hit rate for catching unsolicited e-mail. It uses wizards to help users set up the program and add new filter rules. It allows users to reject messages that exceed a certain size and even allows users to reject e-mail messages that fail to include addresses in the e-mail header. SpamEater works with POP3 e-mail accounts, but current versions do not work with

Web-based e-mail accounts or AOL™ and MSN™ proprietary e-mail accounts.

SpamMotel by SpamMotel.com (free at http://www.spam motel.com) does not rely on spam filters to block unsolicited e-mail. Instead, it uses a patent-pending technology that allows the user to know where the sender obtained the user's e-mail address and then allows the user to block all future e-mail from that source. Since it is a Web-based utility, there is nothing to install on the user computer, and it works with all e-mail clients.

Passwords

A password is one of the simplest and most ubiquitous forms of authentication. Composed of a sequence of characters, passwords identify a user before that user is allowed access to a system or its resources. By using passwords effectively, you can help prevent unauthorized access to critical areas of a computer. By using a BIOS password, a user can ensure that no one (hackers included) has access to this important component. The BIOS, short for the Basic Input-Output System, provides the rudimentary computer code that allows a computer to boot up when the computer is powered on. The BIOS can be seen at work on the computer monitor before Windows™ or any other operating system begins to load. After the operating system loads, it is the BIOS, working as the middleman with the help of the processor, that gives software programs access to all the specific features of the computer. Anywhere passwords are used, one must consider several important factors, including these:

- ✓ *Do not* use patterns such as ABCDEF, ASDFGH, or 123456.

- ✓ *Never* use a word that can be found in a dictionary, English or otherwise.

- ✓ *Do not* use specific, personal words or dates such as names, birthdays, or anniversaries.

- ✓ *Never* grant requests for passwords by phone. Even junior hackers often use this technique to obtain passwords by claiming they are the network administrator or other authorized person performing routine maintenance (more on this in Chapter 10).

✓ *Do* use a mix of both upper case and lower case letters.

✓ *Do* use a mix of numbers, letters, and punctuation characters.

✓ *Change* your passwords *often,* and **never** reuse an old password.

If you are not sure how to access the BIOS on your computer, consult your computer manual for more details. Most computers allow users to access the BIOS by pressing a key such as "Delete" or "Escape" during the boot-up sequence.

Even though passwords provide a secure means of identification, they can be cracked by a relatively inexperienced hacker. Several software tools are available that allow anyone with a standard desktop computer to crack password codes. These programs are often used internally by corporations (using "password crackers") to test employee compliance with their own password policies. In organizations that require a high level of security, employees are often terminated for violation of password policy.

Watch Your IRC and ICQ

IRC and ICQ are two popular online chat forums. These applications are used by hackers to gain access to or to harm some of the unsuspecting users of these services. IRC in particular has been the subject of Internet security problems since its inception. Some of the common hacking events used via this service are:

✓ *Packet Internet Groper (PING) Floods.* These cause the client machine to disconnect from the service by flooding the client computer with excessive PINGS.

✓ *Nuke.* These can crash the client computer.

ICQ is a very popular instant messaging service that is widely used. ICQ can suffer from the following types of attacks:

✓ *Message Spoofing*—Fake messages that appear to come from a different user.

✓ *Cracks*—Flaws in the ICQ code that allow hackers to view a user IP address even if the user has this feature disabled.

If you use these services, be sure to check the program manufacturer's Web site for any security patches. Regular updates of the programs used to access these popular services will ensure that any bugs or holes present in the software are corrected. Since these types of services are breeding grounds for hackers, when they're in use, software firewalls like BlackIce Defender are mandatory equipment.

Children and the Internet

For those with young children who regularly surf the Internet, online security becomes a paramount issue. As mentioned earlier, you can adjust the browser settings to increase your security. You can also adjust the browser settings under Internet Explorer to control the content you or your children are able to view while surfing the Web.

By selecting the "Content" tab under "Internet Properties," users can control what content may not be viewed (what content is to be blocked). The big drawback in using this feature is that it requires Web sites to "go along" and comply with the rating system checks. The sites are supposed to comply by rating their own content. This leaves room for too much subjectivity. Because the system is not foolproof, users may wish to purchase a third-party software product to control content. Several software products exist that can provide protection against inappropriate content. Two of the most popular products are:

• *Net Nanny* by Net Nanny Software, Inc. (http://www.netnanny. com), which provides content filtering for up to twelve users. According to the manufacturer, this flexible program can control what content may be viewed and can also monitor and limit the amount of time a user spends online. It can log and even record online chat sessions and can prevent personal information from being sent out over the Internet.

- *CyberSitter* by Solid Oak Software, Inc. (http://www.cybersitter. com), which provides the same basic features as Net Nanny. It supports all major browsers, including proprietary ones like AOL, and it works with dial-up, digital subscriber line, or cable modem connections. CyberSitter boasts an intelligent content recognition system that can even recognize new objectionable sites.

Backing Up Data

Backing up data is something everybody needs to do but many of us neglect to do regularly. When disaster strikes, a backup may be the only hope of retrieving some original data. Some antivirus and Internet security products automatically back up critical data, and some even place those data on protected areas of the user's hard drive. Some hackers, however, are so sophisticated that even the best security measures may not be sufficient to thwart an attack. When a savvy hacker succeeds at destroying data, well-planned regular backups can save a great amount of time, money, and aggravation. Critical data should be backed up more frequently, perhaps daily or even more often for vitally important data. Noncritical data can be backed up less frequently; a weekly or monthly backup is sufficient if the bulk of the data don't change frequently. The three types of backups commonly used are these:

Normal. Normal backups copy all selected files and then mark all the files as backed up. The advantage to this type of backup is that it allows you to quickly restore files with minimal amount of data loss because all current files are on the backup. The drawback to this type of backup is that it is very time-consuming.

Differential. Differential backups copy only files that have been added or changed since the last differential backup was performed but do not mark the files as backed up. Restoring files requires only that you start with the last full backup, then move directly on to the last differential backup. The advantage to this type of backup is that it is faster; the disadvantage is that it requires longer file restoration because files are not in one continuous piece.

Incremental. Very similar to differential, incremental backups copy only files that have been added or changed since the last full or incremental backup. Unlike differential, however, it does mark the files as backed up. To restore files, one need only start with the last full backup, then perform the increments in their respective order. The advantage to this type of backup is that it consumes the least amount of time and space.

Users can back up data using several different approaches. The most popular devices for backing up data are tape drives and removable media drives (e.g., Zip™ or Orb drive). Tape drives are the slowest at backing up data. When data need to be retrieved, they must be transferred back to the user's hard drive before they can be used.

Removable media drives typically hold less information than tape drives but do allow for data use directly from the drive itself. One type of removable media drive, by Iomega (http://www.iomega.com), is the Zip drive. Zip drives come in internal and external (USB or universal serial bus) versions and can hold either 100 or 250 megabytes of information, depending upon which size you purchase. Because modern hard drives hold much more information than a single Zip disk can accommodate, users should use this system only to store smaller amounts of critical data. It is possible to have the entire hard drive backed up and spanned across several Zip disks, but this is not the most convenient or most cost-effective alternative.

For larger amounts of data, a better option might be to purchase the higher-capacity Orb drive by Castlewood Systems, Inc. (http://www.castlewood.com), a relative newcomer on the removable media landscape. The Orb drive also comes in both internal and external versions, and the disks come in 2.2-megabyte capacity. The internal version of the Orb drive features a fast data transfer rate and can even be substituted for a hard drive for storing and retrieving information. Most tape or removable media drives come with excellent backup and retrieval software as part of their package, obviating the need for purchasing third-party backup software.

For those who have broadband Internet connections, online storage options are available. Several companies provide users with online data storage for a fee. For users with large amounts of data that require backup, a high-speed connection is best for use with these services. Unless the backup requirements are small, using standard analog dial-up modems is not practical with this type of service. Those who are interested in using such a service are urged to visit Xdrive Technologies (http://www.xdrive.com) for additional details (see Figure 3-8).

By performing regular backups, the user ensures that, in the event disaster strikes, data will always be retrievable.

Figure 3-8. Screen shot of Xdrive.com Web site.

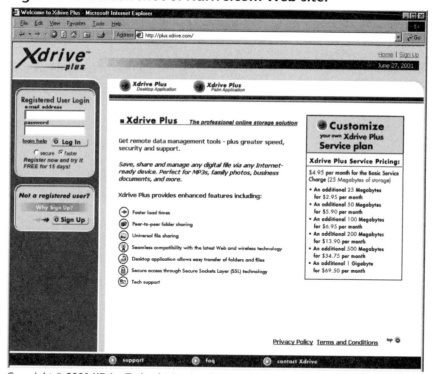

Always On, Always Vulnerable

4

Let's face it; the Internet is here to stay. As the media on the Web become richer in content (i.e., audio, video), the need for speed increases. The faster your connection to the Internet, the faster these media-rich Web pages will download and pop up on your screen. As discussed in Chapter 2, technology has responded to consumer demands by bringing affordable broadband connections to all computer users. Although this chapter focuses mainly on broadband connections, many of the principles outlined can be applied to computers that use standard dial-up modems for Web access and online transactions.

Digital subscriber line (DSL) and cable Internet access are two of the biggest and broadest means to the Internet. In addition to offering speed, they eliminate the wait for dial-up or disconnect dialogs because the Internet connection is always on. While convenient, this type of connection leaves your computer vulnerable to attack, because your Internet Protocol (IP) address (as discussed in Chapter 1) is static (fixed) and always remains the same. A static IP address makes your computer susceptible to port-scanning programs used by hackers to probe IP addresses when they're looking for an entrance into your PC.

Why is there such a risk? The answer lies in the low-cost hardware Internet service providers (ISPs) are installing in many computers. Cheaper DSL and cable modems act as a bridge, essentially a simple pass-through device. When your ISP assigns a bridge an IP address, that address simply passes through the bridge and becomes linked directly with your PC, making your computer visible to anyone on the Internet.

Two-Way Street

Many people forget that the Internet is like a two-way street. You connect to the Internet, and it connects to you. In essence, *anyone with an Internet connection can potentially access resources on your PC when you are connected to the Net.* This applies to all types of connections to the Internet, including standard dial-up access. Most consumer operating systems were not designed with Internet security in mind, leaving them open to attacks. To make matters worse, many new software technologies, such as Java or Active X applets, can interact directly with the operating system. This creates a potentially serious security risk. As recently as a few years ago, many hackers avoided home Internet users since they were few in number. As more and more individuals connect to the Internet, hackers are targeting both home and business users in increasing numbers. Having a computer connected to the Internet is a potential resource for hackers. Without your acknowledgment or permission, your computer can be used as:

- A relay for unsolicited commercial e-mail (spam)

- An arena for the exchange of pornographic material

- An unwilling participant in a distributed denial-of-service (DDoS) attack

After hackers enter a system, they target the programs that they find attractive. They ply their "trade" and do their damage, sometimes for long periods of time without the legitimate user's knowledge. Whether for fun or profit, a computer can be used by others in criminal and felonious activities. Often legitimate users do not become aware that there is a problem until they are charged with a criminal offense.

Note that, unlike denial-of-service (DoS) attacks, which are carried out by a single computer against another single computer or Web site, DDoS are the result of many computers attacking a single victim or Web site. Hackers can exploit the power of hundreds of computers (unsuspecting victims) commandeered to inundate a particular computer or Web site with so many data requests that it either crashes or has to be taken offline. For more information on this type of attack, and what the U.S. government's response is, see Appendix D.

Minimize the Risk

One of the easiest ways to minimize your security risk is to turn off your PC when you are not using it (this is not such a big issue if you use a standard analog modem to connect to the Net). Many people are under the impression that they should leave their PC on all the time to prolong its useful life. The premise is that the "shock" of turning the computer on and off will cause premature failure of sensitive electrical components. This is simply not true. Frequently powering a system on and off does *not* cause deterioration or damage to components.

Disable File and Print Sharing

If you are not using your PC in a networked environment, there is no need to have file sharing and printer sharing installed and no need to have Microsoft networking installed. Your stand-alone computer will boot up and run faster and you will have a marked increase in Internet security without them. "Client for Microsoft Networks" is used primarily to connect your Windows computer to other Windows-based computers. It serves no purpose in connecting a computer to the Internet.

Disabling file sharing and print sharing can also help defend your computer against an Internet Trojan horse program called Back Orifice. A user computer infected by this "back door" program will allow outside hackers to have full access to its systems. Hackers regularly scan the Internet looking for computers that have been compromised by a Trojan horse.

You can disable file and print sharing and/or remove the "Client for Microsoft Networks" by:

1. Opening up the control panel and double clicking on the "Network" icon

2. Selecting the "File and Print Sharing . . ." button (see Figure 4-1)

3. Disabling (unchecking) the two resulting options (see Figure 4-2)

Many new computers use the "Microsoft Family Logon" as the default client software. You may notice that your system has the Transmission Control Protocol/Internet Protocol (TCP/IP) protocol "bound" to the Microsoft Family Logon. By unbinding your TCP/IP adapters from either the Microsoft Family Logon or "Client for Microsoft Networks," you increase your Internet security by not allowing your files to be accessed via the Internet using the NetBIOS file sharing system. (NetBIOS is a protocol used in primarily small computer networks and was never designed for the use with the Internet.) To "unbind" your TCP/IP adapters in Windows 95/98/ME, follow these three simple steps:

1. Open the "Network" icon in the control panel. (This can be found in your "Start" menu under settings or by opening the "My Computer" icon on your desktop.)

2. Under the "Configuration" tab, double click on the TCP/IP adapter you wish to "unbind" (Note: your PC may have several from which to choose) (see Figure 4-3).

3. Click on the "Bindings" tab and be sure the "Microsoft Family Logon" or the "Client for Microsoft Networks" box is disabled or unchecked. Restart your computer so that the changes you made can be put into operation (see Figure 4-4).

Figure 4-1. Windows ME Network configuration screen.

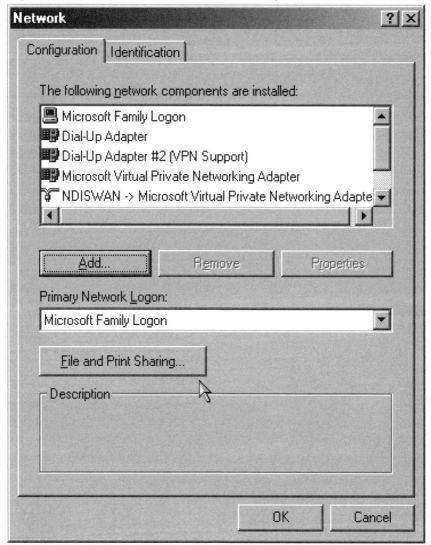

Note: This tip is only for stand-alone Internet-enabled computers! Disabling file and print sharing *should not* be done in a home or business local area network (LAN) environment. If you disable file and print sharing, computers on your network will not be able to communicate or share network resources. If your computer is used in a networked

Figure 4-2. Windows ME File and Print Sharing screen.

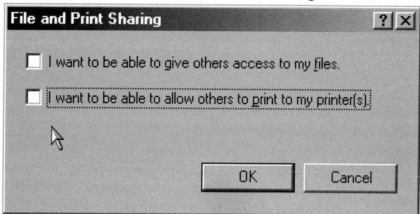

environment and you need to share files, you must purchase and install a third-party firewall product to adequately secure your PC.

A Quick Word About NETSTAT

The NETSTAT command is used to display the status of all TCP and User Datagram Protocol (UDP) ports on a computer. Hackers can use this command to "discover" open TCP and UDP ports on your computer. One of the easiest ways to defend your networked computers against this command is to block TCP port 139 and UDP ports 137 and 138 at the router used to connect your network to the Internet (see Figure 4-5).

Install a Firewall

For those who use Internet-enabled computers in a networked environment, a firewall is essential for security. A firewall is, in effect, software or hardware that protects your computer from external threats *by limiting or controlling access*. Most stand-alone computers use only a software-based firewall, while networked computers might use a combination of both hardware- and software-based firewalls.

Hardware-based firewalls are a bit more time-consuming to set up

Figure 4-3. Windows ME Network configuration screen.

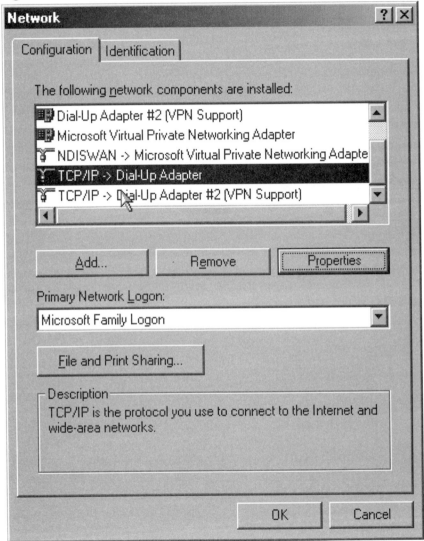

but offer excellent protection, particularly in an LAN environment. If you have a network of two or more computers and wish to have all your PCs share a single Internet connection, I strongly recommend that you use a hardware-based firewall.

The simplest forms of hardware firewalls are small, inexpensive

Figure 4-4. Windows ME TCP/IP Properties configuration screen.

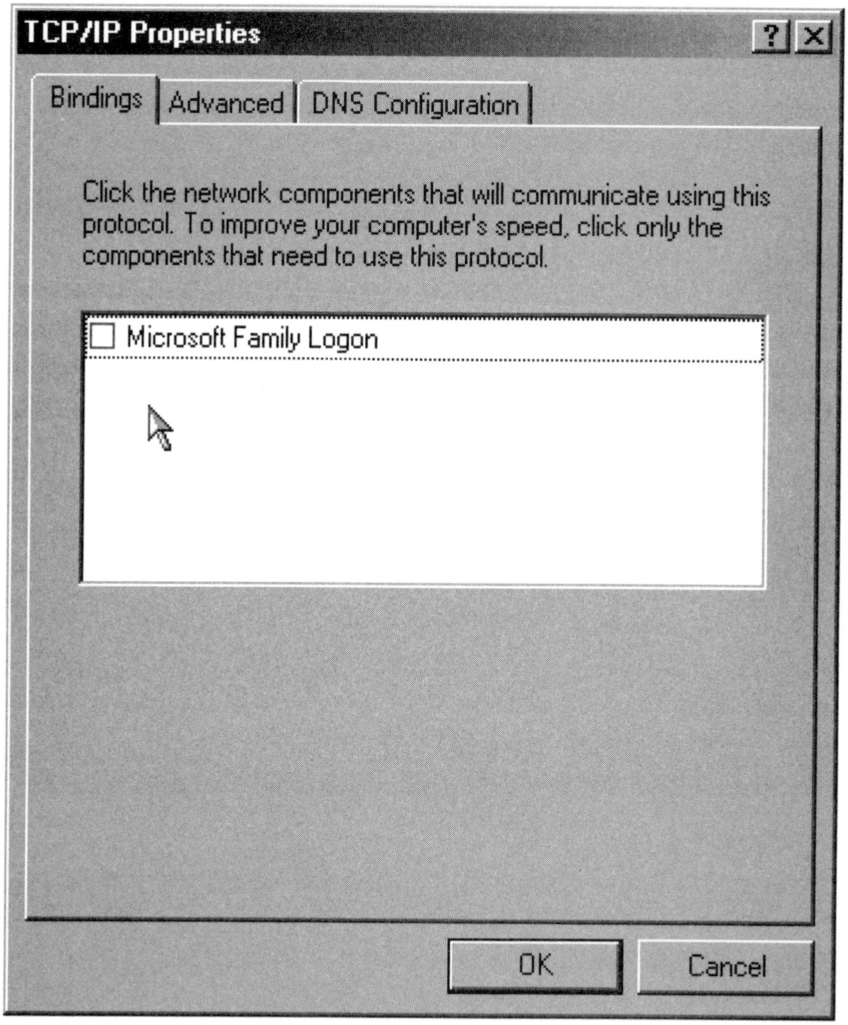

routers that are available specifically for this purpose. These routers provide excellent protection by keeping your trusted network (your LAN) isolated from the untrusted network (the Internet). This "separation" is achieved using something called network address translation (NAT). (NAT is addressed later in this section.) By using NAT, you make

Figure 4-5. "Netstat" command running in MS-DOS Prompt.

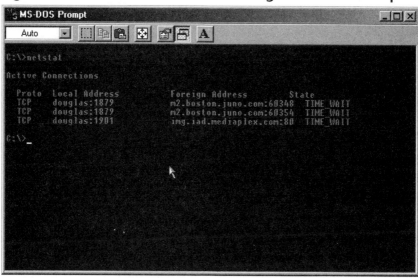

the router the only externally recognized device on your network and keep your computers "hidden" from the Internet. Many of these routers cost less than $200 and come with easy-to-use instructions and excellent vendor support.

One such router, the Linksys EtherFast—Cable/DSL router (http://www.linksys.com), is quite popular in the Internet user community. It costs around $150 (4-port) and comes equipped with a built-in 4- or 8-port switch; it allows up to 253 users to share a *single* cable or DSL connection. (As described earlier, a switch is a layer 2 device used in an ethernet network to link computers. It performs the same functions as a hub, only more quickly, and is therefore superior in an LAN environment that shares an Internet connection.) If you already have a hub or switch on your LAN, you can purchase this router without the built-in switch and save yourself around $50.

This router not only allows all the computers on your network to share a single high-speed Internet connection but also includes a firewall that uses NAT to protect the computers on your network from potential hackers.

If you are interested in purchasing a router, you can visit your local computer retailer or log on to the Web and check out Data Comm Warehouse at http://www.warehouse.com or Computer Discount Warehouse at http://www.cdw.com for information and current prices on routers and Internet security appliances. Keep in mind that most low-capacity routers support up to 253 users. If your company has more than 253 users, you should consider using a higher-capacity router designed for this purpose.

Integrated Service Digital Network/Plain Old Telephone Sysytem

Despite the fact that more and more users are jumping on the broadband-wagon, many still use the plain old telephone system (POTS) to log on to the Web. For those who wish to install a hardware-based firewall, several products are available specifically designed for analog and digital dial-up connections.

With the advent of unlimited Internet access for a flat fee, many users log on once and remain connected for extended periods. Consequently, their network computers are at greater risk, and a hardware firewall is necessary as a first line of defense against hackers. For those wishing to purchase a router/hardware firewall for their dial-up or integrated service digital network (ISDN), several companies make products designed for this purpose. Netopia (www.netopia.com) and Lucent Technologies (www.lucent.com) both produce small ISDN/analog routers that have firewall and remote access capabilities. Intel (www.intel.com) also produces inexpensive routers designed for those who use ISDN/POTS for Internet connectivity. One such product is marketed under the name InBusiness™ Internet Station. It contains built-in security features such as NAT and port filtering and can aggregate or combine two analog phone lines, allowing higher bandwidth for your company. (Because of the dynamic nature of the Internet, readers interested in learning more about these products can visit the manufacturers' Web sites for more details about these products.)

Internet Security Appliances

Hardware-based Internet security appliances are becoming popular because of their ability to provide both a hardware firewall and virus protection in a stand-alone hardware product. More expensive than most router/firewalls, these products usually require that users purchase a license for using their product. The user license allows only a certain number of users to access the product (usually in blocks of ten, twenty-five, or fifty users). Companies should choose a size that meets their current and future needs. Both WatchGuard Technologies (www.watchguard.com) and SonicWall (www.sonicwall.com) produce Internet security appliances that offer home and business users a robust Internet security device in a single hardware product.

Dynamic Host Configuration Protocol and NAT

As explained in Chapter 1, before a client can obtain access to the Internet, an IP address must be obtained. Dynamic Host Configuration Protocol (DHCP) provides for the automatic issuing of IP addresses. NAT is a method of connecting several computers to the Internet using only one IP address and is often used along with DHCP. Most routers act as DHCP servers and automatically assign a special "fake" internal IP address to each computer on a TCP/IP-based LAN. When one of the network computers makes a request destined for the Internet, it is automatically sent to the router. The router then forwards this request directly to the ISP, using the static IP address that was assigned by the ISP. NAT is the process used to convert requests from a "fake" internal IP address to the "real" static IP address issued by the ISP. In other words, the router acts as a kind of old-fashioned switchboard operator by keeping track of all Internet requests from each of the networked computers and routing them to the ISP. To the ISP, it appears as if all requests are coming from only one computer!

Personal Software Firewalls

Personal firewall software isolates your PC from the Internet. Unlike its industrial-strength brethren (used by large company networks), you won't have to shell out a few thousand dollars to achieve a sufficient level of protection from this software. Several vendors produce excellent software well suited to the task. Some of these software products act only as firewalls, while others have additional features you may find useful for Internet security and privacy.

One of the most popular software firewalls is actually available at no cost. *ZoneAlarm 2* (a free download for personal use at http://www. zonelabs.com) is a powerful software-based firewall that can block intrusions from Active X applets and Trojan horse programs and prevents port probes from hackers.

Another free software firewall is *eSafe Protect Desktop* by Aladdin Knowledge Systems, Ltd. (available for personal use only) at www. esafe.com. This powerful software not only has firewall capabilities but also offers antivirus protection and content filtering, as well. Unique to this software is a security "sandbox" feature, which provides safe environments for running downloaded files without letting them cause harm to your computer. This product also has the ability to permit or deny various types of content on the Web from being displayed on your browser. eSafe Protect Desktop is probably one of the most complete Internet security products available for personal use. For home or business users who operate in a networked computer environment, Aladdin Knowledge Systems (www.aks.com) also offers products for securing your enterprise servers and workstations from Internet threats and vandals. Visit the manufacturer's Web site for a list of local distributors and pricing information.

Tiny Personal Firewall by Tiny Software, Inc. (free for personal use at www.tinysoftware.com), is an easy-to-use personal software firewall. Its features include multilayer security, MD5 signature support, and stateful filtering based upon ports, addresses, or applications. This firewall also provides remote access to log files, monitoring of suspicious activity, and intrusion detection.

BlackICE Defender by Network ICE Corporation (http://www. networkice.com) is a personal firewall solution that not only blocks malicious port scanning but can actually capture the domain name system (DNS) or IP address of the computer attempting to "hack" into your PC and place it in a log file for future reference. It offers simple explanations of the different types of hacker attacks and alerts you to an attack with a small flashing icon on your Windows taskbar. A nice feature of this product is its ease of installation and the fact that it requires very little user input during the install process.

For those who wish to protect a home or business network using software-based firewalls, *WinProxy* may be a good choice. Manufactured by Ositis Software ($100 for the five-user version, www.ositis. com), this product allows several computers on an LAN to share one Internet connection, provides antivirus protection, and goes a step further by allowing one of the computers on the LAN to act as a proxy server. One of the functions of a proxy server is to provide firewall protection between a LAN computer and the Internet. Proxy servers also provide performance improvements by holding frequently viewed Web pages in a special storage file (called a cache) on the server computer. Web pages that are viewed frequently will "popup" much faster if they are found in the special cache file than if the LAN computer must go out to the Internet to retrieve them each time they are requested.

In order to use WinProxy, you will need a functioning LAN in your home or office. One of the computers must be designated as the server, and it is only on this computer that WinProxy is installed. The server computer must be the computer that will be directly connected to the Internet. All other computers on the LAN receive their Web data by going "through" the proxy server to reach the Internet. Using DHCP and NAT, the proxy server acts much like a router. It goes a step further by providing virus protection and even allows for the filtering of objectionable Web content. Less expensive than many routers, the firewall protection it provides can be used in conjunction with a hardware-based firewall for an added layer of protection. A possible drawback to using this method is that in situations where the server is underpowered, you may have to sacrifice the use of one computer in your network, since its primary function will be to direct and filter Web requests. Please note that Windows 98 SE and Windows ME also allow for Internet connection sharing through a feature that was built into the operating system. Using the Internet Connection Sharing Wizard, you can have all of the computers on your LAN share one Internet connection. The Wizard allows one computer on the LAN to act as a proxy server, much as WinProxy does, but it doesn't have firewall, content-filtering, or antivirus capabilities. Since it does not provide adequate Internet security, it is not addressed further.

Are You Safe?

Now that you've followed some of these tips and tricks, you can test your security by having a vulnerability scan performed on your computer. There are several Web sites that can test your computer to see whether the security measures you've implemented are in working order. One such site is www.grc.com, the home of Gibson Research Corporation. The site is one of the finest online resources regarding Internet security. Steve Gibson has created some of the best online tools to test your PC for any existing Internet security holes. This site is an indispensable resource in the realm of Internet security. Anyone wishing to gain an in-depth knowledge of Internet security is urged to visit this fascinating site.

Two other important Web sites that cover Internet security and broadband connections are SecureTips.com (www.securetips.com) and Symantec Corporation (www.symantec.com), makers of the well-known *Norton Utilities*™ and other antivirus and Internet security products. At SecureTips you will find a wealth of resources about Internet and broadband security issues. This site also includes a port-scanning utility you may use to test your computer for security holes. At Symantec's site, you will find a link to Symantec's Internet security test page, where you also can test your PC or network for Internet security holes. You will also find details about some of the products Symantec offers to home users and businesses to help protect Internet-enabled PCs from viruses and vandals.

Secure Your Business

5

Whether you're a financial planner wishing to access client information from your local area network (LAN) or a home-based worker performing billing for a medical practice, sending sensitive data across the Internet has serious security implications. Account numbers, billing numbers, and Social Security numbers are some of the types of data hackers lift on a regular basis.

Companies are increasingly using the Web to conduct their regular business activities. Because of this increased use, businesses have an obligation to protect sensitive data from loss or theft. Not only must they see to the security needs of their employees; they must also encourage in their employees a sense of respect for the privacy of their customers. Organizations need to be concerned with protecting private customer information and business secrets. Companies may wish to allow only certain users access to specific resources on their company networks.

This chapter focuses on the essential and critical steps necessary to secure the Internet-enabled computers that populate your company LAN. It looks at some of the specific security measures businesses must follow in the Internet era. Many of the topics discussed in Chapters 3 and 4 can be applied to both the single user and the company LAN environment.

Assess Your Needs

To protect your business from Internet threats and vandals, you need to know where your business computers are most vulnerable. By performing a security audit, you will able to determine what your needs are, thus making it easier to map out your defense. There are software products that perform this function, but they are expensive and may be complicated to use. If you are uncomfortable carrying out this task, there are third-party security specialists who will do it for a fee. At the end of this chapter, we mention some of the places to contact when outsourcing becomes necessary.

Vulnerability scanners are often used by professionals to look for openings that could lead to security violations and breaches in your network. These scanners often examine both server and client computers for commonly overlooked items, such as inactive user accounts, weak passwords, or software that has not been updated. Often enough, human error or neglect leaves a network vulnerable, accounting for a large percentage of network security holes. Here are two programs that can be useful to organizations that wish to perform in-house Internet and network vulnerability scanning: *WebTrends Security Analyzer* by WebTrends Corp. (www.Webtrends.com) and *CyberCop* by Network Associates, Inc. (www.nai.com).

Anyone wishing to explore performing his or her own computer or network vulnerability scanning is encouraged to first visit the Packet Storm Web site at www.packetstorm.securify.com/pssabout.html. This Web site is completely dedicated to Internet and network security. On this Web site you will find a collection of both freeware and shareware utilities and tools specifically designed for network monitoring and vulnerability scanning.

Creating a Network Security Policy

There are several steps you can take to create a network security policy for your company. They include the following:

1. *Identify and locate your company's assets.* This pertains to both information (data) and physical assets (hardware). Assess the importance and value of these assets. For example, a network server might cost $2,000 to replace. The information contained on that server might have a replacement value of $50,000. The losses might even be costlier if those assets were to fall into the hands of your competition.

2. *Perform an assessment of the risk of a threat.* Consider the possibility of company assets being crippled or stolen, and then identify the damage that would result to the company if these were to occur. For example, if a company has a public Web server that is used to distribute information, the cost of the server crashing from a "denial of service" attack would have to include the time required to bring the system back online (e.g., two hours from the MIS department). If this Web server is used to perform financial transactions, then the cost must also include the number of purchases lost during the period of time the server is down.

3. *Adopt a "need to know" approach.* You should never use the rank or importance of an employee in determining network access or privileges. Just because she's the head of the sales department does not mean an employee should have a password that will gain her entry into all the company systems when all she actually needs is access to the accounting system. If she has such a "global" password and someone learns her password, it can be misused.

4. *Visually gauge your organization's layout.* Depending upon the results you had in the first step, you may find more secure areas for some (or all) of your valuable assets or protect these assets in other ways. You may need to increase your security personnel force or issue smart cards to employees, maybe even attaching locks where needed. Drop ceilings can be easily opened and penetrated to gain entry into an adjoining (and locked!) room. For obvious reasons, valuable assets should not be stored in very isolated or unused divisions of the organization. Wiring paths and cable drops can be tampered with and must also be adequately protected. For example, companies often house all of their most valued servers in one highly secure area or room with

limited access. Limiting access eliminates the possibility that nonauthorized employees can eavesdrop on colleagues entering passwords or generating confidential printouts.

5. *Categorize all information.* All data should be labeled according to their sensitivity (private, public, unclassified, confidential). The information's classification determines which employees are to be allowed access to it. A method should be in place that identifies which employees have access privileges. Thus, a list of potential clients would be restricted to the sales department. Employee pension plan statements might be restricted to the accounting department. For highly classified information, individual files and even single documents may have to be tracked at every change of hands. A company policy could be put in place that requires authorization before certain documents can be photocopied or reprinted.

6. *Determine who should access outside data.* Outside data are available through the Internet or dedicated wide area network (WAN) line such as T-1 or Frame Relay network. Limitations should be put on what information can be accessed and by whom. External users such as customers or the public, and even the company's own employees and officers (when they are working off-site), need to have access to internal data. Conversely, internal users need to have access to external data. What information is accessible must be limited for both security and productivity purposes. When employees are not prohibited from downloading software or visiting nonwork-related sites, the company should be sure adequate antivirus software is in place. For example, employees often visit recreational sites (news, weather, pornography, sports, entertainment), which interfere with work time. In an effort to reduce the loss of productivity, a company can restrict access to the Web by the use of a firewall that allows access only to certain sites or only during certain hours.

7. *Prepare for crisis.* Preparing for a possible disaster includes being sure that backups are performed systemwide on a consistent basis. For added safekeeping, backup information should be stored in a location separate from the company. Preparedness includes determining in advance what should be done in case of the loss of assets. Imagine, for example, that your company building suffers an explosion. Being prepared means having already in place a way to continue serving the needs of your clients. You should determine what the bare-bones requirements are for your organization to remain functional and how long you will be able to stay in business either at full or at partial capacity.

8. *Name a security officer.* This person or group of persons is responsible for enforcing company security policies. Using several groups of people can in some instances provide "checks and balances" among the group(s). For example, the office manager may be the person who oversees Internet access, while the head of accounting might be responsible for the accounts receivable and payable databases.

9. *Anticipate how changes in policy will affect your employees.* Employees are not always able to adjust to frequently changing passwords, use password-activated screen savers, or activate and deactivate alarm systems. Educational courses and in-house training allow employees to adapt to changes in security policy. Such training helps to instill in employees an understanding of the need for heightened security at the individual level. In any case, if security is still in question, the use of forced password changes and the running of screen saver programs may be required.

10. *Periodically check to see that your security policy is applied appropriately.* Security audits should be routinely carried out to establish whether the policy continues to be effective. When the policy is deemed ineffective, you should implement changes. If you assess your security policy a few months after implementation, you may discover several major flaws and a few less serious defects. The major flaws should be addressed immediately and the lesser ones fine-tuned with less urgency.

Keep Operating Systems Current

Keeping your software up to date is one of the easiest ways to ensure that software bugs won't leave you open to attack. When a software flaw is found, the manufacturer usually sends out a bulletin (via written letter or by e-mail) to registered users alerting them to the problem. The manufacturer usually posts "patches" or bug fixes on the Web as a free download. All companies should implement a procedure for ensuring that updates and bug fixes are obtained on a regular basis.

Restrict Access

It is important to remember that threats can come from both outside and inside your organization (more on this later). Server computers that contain sensitive data should be inaccessible to all except authorized personnel. Routers and switches should be placed in locations that are out of reach of unauthorized personnel.

Capture and Guard Logs

Auditing is the procedure for recording and identifying security-related events. Audit logs provide companies with written records of Internet and network activity. Keep all audit logs in a safe location; this way, you'll have evidence should someone choose to infiltrate your system. Some auditing programs have a feature that can (in real time) alert those responsible for network operations to the occurrence of a security breach.

Suspicious Activities

In order to provide Internet security for your company, it is essential that you be able to distinguish and understand the different types of attacks and suspicious activities that can arise. Following are descriptions of some of the most common:

Denial-of-Service (DoS) Attack. DoS attacks are premeditated attacks with the intent of denying legitimate access to a particular computer or service. This type of attack can be compared to continuously calling a business and tying up the phones, thereby preventing legitimate customers from getting through. Higher-quality routers and switches have the ability to sense a DoS attack and are often used by organizations as their first line of defense.

Smurfing or Packet Internet Groper (PING) Floods. A ping flood is an attack of many pings over a small period. PING is a utility often used by network administrators to see whether they can reach another remote host on an Internet Protocol (IP)-based network. Since a PING request requires a response from the remote computer, the remote host is tied up "responding" to the repeated PINGing and is unable to carry out any other functions.

Mail Flooding. Similar to spam, mail flooding occurs when large amounts of e-mail are sent to one account with the intention of over-whelming and crashing a computer. Because this can result in the loss of revenue to a business while its computer is down, this type of attack is considered a criminal offense.

Network Operating Systems

Companies that conduct business on the Internet should carefully consider the type of operating system that is installed on their network workstations and servers. Many operating systems were designed for home use and do not have any significant built-in features for Internet security. Network operating systems provide additional incorporated features that allow for tighter security for both LAN and WAN environments. This section explores a few features of the two most popular network operating systems.

Windows NT Server. Windows NT (New Technology) 4.0 was Microsoft's premier operating system for the networked LAN/WAN computer environment. It is no longer in production and has been replaced by Windows 2000, which comes in several varieties (such as Professional, Server, and Advanced Server). Many businesses are slow to upgrade and prefer to wait until the new operating systems have been used by consumers for some time. Numerous companies still use NT 4.0 Server and Workstation, yet may not be fully aware of all its capabilities. Using the same recognizable interface as Windows 95/98, NT 4.0

offers control over and includes many features that are not available in Windows 95/98. Some important features are:

- **Remote Access Service (RAS).** This service allows users to connect into the domain for a shared modem and provides users with secure access to network services.

- **Dynamic Host Configuration Protocol (DHCP).** Windows NT4.0 is able to act as a DHCP server, allowing it to assign IP addresses to workstation computers or other network devices.

- **Domain Name System (DNS) Server.** Windows NT 4.0 has DNS server capabilities that allow it to resolve or convert Transmission Control Protocol (TCP)/IP numerical addresses to fully qualified domain names (FQDN), worded Web addresses. This is the same as the DNS servers on the Internet (those that allow for the resolution of Web addresses to TCP/IP addresses).

- **Internet Information Server (IIS).** Windows NT 4.0 gives you the ability to publish Web content and even host that content on the Internet. This service is an integrated and standard component of the NT 4.0 server operating system.

- **Logging Functions.** Windows NT 4.0 includes important logging functions that are key for troubleshooting and security. These include:

  —**Security Logs.** These show security-related events generated by the built-in security subsystem, such as failed login attempts and unauthorized network resource use.

  —**Application Logs.** Application logs record warnings and errors caused by the condition of software applications and those that failed to install properly.

  —**System Logs.** These contain information regarding the status of hardware items, including their condition.

Novell NetWare. Novell NetWare (currently in version 5.1) is a powerful and secure network operating system. Netware was designed to provide secure network access to both LAN and WAN environments and includes features that help ensure security and proper Internet-integration. Following is a short list of its Internet-related features:

—*DHCP and DNS Services.* Like Windows NT, Netware provides DNS and DHCP network services and capabilities. Through a built-in management utility, it combines all network resources into a single secure proprietary directory service known as Novell Directory Service, or NDS. NDS includes support for Java and Microsoft ActiveX and integrates the management of DHCP and IP addresses into the NDS architecture.

—*Manage the costs and congestion of WAN traffic with the WAN Traffic Manager.*

—*Support all leading File Transfer Protocol (FTP) clients with NetWare built-in FTP Server.*

—*Securely develop, deploy, and manage Web applications with IBM WebSphere Application Server 3.5 Standard Edition for NetWare 5.1.*

While both of these operating systems provide the added security essential to business on the Web, individuals and companies should be aware that network operating systems can be difficult to set up and administer. Most companies contract outside help or have network administrators on staff who specialize in one of these operating systems. Their purpose is to handle the day-to-day needs of network administration and the security of these complex operating systems.

Industrial-Strength Firewalls

Companies that wish to use the Internet to conduct business face an important challenge: how to meet their need for Internet security while staying within their budget. The gatekeepers of the Internet are firewalls. While most of the hardware and software products covered in Chapter 4 provide advanced levels of Internet security and can be used by most companies, more sophisticated (and expensive) products are available. These hardware or software products can provide larger companies that have highly sensitive data with a corresponding high level of Internet security. While the price of these products often runs in the five- to ten-thousand-dollar range, many companies find that when the safety of critical or sensitive data is concerned, no price is too much to pay. Most of these products are designed for larger organizations with higher security needs.

Several popular and powerful software-based firewall products are available. Three are presented, with brief explanations of their most advanced features.

FireWall-1 by Check Point Software (www.checkpoint.com) offers a mix of both application proxy server features and stateful inspection firewall capabilities. Stateful inspection is the process by which packets coming in from the untrusted network (Internet) are examined and compared to the packets that are known to be trustworthy. This is achieved by identification of the port numbers of the source or destination addresses. A proxy service firewall can hide your internal trusted network (LAN) from the untrusted network. By applying a set of rules, it permits or restricts the exchange of data packets between the two networks. Data packets that comply with the rules are allowed to exit the LAN and are then restructured (have their internal IP address stripped) and sent out using the IP address of the firewall. [Here is an analogy: John takes his neighbor Jim's return address off Jim's letter and replaces it with his own address. John then hands the letter to the letter carrier. When a reply letter arrives, it comes addressed to John, who then (privately) forwards it on to Jim. Jim's address is never revealed.] The same rules apply to data packets received from the Internet; they are restructured (have their external address stripped) and are sent out to the LAN using the firewall's IP address. To both the LAN and the Internet, all data appear to have originated from the proxy server firewall.

A nice feature of FireWall-1 is that it uses a single point of management for all firewalls. Its security policy interface clearly illustrates all the rules on every firewall in an easy to read tabular format.

Gauntlet is another software-based firewall solution by Network Associates, Inc. (www.nai.com), a major player in the field of network security. This product uses mostly application, proxy-type firewalls. It uses policies and policy maps to create firewall rules.

WinRoute Professional by Tiny Software, Inc. (www.tinysoftware. com) is a software-based Internet router and firewall solution that makes it virtually effortless to set all computers in your network to a single Internet connection. WinRoute Pro is an award-winning, ICSA-certified firewall for networks of any size. For current pricing and detailed information about any of these products, visit the product manufacturers' Web sites.

Aside from packet switching and path determination, routers also provide for the filtering of Internet traffic by the use of access lists. More powerful and sophisticated routers like those produced by Cisco Systems supply advanced firewall capabilities in the form of IP Access Control Lists. Simply put, IP access lists are used to permit or deny specific traffic into or out of a router interface. IP access lists come in two types: standard and extended.

Standard access lists are used to filter IP traffic based upon the source address or address range. They are often employed when you want to restrict access to a specific user but allow access to others. Extended access lists, like standard access lists, filter traffic based upon the IP address source, but they dramatically extend its capability. Extended access lists allow for a more precise filtering of IP traffic through the router interface. Additional features of extended access lists are as follows:

- Source and destination IP address filtering

- Filtering based upon ports

- Filtering based upon type of protocol

While providing a powerful tool for filtering traffic, access lists or routers in general should not be relied upon to provide all of your Internet security requirements.

Cisco Systems produces Secure PIX Firewall, which delivers strong security and creates little or no negative impact on network performance. Cisco Secure PIX Firewall is the dedicated firewall appliance in Cisco's firewall family. The Secure PIX product line enforces secure access between an internal network and Internet, extranet, or intranet links. The Cisco Secure PIX Firewall scales to meet a range of customer requirements and network sizes and currently consists of five models. Readers may visit www.cisco.com for a complete list of Secure PIX products.

Keep in mind that high-performance routers are often tricky to configure. Many companies outsource this task to professionals who are specifically trained in the product. Once the initial configuration of the router is set, the router can be reconfigured remotely (using Telnet) if subsequent upgrades or configuration changes are needed.

Two-Tiered Approach

One approach often used to provide Internet security is to employ a multifirewall approach. By using a combination of hardware and software firewalls, companies connected to the Internet can ensure a high degree of safety for their data. To better illustrate this point, consider the following real-world situation.

Recently, a business acquaintance had an Internet security concern. She is the network administrator of a small consulting firm, and her main concern was protecting her company's eight-workstation LAN from Internet threats. She recently had DSL service installed by a local provider and wished to "share" this connection among all the users on her peer-to-peer network. As she was advised, she installed a DSL router to separate her LAN from the "untrusted" network of the Internet by using network address translation. Because some of the data on her network contained sensitive client information, a software-based firewall was also suggested. By using a combination of both hardware and software firewalls, she markedly increased the safety and integrity of her network data.

IP spoofing (explained in more detail in Chapter 10) is one method hackers use to gain access to a network. By falsifying an IP address, hackers are able to "spoof" or fool a firewall into thinking the packets came from a trusted source. Examples of spoofing are man-in-the-middle, blind spoofing, and source routing. The use of multiple firewalls can help to reduce the risk of this type of attack.

Monitor Traffic

The hallmark of a good security plan is that it covers all aspects of security. One important but sometimes overlooked point is intrusion detection. A second point to consider is intruder alert. If alarms are in place and there is automatic notification of security breaches, those in charge of network security will be aware when security is compromised and can act on security problems as they arise. Using multiple notification methods (such as e-mail or pager) also ensures that security personnel are always kept up-to-date. Software programs like NetProwler and Intruder Alert by Axent Technologies (www.axent.com) provide intrusion detection and automatic notification.

Outsourcing

Internet security challenges are vast, and there are few qualified people to deal with them. Because of this shortage, there has been a large increase in the number of companies seeking to outsource Internet or network security. When security needs outgrow a company's abilities, outsourcing may be necessary. Research firms predict that the number of organizations providing outsourced security will increase dramatically over the next few years. Companies like IBM Global Services are vying for a leading position in this security market. Following is a partial list of some of the larger companies dedicated to providing network or Internet security services:

- *IBM Global Services* (www.ibm.com) has scores of people devoted to providing outsource services for all aspects of Internet and network security. IBM also offers firewall and intrusion detection packages.

- *Checkpoint* (www.checkpoint.com), the makers of FireWall-1, offers Internet security outsourcing and has trained professionals available to install and support all its products.

- *Network Associates (NAI)* (www.nai.com) manufactures and provides training for dozens of security products. Like CheckPoint, the organization specializes in and is dedicated solely to network security. NAI provides outsourcing and training services for its products.

- *RSA Security* (www.rsasecurity.com) is a network security firm that provides both enterprise software and outsourcing services for all aspects of Internet security. This company also offers seminars and educational materials for individuals or companies that wish to improve in-house network security.

Other companies that specialize in security audits are InfoSysSec (www.infosyssec.com), NetraCorp, LLC (www.secnet.com), and E-Soft, Inc. (www.esoft.com).

Independent Information Technology Contractors

Because outsourcing Internet security can be an expensive endeavor, many companies may find it is easier and less expensive to hire an independent Internet security specialist. These specialists usually charge much less than the larger companies and can provide very specialized services. I include a few Web addresses where independent IT consultants can be found. Many of these consultants have gone through a screening process to ensure their qualifications. Companies interested in hiring an independent consultant can browse through these sites to locate a specialist in their area: www.freelance.com; www.guru.com; www.prosavvy.com.

Security Summary

Some of the more common causes for security holes:

- Having weak passwords or no passwords

- Failing to upgrade operating systems and browsers

- Failing to apply patches

- Leaving computer continuously logged on or logged in to the network

- Allowing users access to more network resources than they need

The following suggestions address these flaws:

- Make passwords six to eight characters long, and be sure to use both numbers and letters and special characters.

- Utilize operating system security techniques, such as password expirations and minimum password lengths.

- Institute a lockout after three login tries.

- Eliminate inactive user IDs.

- Change default configurations and passwords.

Making Your Web Server Secure

6

If you maintain a Web server with a Web site, you know that it is a potent tool for carrying out business on the Internet. In today's environment, almost any trade, no matter what its service or product, whether it is large or small, can benefit from maintaining a Web site. Companies are increasingly expending large amounts of both time and capital in the creation of striking Web sites that are progressively more eye-catching and more arresting, with state-of-the-art video and audio content. Security must also be considered as an equally important component of the design and development of Web sites. Proper security is a valuable asset that becomes a costly expense if it is ignored by site creators.

Prepare for Securing Your Server

After being hit by a virus or hacker, businesses usually suffer little more than embarrassment. In some instances, however, that embarrassment is coupled with severe debilitation and economic loss. Security on the company Web site should be a basic part of operating procedure. Just as no organization would think of leaving its entrance unlocked and unattended after hours, neither should the company Web site designers leave their site open to intrusion. Some organizations do leave their doors unlocked after hours *when protected by a guard.* In the same way, your site may be left open for visitors, provided that you are watchful of all who enter.

Assessing your company's sensitivity to risk will help you determine what plan you will implement for security. Economics inherently plays a large role in the conduct of your business. The amount of capital your business has available must be weighed against the cost of potential security breaches before you decide on a security plan. Outlays for protective security procedures should be concentrated on the areas considered most sensitive to your business.

The following are methods of applying security to your Web server:

Level 1: Minimum Security

1. Upgrading software/installing patches

2. Using single-purpose servers

3. Removing unnecessary applications

Level 2: Penetration Resistance

1. Items 1 through 3 in Level 1

2. External firewalls

3. Remote administration security

4. Restricted server scripts

5. Web server shields with packet filtering

6. Education and personnel resource allocation

Level 3: Attack Detection and Mitigation

1. Items 1 through 6 in Level 2

2. Separation of privilege

3. Hardware-based solutions

4. Internal firewalls

5. Network-based intrusion detection

6. Host-based intrusion detection

Securing Your Web Server

The methods used most frequently by businesses when protecting their Web servers and sites are:

- Deleting unused, extraneous software

- Repairing software flaws and shortcomings

- Recognizing attacks to the Web site

- Limiting an intruder's movement once he is recognized

- Safeguarding the rest of the network after an attack is detected

Upgrading Software/Installing Patches

As mentioned earlier, one of the simplest yet most effective methods for minimizing security risks to your server is to install the latest available software updates and patches. Regular maintenance of your server includes inspecting your software to see what requires patching or updating. Certain software systems that might be used by an intruder to infiltrate the server require frequent updating. These include servers, the operating system, and any software that accepts network packets, security software, or software that operates with full administrative rights.

Proceed with the following course of action:

1. Create a written inventory of all such software in use by your system. Be sure to include which versions you have.

2. Visit the Web site of the manufacturer of the software. Install the latest version if your software is not already up to date.

3. If patches are available for your version of the software, be sure to download and install them. Vendors supply detailed instructions for the installation of these patches. Follow the directives specifically, as patches often require installation in a sequential order.

4. Run the updated software to be sure that it performs properly.

Use Purpose-Specific Servers

When possible, you should limit Web servers to a single task. Companies should attempt to dedicate computers that provide specific services (i.e., Web servers, mail servers, and print servers). It is possible to run more than one server on a single host, and this is often done as a cost-saving measure; a Web server, database server, and e-mail server can all be put on one computer. The monetary savings, however, are not worth the added security risk. Security is severely compromised in this scenario, since each server on such a system opens another door for attackers. By adding additional functions to an already taxed server, you increase your company's dependence on that single host while at the same time decreasing your level of security. With the passage of time, technology becomes more affordable as the price of computers and servers decreases. Since customer satisfaction is an all-important part of e-commerce, a fast, dedicated Web server is a wise investment. This same principle can be applied to any server dedicated to performing a specific function. If the server has only one task to perform, it can do it more efficiently than if it is overloaded with other functions. In situations where a Web server must regularly query a database for information, it is wise to have two separate computers performing these functions.

Remove Dead Wood

Any software not required for the proper function of the Web server should be eliminated. Certain software programs can operate with special administrative privileges. (Administrative privileges are special rights that allow access to critical system resources.) Operating systems often run a variety of privileged programs by default. Sometimes, network or Web administrators aren't even aware of the existence of these surreptitious programs on their servers. In Unix or Linux, for example, an administrator can log into the system as a root or "superuser." These "superusers" have unique rights that allow them to have complete control over system settings and resources. Sometimes it is difficult to ascertain which programs present a potential security threat on a Web server. It is for this reason that some network administrators remove any extraneous software not immediately required for that server to perform its function.

Employ External Firewalls

Whenever possible, Web servers that serve the public should be located outside a company's firewall. With this type of arrangement, the firewall will prevent the Web server from sending potentially dangerous packets into a company's trusted internal network. When hackers on the Internet attempt to infiltrate the external Web server, they will have no access to the company's internal network. In contrast, when a Web server is located on the company's internal network side of the firewall and is infiltrated by a hacker from the Internet, the hacker can then use that Web server as a launch pad for assaults on the entire internal network. Under this setup, external attacks completely circumvent any security provided by the firewall.

Remote Network Administration

System administrators often install special software that allows them to administer the network from a remote location. It is far more convenient to utilize this type of approach than to have to be at the same location as the computer that requires management. From the standpoint of security, however, this is a potentially risky practice and should be avoided or eliminated where possible.

In the event this type of practice is unavoidable, the following precautionary steps should be taken to augment your level of security:

- Use encryption on all remote administration tasks. This will prevent hackers from monitoring network activities, preventing them from acquiring passwords or placing malevolent commands into communications.

- Use packet filtering that allows the use of remote administration from only selected computers or hosts.

- Maintain this designated set of hosts with a higher degree of security than you use for standard hosts.

- Never use packet filtering as a substitute for strong encryption. Hackers have sophisticated ways to "spoof" an Internet Protocol (IP) address. As discussed earlier, IP spoofing occurs when a hacker lies about his or her true whereabouts by sending packets from an IP address other than the hacker's actual location.

Restrict the Script

Many Web sites use small programs called scripts. These are usually created by the programmers who developed the Web site. The Web server runs these scripts when a user requests a particular Web page. Hackers can use scripts to penetrate Web sites by finding and exploiting any flaws known to exist in the program's code. To uncover such flaws, a hacker does not necessarily need the source code of a particular script. Scripts must be carefully written with the security of the Web server in mind. Those charged with the administration of the Web server should scrutinize scripts before placing them directly on a Web site. Do not allow scripts to run arbitrary commands on a system or to launch insecure (or nonpatched) programs. Scripts should be utilized only to restrict users to doing a small set of distinct tasks. Administrators should carefully restrict the size of input parameters so that an attacker cannot give a script more data than it expects. If an attacker is allowed to do this, he can often penetrate the system using a technique called buffer overflow, in which the attacker overloads a Web server by giving it far more information than it had anticipated. Running scripts with limited user privileges prevents a hacker from compromising the security of the entire Web server in the event that a script does contain some kind of flaw.

Shield Your Web Server

A router is often used to separate a Web server from the rest of the network, thereby protecting the server from various types of attacks. The router can prevent attacks before they reach the Web server by dropping all packets that do not meet certain criteria for valid Web server services. Routers are often programmed to drop all IP packets that are not specifically destined for either the Web server (remember port 80) or the remote administration server being used.

For added security, you should limit access to all but a predetermined list of hosts. Allow only these restricted hosts to send IP packets to the remote administration server. By doing this, you ensure that a hacker can compromise the Web server (using the remote administration server) only by way of a restricted network path. The router offers protection similar to that achieved by removing all unnecessary software from a host, since it prevents a hacker from requesting certain services that are often open to attack. Be advised that setting up a router with too many filtering rules can noticeably slow down its capacity to forward packets.

Educate Those in Charge

Hackers are often able to penetrate Web servers because the network or Web site administrators were either ignorant about Web server security or did not take the time to carefully and properly secure the system. Web site administrators must be adequately trained in Web server security and the various techniques that are currently available to achieve it. Numerous resources exist to assist network and Web site administrators in this task.

Divide the Server's Duties

No matter how many precautions you take or how many security measures you put into place, your Web server may still be infiltrated. Hackers are becoming more knowledgeable and increasingly more brazen as the Internet continues to grow. Web sites that provide knowledge and the tools of the trade required for hacking are expanding, too. On the rare occasion that a hacker bypasses all your security measures and manages to break into your Web server, you must have some sort of contingency plan in place.

Your first line of defense is to limit the hacker's actions on the infiltrated host. Separation of opportunity is a key concept for restricting actions once a part of the host has been penetrated. To establish such control, you must partition the various server resources among a mix of different types of user accounts. In Windows 4.0, for example, you can use the file manager utility to restrict a particular user, department, or application from access to certain files or directories. A hacker who manages to infiltrate a Web server and take control of one of the running programs will then be limited to acting only within that single user account. This spares the rest of the entire Web server from the hacker's control. For example, a Web server can be set up to run as one specific user's account, while the Web pages on that server can be given read-only access and be controlled by another user's account within the Web server. Then, if hackers manage to penetrate the Web server, they will not be able to modify or make changes to the Web pages that are under the control of the other users' accounts.

Similarly, any third-party intrusion detection software can be set up and run as another user account (with its own ID and password) to prevent it from being modified by a hacker who has penetrated the Web server. For the best security, run the Web server processes with a user who has only write privileges, and then run these processes in a few designated temporary directories. This requires *storing* the Web server software as read-only under one user but *running* it as a different user.

Implementing Hardware Solutions

One of the advantages of using a hardware solution for security is that it cannot be modified by hackers as easily as software can. Hardware can implement the partitioning of user privileges with a greater degree of security than can software. If the operating system is protected only by a software firewall and the Web server is successfully infiltrated, the hacker will then have total control of all files located on the Web server. By setting up the hard drives in the server to access files on a read-only basis or by using CD-ROMs on the server to store data, you can store Web pages and even some of the vital software in such a way that hackers cannot modify these files. The standard configuration for many Web servers is to have a read-only port to an external hard drive, while another well-protected and highly secure computer has a read-write port open. In this manner, Web pages can be continuously updated. Even with this type of setup, a hacker who manages to penetrate the well-protected Web server will be able to copy data, alter the copied data, and then send the "modified" data right back to the Web server.

Internal Firewalls

Most contemporary Web servers serve as entry points or "front ends" to a set of complex and distributed applications. In this situation, a Web server often communicates with several computers, each of which contains particular data or performs a particular function. It is tempting for hackers to zero in on these computers when they are located inside an organization's firewall. They are sometimes situated on the internal network side of a company's firewall for ease of routine maintenance. However, if a hacker can manage to compromise security by infiltrating a "front end" Web server, the "back end" computer systems could be affected, since the Web server is being used as the hacker's launch pad. It's therefore wise to separate the "back end" Web servers from the rest of the company's network by using an internal firewall. This way, if a hacker infiltrates the "front end" Web server and then eventually makes it to the "back end" systems, the hacker will not have any access to the rest of the company's internal network because of the placement of the firewall.

Network-Based Intrusion Detection

Despite all attempts to patch a Web server and to securely configure it, the system may still have vulnerabilities. These are well known to hackers. In addition, a Web server may be completely secure, but a hacker may cunningly overwhelm that server in such a way that it can no longer perform its required function. In this situation, it is imperative to know when your Web server has been compromised by hackers or shut down so that Web services can be rapidly restored.

Network-based intrusion detection systems continuously monitor all network traffic to determine whether a Web server is under attack or has been compromised or rendered inoperative by a hacker. Most contemporary intrusion detection systems have the capacity both to launch a counterresponse to attacks and to notify appropriate parties (network security personnel) by the use of e-mail or pagers. Typical automatic intrusion detection responses include the severance of certain network connections and the blocking of certain unrecognized or unauthorized IP addresses.

Computer-Based Intrusion Detection

Computer-based intrusion detection systems are usually located directly on the Web server itself. From this perspective, they are in a better position to determine the state of the Web server than a network-based intrusion detection system. They provide many of the same benefits as network-based intrusion detection systems and in some cases can detect attacks even better because they have more sophisticated and closer access to the condition of the Web server.

On the other hand, there are some disadvantages to this type of setup. A hacker who infiltrates a Web server can often disable a host-based intrusion detection system, thereby preventing it from providing a warning. In addition, remote denial-of-service (DoS) attacks often disable host-based intrusion detection systems by disabling the Web server. Remote DoS attacks enable an attacker to remotely shut down a Web server without actually penetrating it. Host-based intrusion detection systems are quite valuable but should be used in combination with the characteristically more secure network-based intrusion detection systems.

Software and Hardware Limitations

Much research is done to ensure that software is secure. In some cases, this requires significant expenditures of time and money. Usually by the time software is time-tested and proven to be secure, it is rendered out-of-date and replaced with a new (and unproven) version. Much software produced today is not time-tested, bug free, or *proven* to be secure. As a result, the application of standard Web security techniques won't guarantee that a Web server will be safe from infiltration by hackers. On the other hand, a Web server can be made quite resistant to hackers by using the stated Web server security techniques *in addition* to trustworthy software. Trustworthy software means that the software that can be confirmed by some measure to be secure. Software packages can be assessed for security in the following ways:

- Studying its past vulnerabilities

- Using software specifically created with security as its principle goal

- Using software evaluated by trusted third parties

You may gain some level of assurance about the quality of particular Web server software by looking at its past record of vulnerabilities. The number of past vulnerabilities can be used to gauge the likelihood that future vulnerabilities will be found, since it reflects how well the software was crafted. Trustworthiness is directly related to the quality of the software product. A poorly designed software product, even if built specifically to meet security needs, remains a poorly designed product and gets poor reviews by those who test such products, since it cannot be considered trustworthy.

You can also read the company's own literature. Some companies specialize in creating very secure Web server software and even tout their product as one in which no vulnerabilities have ever been discovered. Users have to balance the security claim of the vendor's product against any security-performance tradeoffs that have been made.

A third way to gain a level of assurance in software is to use evaluated and validated software. Many companies obtain third-party evaluations of their commercial firewall and Internet security products in order to verify a particular level of security. Many popular computer magazines regularly test both hardware and software products to determine whether the manufacturers' claims can be backed up and quantified. At the Web site of Gibson Research Corporation, www.grc.com, Steve Gibson, a pioneer in the field of Internet security, posts some of his independent findings and the results of tests that he has performed on various software-based firewall products. While many of these products from big-name vendors are personal firewall products and are designed for home users, his test results can give prospective buyers an idea of which vendors produce the highest-quality Internet security goods.

Public Key Infrastructure

7

The First Amendment is the cornerstone of our free and open democracy and gives us the right to freedom of speech, which is the hallmark of a free society. There can be no free speech in today's digital world without the use of encryption. Encryption is the process of turning ordinary text communications and images into indecipherable material in such a way that the encrypted material can be turned back into a readable message by the intended recipient. Why is encryption so important? Because hackers are out there, ready to intercept your messages. Sometimes, even our own government may be eavesdropping. Most of the time, the Feds are inconspicuous to the average American, but, nevertheless, they're there. Your right to privacy can be compromised in many ways. It is not always possible to easily anticipate intrusions, which can take the form of a computer program searching for keywords, or a hacker intercepting and reading your e-mails. Whatever the cause, public key infrastructure (PKI) helps by offering a solution to the problem of privacy violations.

Public key infrastructure provides the essential security required for the safe and secure transmission of critical or highly sensitive data across the Internet. It can be used for less sensitive information as well. At times users simply want to ensure privacy regardless of the content of their data. Whether you're a doctor needing to send medical records across the globe or an accountant electronically filing a client's personal tax return, PKI provides the tools necessary to complete the task securely.

In the age of telecommuting, virtual private networks (VPNs) are becoming common. Many businesses are setting up intranets and extranets to conduct e-commerce activities with both customers and vendors. The one aspect common to all these types of networks is the need for strong, effective security.

Cryptography

Cryptography supplies the framework for providing confidentiality, data integrity, and control. Cryptography is an essential component of the PKI system. It uses special mathematical formulas called algorithms to convert plain text (the kind you're reading now) into indecipherable text for safe transmission across a network. Cryptography also has the ability to reverse this procedure, converting indecipherable text back into plain text when the data have reached their destination.

Two types of encryption methods are commonly used on the Internet: symmetric key cryptography and asymmetric key cryptography.

Asymmetric (Public) Key Cryptography

In asymmetric key cryptography, a pair of digital keys is created. The first of these keys is known as a public key. The public key is distributed to a specific recipient. The second is known as the private key. The private key is known only to the person holding that key. The two key types have a reciprocal relationship. Data encrypted with the public key can be deciphered only by the private key. Data encrypted with the private key can be deciphered only by the public key. What the one key does, the other undoes, and vice versa.

The most common asymmetric algorithms in use today are:

- Diffie-Hellman

- RSA (named after Rivest, Shamir, and Adelman, developers of this algorithm)

- ECC (Elliptic curve cryptosystem)

Symmetric (Secret) Key Cryptography

Just as in asymmetric key cryptography, in symmetric key cryptography a pair of digital keys is created. In the case of symmetric cryptography, however, both the sender and the receiver use the exact same secret key pair. The main concern with this type of service is how to present the secret key to the recipient. It must be provided to the recipient without being intercepted in the process. Trusted couriers are often used to hand deliver the secret key to recipients with whom the sender wishes to correspond in complete security.

Because of the increased use of the Internet for business purposes, more and more companies are finding it necessary to use public key cryptography. Automated teller machines (ATMs) present a good analogy to symmetric key cryptography. When you wish to perform a transaction, you must insert your magnetized card into the ATM and then enter your personal identification number (PIN). Both are required in order to gain direct access to your account or your account information. After you have keyed in your PIN, the ATM authenticates your identity by the PIN you've entered and the card you've inserted. If your information is confirmed, the ATM then allows you to proceed with the desired transaction on your account. Your PIN is the "secret key" that allows you to have this access.

Some common symmetric key algorithms in use today are:

- DES (Data Encryption Standard)

- IDES (International Data Encryption Standard)

- RC5 (Rivest Cipher 5)

Nearly all cryptographic keys can be broken given adequate resources. The most common approach to breaking a cryptographic key is a "brute force attack." In this type of attack, a powerful computer is used to test every possible key combination. It continues to test until the correct key has been obtained. The longer the bit length used in the key's cipher strength, the longer it will take a hacker to crack it. The main drawback to an excessively long key length is that it also dramatically increases the time required by the recipient computer to decipher it.

PKI Applications

Two common applications of the PKI system that use cryptography are digital certificates and digital signatures.

The three main components of a PKI are:

1. *The Certificate Authority, or CA*. This authority consists of the entities that issue digital certificates. Several companies issue digital certificates. All of these companies offer services to assist users with certificate utilization and management. Two popular certificate authorities that offer digital certificates for users to purchase (for either personal or business use) are *VeriSign* (www.verisign.com) and *Baltimore Technologies* (www.baltimore.com). *Thawte Consulting* (www.thawte. com) was purchased by VeriSign in 1999 and offers users a free personal digital certificate for secure Internet e-mail purposes.

2. *The Repository*. The repository holds the digital certificates or keys. This repository is usually based upon the Lightweight Directory Access Protocol (LDAP). LDAP is a set of protocols used for accessing information directories. It is based upon a standard known as X.500. CAs often provide this repository service for their customers as part of a complete PKI implementation package.

3. *Management of the Certificates*. Besides VeriSign and Thawte, other companies, including Netscape and Microsoft, also provide for the implementation as well as the management of PKI.

Digital Certificates

Digital certificates provide a method of guaranteeing the identity of an individual or business. These certificates can be thought of as the

equivalent of an online "passport." Ensuring the validity of data transferred over the Internet, intranet, or extranet, these online passports
positively identify all parties involved. Figure 7-1 shows an example of
a digital certificate. Digital certificates are often used by an organization or by individuals for validation purposes, and software developers
often use digital certificates as a means of ensuring the authenticity of
their products. One common trait among all digital certificates is that

Figure 7-1. Windows ME Certificate information screen (IE 5.5).

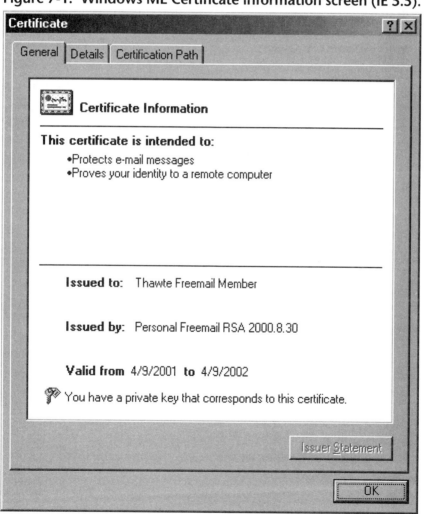

they are issued by certificate authorities (CAs). Before she can issue a certificate, a CA must validate the identity of the individual or organization requesting the certificate. The CA signs the certificate and authenticates the identity of the user. The CA then places an expiration date on the certificate.

Digital certificates use public key encryption, as described earlier. The tools that are needed for the authentication and encryption are provided by the CA. Digital certificates provide a means of authentication that cannot be repudiated. Nonrepudiation proves the originality of the message so that the message cannot later be denied or claimed as erroneous. If you use a brokerage account to perform online stock trades, the brokerage firm may request that you use a digital certificate to perform the trades. The purpose of using a digital certificate in this case is to ensure the validity of the trade. A digital certificate also provides a means to prove it was you that requested the trade. Accountants, financial planners, and lawyers often use digital certificates for documents sent over the Internet when integrity and security of information are critical.

Sometimes a digital certificate must be intentionally invalidated prior to its expiration date. There are any number of reasons for this, such as a change in employment status. If an employee is laid off, for example, the CA must revoke the employee's digital certificate to prevent a possible compromise in security. When a digital certificate is revoked, it is added to a certificate revocation list (CRL) maintained by the CA. Placing a digital certificate on the CRL keeps it from being reissued.

Digital Signatures

Like their handwritten equivalents, digital signatures are used to validate the identity of the sender. Digital signatures even go a step further by also ensuring the integrity of a message.

A digital signature is not a digitized version of a handwritten signature. (When the FedEx delivery person has you sign for your package on the electronic keypad, that signature is indeed digitized; however, it should not be confused with a digital signature.) Digital signatures are issued by a CA. They are often used in conjunction with digital certificates to validate the identity of the sender. Unlike a digital certificate, a digital signature does not encrypt the contents of a message. What a digital signature does do is ensure that the message was not altered or modified in transit. If a user wants to encrypt the contents of a message in addition to sending it with a digital signature, she must do so by using a separate program such as Pretty Good Privacy (PGP) prior to sending it. Digital signatures are legally acceptable for use in a number of states already and will probably be legally recognized nationwide and worldwide in the near future.

Digitally Signed Programs

Many software vendors now allow customers to first pay for and then download software programs directly from the Internet. Popular tax preparation software vendors now allow those who purchase the federal version of their tax program to download their appropriate state tax module at a reduced fee. While this is convenient to the user, it does pose some security risks, such as Internet-borne viruses. By using a PKI solution such as Microsoft's Authenticode, customers can be assured of the safety, authenticity, and validity of these types of downloads.

Other Common Uses of PKI

In addition to software downloads, PKI has many other pertinent and important uses. As mentioned earlier, many Web browsers have built-in encryption features that allow users to conduct transactions (e.g., online shopping or banking) with safe, secure connections. PKI is what enables a VPN to use the public Internet for the safe remote access of data. PKI is also often used for sending and receiving secure e-mail and e-mail attachments.

Secure Multipurpose-Mail Extensions

Secure multipurpose-mail extensions (S/MIME) is a secure version of the common MIME, or multipurpose-mail extension e-mail protocol.

MIME was initiated by the Internet Engineering Task Force (IETF) as a method of specifying the way nontext messages (e.g., video files such as QuickTime™ and audio files such as MP3s) are to be transported across the Internet. MIME defines how the body of an e-mail message is structured. MIME is what allows the body of an e-mail to contain special text and graphics. Widely supported by all modern Web browsers, MIME is a very flexible specification. It supports a host of media types. The users of MIME can even develop their own MIME extensions if they choose to do so.

S/MIME is nothing more than an enhanced, more secure version of MIME. The added security comes from the use of public key encryption developed by RSA (Rivest, Shamir, and Adelman). The current version S/MIMEv2 supports the encryption of messages and allows for the use of digital signatures. It is endorsed by many major Internet players, such as Microsoft, Novell, Netscape, and VeriSign.

Pretty Good Privacy

PGP is a program used to digitally sign and encrypt messages, developed by Phil Zimmerman. Zimmerman was the subject of a three-year federal investigation because of the alleged distribution of his strong encryption software outside the United States. Strong encryption is a politically charged technology. Governments have always used cryptography during times of war. Strong cryptography at the hands of criminals poses serious threats to both the government and civilians. The United States has recently relaxed some of its export limitations and now is concerned primarily with export to countries that are subject to certain sanctions.

PGP software uses public key cryptography, discussed earlier. PGP software is available at no cost on the Internet. By using PGP software, you can encrypt messages using your recipient's public key so that only the recipient can decrypt the message using his corresponding private key. Consider this real-world scenario: Accountant Lewis needs to send a client's personal financial information across the public Internet to a pension consulting firm. One way for Lewis to ensure the privacy of the client's information is to encrypt it. He may do so by using the pension firm's public key (previously supplied to him by the pension firm). The recipient, the pension-consulting firm, then decrypts the message using its private key. The keys used in the exchange of data come in pairs. When the pension firm needs to use its private key, it does so by using the private key that matches the public key used by Lewis to encrypt the data he sent.

Because this program is widely available, any one of the millions of people who regularly use the Internet can now send and receive secure private messages. You may wonder why using a widely available program is safe. Because there is safety in numbers, the more people that use this program, the better it serves all. The basic premise behind this is as follows. Imagine that everybody sent letters without first putting them into envelopes. If this were standard procedure and one day a person decided to send a letter sealed in an envelope, it would raise suspicions that the person had something to hide. If more people started using PGP (envelopes), hackers wouldn't know which targets to choose, as they would not be able to tell which had the kind of information they were seeking. PGP makes sending digital messages safe and secure.

PGP has increasingly found its way around the world. Rumor has it that it is being used by human rights activist groups in dictator-run countries to allow activists to send and receive private messages without fear of repercussions from their governing bodies. The latest non-commercial freeware version of this program can be found at the following Web sites: Web.mit.edu/network/pgp.html and www.eudora.com. The commercial version is available at www.pgp.com for a cost.

Secure Sockets Layer

Secure Sockets Layer (SSL) is a protocol that was originally developed by Netscape Communications Corporation to ensure security and privacy over the public Internet. One nice feature of SSL is that it is not application independent, that is, it can function with many of the common protocols in use, such as Hypertext Transfer Protocol (HTTP) and File Transfer Protocol (FTP), while providing client and server authentication.

A secure connection between a client and a server using SSL requires the server to send its digital certificate to ensure that the client is communicating with a trustworthy source. SSL runs on top of Transmission Control Protocol/Internet Protocol (TCP/IP) but below protocols such as HTTP or FTP. It uses TCP/IP on behalf of the higher level protocols and allows an SSL-enabled server to authenticate itself to an SSL-enabled client. SSL also allows the client to authenticate itself to the server, permitting both machines to establish an encrypted connection. This encrypted communication is completed using the Secure Sockets Layer Handshaking Protocol. This procedure consists of a series of phases. A brief summary of these handshaking phases is as follows:

- Various data are needed by the server to communicate with the client using SSL. The server receives the client's SSL number (one of several versions), cipher settings, and other data needed in order for the two to communicate.

- The client then receives the server's SSL version number, cipher settings, and the other data and information the client needs in order for the two to communicate. In essence this is the same as the preceding step, except in the opposite direction. It is during this phase that digital certificates are exchanged (including public keys), if required by the nature of the data being transmitted.

- After receiving a digital certificate, the client must authenticate the server. The client does this by applying certain parts of the information the client has received from the server. When the server has been effectively authenticated, the client goes to the next phase in the protocol. In the case of a failure to authenticate the server, a warning is issued to the user. The user is notified about the failure and warned that an encrypted, authenticated communication cannot be completed.

- With the information already received during the handshake, the client generates what is called the "premaster secret" for the communication session. The premaster secret is encrypted with the server's public key. The client then sends the key encrypted premaster secret to the server.

- Sometimes the server wishes to secure client authentication, as well. This is not mandatory. When such authentication is requested, the client also sends an additional piece of information (known by both the client and server) that is exclusive to this handshake. The client sends the additional information as well as the client's own digital certificate and the key encrypted premaster secret to the server.

- Once it is determined that client authentication is required, the server tries to generate the authentication. If authentication of the client fails, the communication is ended. In the case of a client suitably authenticated, the server then unencrypts the premaster secret (using its private key). At this time both the client and server use their premaster secrets to start a sequence of steps that lead to the creation of what is known as the "master secret."

- During this phase, the master secret is used (by both the client and server) to produce what are known as "session keys." These keys are symmetrical. Session keys are used to both *en*crypt and *de*crypt data shared during the SSL session. They are also used to validate the reliability of the exchanged data. Reliability is ensured when no changes are detected in the information during the time it was sent and received via the SSL connection.

- The client sends information to the server, notifying it that future messages sent by the client will be encrypted with the same session key. The client then sends a separate and encrypted message reporting that the handshake has been completed (on the part of the client).

- The server sends information to the client, notifying it that future messages sent by the server will be encrypted with the same session key. The server then sends a separate and encrypted message reporting that the handshake has been completed (on the part of the server).

- With the handshake portion now concluded, the SSL session commences. As information is sent and received by both the client and server, it is encrypted and decrypted with the use of the session keys. The session keys also endorse the integrity of the information.

In summary, during the handshaking procedure, the type of encryption and the methods of key exchange are negotiated. While the handshaking procedure slows transaction time somewhat, it is a small price to pay for the added security. Now, let's examine the three basic steps of SSL connections. They include:

- *Server Authentication.* This allows the client computer to authenticate the server. SSL client software often uses public key cryptography to determine whether the server has a valid ID issued by a CA (and is therefore trustworthy). This is useful for users who need to send their credit card numbers across the Internet to make an online purchase and need to verify the online merchant's identity.

- *Client Authentication.* This allows the server to authenticate a client's identity. SSL server software checks to see whether the client has a valid ID issued by a CA (and is therefore trustworthy). This is useful for an institution that wants to send confidential information to a client and needs to verify the identity of the recipient.

- *Encrypted Connection.* This ensures that the sending and receiving nodes can send the confidential information via the Internet with a high degree of security. In addition, encrypted SSL connections provide a method for determining whether the data were altered in transit.

In summary, an SSL transaction is performed using a public key given to your browser by the online merchant's server. The digital certificate provider verifies that the key belongs to a valid certificate used by the company located at the domain where the transaction is taking place. Essentially, a three-way transaction is conducted, but each party can access only the information it needs to complete the transaction.

Secure Electronic Transaction

Secure Electronic Transaction (SET) is a protocol that was developed primarily by MasterCard and Visa. It was conceived as a method for performing credit card transactions over the Internet. Like many of the other applications that use PKI, SET uses public key encryption and digital certificates to ensure the safety of the data and the validity of the merchant for online transactions. There are three basic components to a SET transaction:

- *Consumers/Merchants* ensure that credit card data are both encrypted and safely transferred across the Internet.

- *Consumers* confirm that the merchant is authorized to accept credit card payments.

- *Merchants* confirm that the consumer is authorized to use a credit card for the transaction.

Secure Hypertext Transfer Protocol (S-HTTP) also allows for secure Internet transactions. However, S-HTTP uses a symmetrical (secret) key for the encryption of data. Rather than securing the communication link on which the transaction takes place, S-HTTP secures only the messages themselves.

Smart Cards

Smart cards are usually small devices that closely resemble a credit card. Smart cards are thicker than a standard credit card or bank ATM card. While the use of passwords may rely on what a person knows, a smart card adds another layer to the authentication process.

When you use the ATM at your local bank, you must place your ATM card into the machine before the machine will ask you for your PIN. Your account information is stored on a magnetic strip attached to the card itself. Smart cards are much more powerful and sophisticated than the typical ATM card. Smart cards contain small microprocessors and memory cells to hold personal information. Special processors in these cards are used to encode and decode their sensitive information.

While ordinary magnetic strip cards are relatively inexpensive to manufacture, smart cards are a costly product. Smart cards are more widely used in Europe than in the United States. In Europe the cost associated with making a telephone call is typically much higher than it is in the United States. Connecting to a centralized database via a telephone modem for each transaction is therefore an expensive venture. By having the user's personal information embedded on the card itself, banks eliminate the need to contact a central database.

Another nice feature of smart cards is that, unlike magnetic strip cards, smart cards are much more difficult to tamper with because they have chips inside them.

One incentive for banks to increase the use of smart cards in the United States is the prospect that the same card could be used in several ways. In theory, the same card could serve as an ATM card, a personal identification card, a debit card, and even a credit card. The smart card could contain crucial medical information and could act as a cash substitute for transactions over the Internet. Additional smart card uses would be limited only by the public's willingness to accept the technology. Security and privacy concerns need to be addressed in detail before the public will accept smart cards that contain a great deal of private information about their lives.

Biometrics

The use of biometrics for authentication is a very exciting emerging field. Instead of using something the person knows, or something the person has, as the means by which to verify his identity, biometrics uses something totally individual: our biological makeup. By focusing on certain aspects of a person's biological makeup, biometrics permit authentication of a person's identity without concern for forgery. Fingerprints, eyes, and even speech are unique to each individual; no two people possess identical characteristics. Biometrics therefore permits virtually foolproof authentication.

Everyday transactions are now increasingly being handled through electronic means instead of through face-to-face contact. Because of the increased use of electronic transactions, fast and accurate user authentication is essential. Biometric technology is one of the best means of obtaining highly secure authentication. While passwords can be forgotten, paper identification, cards, and keys lost or stolen, your physical traits are always with you and ready to identify you. Biometrics has several potential commercial applications. For Internet security purposes, these might include control of computer access, access to Web site servers, access through firewalls, and physical access to information.

Summary

PKI provides the mechanism for safe and secure communication across the Internet. A list of the key concepts used in its application is as follows:

- ✓ Asymmetric (public) key and symmetric (secret) key cryptography provide data confidentiality and security.

- ✓ While very secure, nearly all cryptographic keys can be broken. Keys with longer bit lengths are harder to crack.

- ✓ Two common PKI applications are digital signatures and digital certificates. Both are used for authentication of individuals and businesses, and to verify that data was not tampered with in transit.

- ✓ PKI is used in VPNs to allow safe and secure communication across the public Internet.

- ✓ S/MIME is a secure e-mail protocol that uses public key encryption to protect sensitive e-mail data in transit.

- ✓ PGP uses strong encryption and public key cryptography to encrypt messages for transport across the Internet. Strong encryption (128-bit or greater) is the subject of legal controversy, and appears on the U.S. munitions list because of the threat it can pose to government and civilians if misused.

✓ SSL protocol was originally developed by Netscape for secure communications across the Internet. It is very flexible because it has the ability to function with many different protocols, and is application independent.

✓ SET is a protocol developed by Master Card and Visa that allows secure credit card transactions over the Internet.

✓ Smart cards and biometrics are gaining popularity as an added means of providing authentication of users.

Secure Remote Access

8

Think of a local area network where all the computers of an organization are connected together sharing and exchanging information. Now imagine that one of the organization's salespeople is at a client's office 3,000 miles away and needs to access some important files on his company's network. Remote connectivity is the means by which he will gain access to network resources from a distant location.

Whether it's the salesperson away from the office for the day or on an extended business trip or a home user connecting to the Internet, the basic procedure for remote connectivity remains the same. With technology making it easier to connect to company networks while out on the road, portability is becoming a central component of many professions.

Connecting to a computer or network from a remote location relies upon several different protocols. It also has some inherent security risks. Before we discuss the potential risks of remote connectivity, it's important to know the remote access protocols and the associated strengths and weaknesses of those protocols.

Serial Line Internet Protocol

Serial Line Internet Protocol (SLIP) is a standard that was commonly used for point-to-point serial connections running over a Transmission

Control Protocol/Internet Protocol (TCP/IP) network. It has not been used as much since the development of the more flexible and reliable Point-to-Point Protocol (PPP). SLIP can trace its roots to the early 1980s. It is merely a packet framing protocol. It essentially encapsulates the IP data packets at the Data Link Layer (layer 2 of the OSI model) and then transports them across a serial (modem) link.

As described in Requests for Comments (RFC) 1055, the TCP/IP family runs over a variety of network media, such as ethernet, Token ring, local area networks (LANS), X.25 lines, satellite links, and serial lines. Standard encapsulations for IP packets are defined for many of these networks, but there is no standard for serial lines. SLIP defines a sequence of characters that frame the IP packets on a serial line, and nothing further. It provides no addressing provisions, packet type identification, or error detection/correction or compression mechanisms. Because the protocol does very little, it is an easy protocol to implement.

In the mid-1980s, Rick Adams implemented SLIP for several companies and then released it to the public. It quickly caught on as an easy way to connect TCP/IP hosts and routers using serial connections.

SLIP is commonly used on dedicated serial links (i.e., LAN) and for dial-up connection purposes. It is often used with line speeds between 1,200 bps and 19,200 bps. SLIP is useful for allowing different mixes of host computers and routers to communicate with one another. Host-to-host, host-to-router, and router-to-router are all common SLIP-type network configurations.

Users would like SLIP to include several features that it lacks. With all due respect, SLIP is just simple protocol designed quite a long time ago when security issues were not of great importance. The following are some of the shortcomings in the existing SLIP protocol:

- *Addressing.* Both computers in a SLIP link need to know each other's IP address for data routing purposes. In addition, when a host computer is using SLIP to dial into a router, the addressing method may be somewhat dynamic (changing continuously) and, as a result, the router may need to inform the dialing host of the host's IP address. SLIP does not provide any mechanism for hosts to communicate IP addressing information over a SLIP connection.

- *Identification.* Only one protocol can be run over a SLIP connection. Note that while SLIP is "Serial Line IP," if a serial line connects two multiprotocol computers together, those computers are able to use more than one protocol over that line.

- *Error Detection and Correction.* Noisy phone lines often corrupt data packets in transit. Because the line speed is usually low when SLIP is used, the need to retransmit data packets can be a costly consequence of such corruption. Error detection is not necessary at the SLIP level because many IP applications can detect damaged packets on their own. Since it takes so long to retransmit a packet that has been corrupted by line noise, it is not efficient for SLIP to provide its own method of simple error correction.

- *Data Compression.* SLIP does not support the use of data compression. Because dial-up connections are usually slow, using data compression greatly improves packet throughput speeds. Usually, streams of packets in a single TCP connection have little changes in their TCP/IP header fields; so simple compression schemes might send only the changed parts of the headers instead of the complete headers, as in the case of Compressed Serial Line Internet Protocol.

Point-to-Point Protocol

First implemented in 1990, PPP was intended to deal with some of the limitations of SLIP. PPP provides a standard method for transporting multiprotocol datagrams over point-to-point links. This means that PPP not only transports TCP/IP traffic but can also transport Novell's IPX protocol and AppleTalk traffic. PPP goes a step further by permitting these protocols to be transported at the same time over the same connection.

PPP is a technology for connecting to networks over standard serial (telephone) lines. In its most common implementation, users connect their personal computers to the Internet with PPP, using a modem. PPP is similar to SLIP but is more full featured and robust. It provides error checking and uses two methods with which logins can be automated. The two methods are Password Authentication Protocol (PAP) and Challenge Handshake Authentication Protocol (CHAP); both of which are discussed later in detail. Both PAP and CHAP provide a means for your system to automatically send your login ID and/or password information to the remote computer.

PPP permits a more direct and flexible connection to the Internet. It is a communication protocol that allows a computer connected to a remote server via a serial line (such as a modem) to become an actual node on the Internet. This allows the user to run network applications on his home computer directly. For instance, PPP allows the user to use e-mail, news-reading, and Web browser programs, taking full advantage of the computer's graphics potential.

PPP comprises three basic components, as described in RFC 1661:

1. A method for encapsulating multiprotocol datagrams

2. A Link Control Protocol (LCP) for establishing, configuring, and testing the data-link connection

3. A family of Network Control Protocols (NCPs) for establishing and configuring different network-layer protocols

Using both the LCP and NCP, PPP has four important phases:

1. *Link Establishment and Configuration Negotiation.* Before any network-layer datagrams (e.g., IP) can be exchanged, LCP must first open the connection and negotiate configuration parameters. This phase is completed only when a configuration acknowledgment frame has been both sent and received.

2. *Link Quality Determination.* LCP allows an optional link quality determination phase following the link establishment and configuration negotiation phase. In this phase, the link is tested

to determine whether the link quality is sufficient to bring up network-layer protocols. This phase is optional. LCP can delay the transmission of network-layer protocol information until this phase is completed.

3. *Network-Layer Protocol Configuration Negotiation.* After LCP has finished the link quality determination phase; network-layer protocols can be configured separately by the appropriate NCP and can be brought up and taken down (terminated) at any time. If LCP closes the link, it informs the network-layer protocols so that they may take appropriate action.

4. *Link Termination.* LCP or NCP can close or terminate the link at any time. Link termination is often done at the request of the user but sometimes it is caused by an outside event such as the loss of transmission carrier or the use of an idle period (inactivity) timer.

Some of the more common uses for the PPP include the following:

- *World Wide Web*—Using Web browsers to visit Internet sites

- *Telnet*—Terminal emulation programs that allow connections to remote machines over the Internet

- *File Transfer Protocol*—Transfer files between your computer and remote computers over the Internet.

- *E-Mail*—Allows the use of e-mail applications such as Microsoft Outlook and Qualcomm's Eudora

You may now be wondering what SLIP and PPP have to do with Internet security. Neither one actually has very much to do with Internet security. This reality, in fact, created a problem. With the increasing popularity of remote connectivity across the Internet, users quickly realized the importance of having a more secure protocol. As more and more companies began to use the Internet to conduct their business, they needed a secure means of allowing their users (such as salespeople) to connect to their company network from remote sites. To meet this need, Point-to-Point Tunneling Protocol (PPTP) and other tunneling protocols were developed.

Point-to-Point Tunneling Protocol

PPTP is a wide area network (WAN) protocol that allows users to access their company networks in security from remote locations using the public Internet. (Tunneling is the process of sending secure, encapsulated, and encrypted packets to a remote computer by routing them over the Internet. Since the Internet is a public network, if data have not been encapsulated and encrypted using a secure method, the possibility exists that they could be intercepted and easily read, resulting in serious security and privacy breaches.) PPTP is often used to create a virtual private network (VPN) across a TCP/IP network such as the Internet. VPNs are discussed in detail later in this chapter.

Like PPP, PPTP allows the simultaneous use of multiple protocols and can encapsulate many different packet data types. PPTP uses PAP and CHAP, which provide for a secure means of data access through the tunnel. PPTP secures the data packets sent through the Internet by encapsulating or covering them with other packets. Encryption is used to further secure the data contained in the packets.

One nice feature of PPTP is that it creates a *tunnel,* allowing it to securely carry other non-TCP/IP protocols such as NetBEUI or IPX across the Internet. Many of the newer versions of the Windows operating system have built-in features that allow remote users to utilize PPTP to safely connect to their private company network using the Internet.

There are three steps in the process of creating a PPTP connection:

1. The client (remote user) uses PPP to establish a connection over the Internet to the internet service provider (ISP).

2. After the PPP connection is made to the ISP, an additional special type of connection is made from the client to the server

located at the remote network with which he is trying to connect. Both the client computer and the server with which it is trying to establish a connection must support PPTP in order for this type of connection to occur.

3. After the remote user establishes the PPTP connection, PPTP then encapsulates or wraps the PPP data packets, turning them into secure IP datagrams. These encapsulated IP packets are then transmitted over the Internet through a PPTP tunnel to the PPTP server that connects the remote user to the company LAN.

As companies use tunneling over the Internet, they gain secure WANs, intranets, and extranets. Tunneling achieves the security they require at a far lower cost than that incurred when using dedicated connections such as T1 lines. Tunneling has proved its ability to achieve essential security at reasonable cost.

Other Tunneling Protocols

Several other tunneling protocols besides PPTP are used for the secure transmission of data across a public network. Like PPP, these additional protocols are essentially extensions of PPP.

IP Security

IP Security (IPSec) is a course of action used in protecting IP communications. IPSec spells out how your confidential data can be sent over the Internet. IPSec provides encryption, authentication, and detection of data tampering (i.e., it prevents the unauthorized resending of the data).

Internet key exchange (IKE), the IPSec key management procedure, is a progression of steps that makes keys that are then used to encrypt and decrypt data. IPSec instructs both client and server as to which language they will use to communicate with each other (using a language familiar to both).

The Internet Engineering Task Force developed both IPSec and IKE.

IPSec and IKE have become the standard means for securing data. As a result, security hardware and software produced by different companies are all able to successfully work together.

The most common way of deploying IPSec is by using what is called the transport mode, that is, sending information protected by IPSec from one user to another. This mode is often used in computers that incorporate IPSec as part of TCP/IP protocol stack (e.g., between two computers that both have IPSec-enabled software incorporated into their operating systems).

The other method of deploying IPSec is by using the tunnel mode. In this mode, Internet data generated by hosts without IPSec support are captured from the line by a special security appliance. The security appliance wraps the entire IP packet with IPSec encryption, including the original IP header. It then appends the IP header of the data packet and sends it across the Internet to a second security appliance, where the information is unencrypted and sent in its original structure to the chosen recipient.

Layer 2 Forwarding

Layer 2 Forwarding (L2F) is a proprietary protocol developed by Cisco Systems. It is similar to PPTP in form but differs in function. L2F is not dependent on any single protocol and thus can be run on different types of networks. This is in sharp contrast to PPTP, which only runs over TCP/IP. Unlike PPTP, which uses TCP, a connection-oriented means for data transport, L2F uses User Datagram Protocol, a connectionless means of transporting data. Like most tunneling protocols, L2F is used in the creation of VPNs.

Layer 2 Tunneling Protocol

Layer 2 Tunneling Protocol (L2TP) has tremendous support from many of the biggest Internet security vendors. Because it can be used with many different vendors' products, it is predicted to become the most widely used tunneling protocol for VPNs. Instead of using the encryption provided by PPP, L2TP uses IPSec to encrypt data sent through the tunnel.

Password Authentication Protocol

PAP entails the use of a two-way handshaking procedure. After establishing a link, the sender forwards his user name and password pair to his server. Once the sender is authenticated, the server notifies the sender of his acceptance. If the sender is not authenticated, the sender is allowed an additional attempt, or the session is terminated.

The PAP method does not provide a powerful means of authentication. The sender may repeatedly send his password if he so desires. Servers that are able however, will choose to negotiate using a stronger means of authentication and will use that method before using PAP. When a simple plain text password is needed to replicate a login at a remote host, using the PAP method is warranted.

PAP allows any Internet user to log in to his dial-up PPP account without having to type in his username and password. The user must, however, first configure his system and connection parameters so that his username and password can automatically be supplied at the beginning of the logon process. PAP works by sending the username and password to the ISPs server immediately after the modem completes the connection. The username and password information is stored in the dialer software (i.e., Dial-Up Networking for Windows 95/98). Since it is stored, the ISP's server no longer needs to request the information through the login and password prompts. PAP is easier to set up and more reliable than a login script, and it requires less updating.

Using PAP to dial in to your account simplifies the dial-up and login process. Because PAP skips certain procedures, it reduces slightly the time it takes for users to log in. This time saving may amount to only one or two seconds, however. The time required for the modem handshake procedures to be completed remains the same. The level of security for the access to your account remains the same, since your username and password are still required for completing the connection. However, since PAP sends your username and password over the line to your ISP, those passwords are not secure from interception by hackers.

Challenge Handshake Authentication Protocol

CHAP is a more secure means of user authentication. Instead of sending passwords over the line, CHAP uses a Three-Way Challenge/Response procedure, which is as follows:

1. The remote server is sent the username of the host that wishes to log on to the network.

2. The server authenticates the host by username only and then gives the host limited access to the server.

3. The CHAP server sends randomly generated data to challenge the client, along with its hostname. The client uses the hostname to look up the appropriate secret, combines it with the challenge, and encrypts the data, using a one-way hashing function. The result is returned to the server along with the client's hostname. The server now performs the same computation and acknowledges the client if it arrives at the same result.

Virtual Private Networks

VPNs are used when private company networks wish to allow remote users access to those networks while using the Internet as the transport medium. As more and more people work from home (or from out on the road), the need to allow mobile workers secure access to company networks is rapidly increasing. Allowing remote access increases productivity, since employees are then able to contribute their talents and resources from almost any distance or location. Business travelers are now able to work with customers or clients no matter where either one is located. In general, remote access to company data helps reduce delays and unproductive work procedures. VPN allows companies to connect with their branch offices, or with other companies, while maintaining a secure VPN connection.

The key to cost-effective, secure remote access over the Internet is to have a VPN in place. The Internet is both ubiquitous and the least expensive of public data networks. This provides the optimal foundation for a VPN. Although the Internet provides a natural and economical path for linking remote users, security concerns have rightly made network administrators hesitant to open their systems to remote access via the Internet.

An Internet-based VPN is "virtual." It only looks as if it is a dedicated private network. In reality, the Internet is anything but private or dedicated. Because users see only their own "traffic" as it is routed to them, it seems that the network is private. Hence the word _virtual_.

Consider this real-world use of VPN: After many years of commuting to work on a daily basis, financial planner Frank decides one day that he would like to _tele_commute to work two days a week. By employing a VPN to tunnel into his office LAN, Frank is able to access all the client data he needs directly from his office while he is at his residence many miles away. On his company LAN, Frank uses Windows NT 4.0 on both his server and his workstations. Frank's objective was to be able to securely connect the two using the public Internet, so he recently installed a broadband connection at both his home and his business. Because VPN is supported and included with Windows NT 4.0 (using PPTP), Frank is able to securely tunnel into his company LAN from home. He achieves this without the added expense of a dedicated connection or the fear of compromising sensitive client data.

A VPN uses a combination of authentication, data encryption, and tunneling to create a secure channel between a user and a corporate network or between two networks. In a remote access situation, the users dial into the local access provider's Post Office Protocol, establish a connection to the Internet, and then identify themselves to the corporate VPN's authentication system. The VPN verifies the identity of the user on the basis of username and password, a hardware token and personal identification number, or some other device. When the user is successfully authenticated, the system sets up tunneling or encryption for all traffic between the VPN client and the VPN server.

Security is vital to a virtual private network. Users, often mistakenly, assume that private networks are, in fact, private. The key is to employ a VPN solution that is as private as a private network would be. With appropriate security, users on the Internet can achieve a high degree of privacy. The key concern is to ensure that the privacy of information is maintained while it is in transit between servers and clients. Protecting data while they are in transit over the Internet requires that they be encrypted. There are many encryption methods, also called algorithms; TripleDES is currently a popular method among high-ranking companies. Tunneling, also known as encapsulation, can be used to transport nonIP protocols, such as NetBEUI and IPX.

Implementing "Built-in" VPN for Windows NT 4.0

VPN in Windows operating systems is based upon the open standard PPTP. Remote users simply dial the local access number of an Internet service provider, then securely tunnel into their corporate network. Companies can use a VPN via the Internet to outsource (subcontract) dial-up access to their company networks. Implementing VPN in this fashion is more expensive. It is secure, easy to put into operation, and, like PPP, protocol independent. In addition, it does not require any changes to the existing network-addressing scheme. Most versions of the Windows operating systems produced after 1996 have the built-in capacity to support VPN using PPTP. VPN allows a corporation to connect with branch offices, or with other companies, while maintaining a secure PPTP connection.

Once PPTP is installed on the Windows NT Server, tunneling is achieved either through a PPTP-enabled client or through a PPTP-enabled ISP. This means that a user with VPN enabled on his laptop or home computer can make a secure, tunneled connection directly to his company's NT Server, even when he is using an ISP that is not PPTP enabled. In the same way, a user without a VPN-enabled computer can make a secure tunneled connection if his ISP has VPN support on its servers.

A remote client using non-dial-up-type connections such as an ethernet card connected to a digital subscriber line or cable modem with a direct connection into an ISP can also use PPTP. As long as both the remote client PC and the server support VPN using PPTP, the user can benefit from a secure connection.

NT 4.0 Server

Setting up VPN using PPTP on a Windows NT 4.0 server follows the same procedures as other remote access services (RAS) under NT.

Since VPN support using PPTP is already built into the operating system, VPN support follows the steps many of us are already familiar with for setting up a dial-up access via RAS. Assuming the server is already set up for WAN access using RAS, you simply add the PPTP protocol to the list of protocols using the RAS setup program. Setting up VPN on Windows NT Server 4.0 is fairly easy. A VPN can be considered just a particular use of RAS, an important feature that is already built into Windows NT. As a result, setting up a VPN under NT 4.0 using PPTP involves many of the same steps any user takes when setting up a server to accept dial-up networking connections using RAS:

1. Set up the network server to use WAN under RAS.

2. Select the protocol or protocols to be used with RAS, for example, IP, IPX, or NetBEUI. PPTP is simply another protocol that can be selected, installed, and enabled in much the same way these other protocols are. Anyone who is familiar with RAS setup will find the small number of screens and dialog boxes needed to set up and use PPTP under NT 4.0 a familiar sight. The user can retain control of who gets access to the corporate network with Microsoft's VPN, even if the company has contracted a third party to provide its VPN service, because the user profiles are preserved on the Windows NT Server so that they can be quickly updated to reflect changes in employee status.

An additional security feature of VPN implementation under NT 4.0 is that filters may be applied so that only those who use a PPTP for remote access will have access to the network resources.

NT 4.0 Client
Users can also enable VPN service on the client computer, allowing the user to connect to the company LAN via any ISP, even those ISPs that do not provide support for PPTP. Please note that the client computer must have the PPTP protocol installed in the same way it was installed on the server machine. Again, PPTP is treated like any other protocols that can be selected.

Once PPTP is installed on the client computer, the user creates an RAS Phone Book entry for the VPN connection. This entry looks like any other Phone Book entry with two exceptions: An IP address appears in place of a telephone number, and the Dial Using pull-down list includes a PPTP option.

This VPN Phone Book entry is activated after the user has connected to the ISP, so it is a two-step process. To make this process even easier, both the ISP connection and the VPN connection can be set up and triggered from one easy automatically dialed Phone Book entry. Once this Phone Book entry has been set up, the user can simply double click on the Phone Book entry icon to automatically dial into the VPN-enabled server through any ISP.

Windows 98/ME Clients

Many laptops and home computers come with Windows 98/ME operating system already installed. As a result, users can implement VPN using PPTP on their computers to connect to a Windows NT 4.0 or Windows 2000 network server located at their company's LAN. To see whether you have VPN support installed on your Windows 98/ME computer, follow these steps:

1. Open up your Windows Control Panel (found under the "Start" menu), and click on the "Add/Remove Programs" icon. A window will open up with three tabs.

2. Access "Windows Setup," then highlight the "Communications" option and click on the "Details" button (see Figure 8-1). In the communications detail options you will see a "Virtual Private Networking" option (see Figure 8-2). If the box is checked, your computer already has support for VPN installed. If it is not checked, then put a check in the box to have Windows install it. You may be asked to insert your Windows 98/ME operating system disk, so be sure to have it available.

Windows will ask you to reboot your computer in order to put the changes just made into effect.

Figure 8-1. Windows MS Add/Remove Programs properties screen (setup tab).

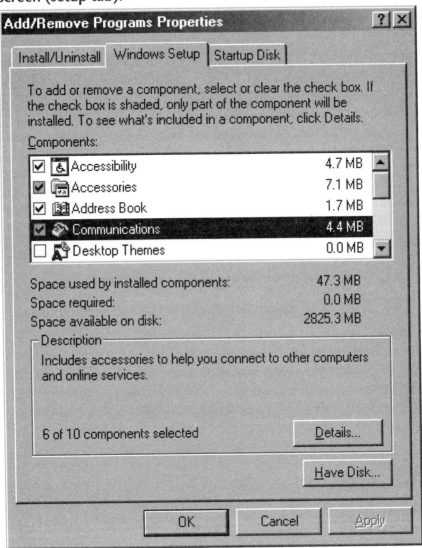

After following these steps, you will want to make sure you have the appropriate VPN software activated and included as part of your networking protocols under the "Networking Options" box. To check whether you have the protocol installed or to add VPN support to your

Figure 8-2. Windows MS Add/Remove Programs configuration screen (communications tab).

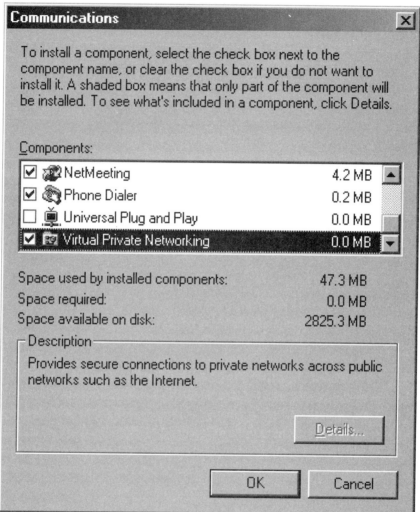

list of protocols, follow these steps (these steps may vary depending on which version of Windows you are using; for this example, we are using Windows ME.):

1. Open up the Windows Control Panel, and click on the "Network" icon. Your networking configuration panel will open. It

will show you a list of the networking components that are currently installed on your computer (see Figure 8-3).

2. As illustrated in Figure 8-3, you should see a "Dial-Up Adapter" and the associated "TCP/IP Adapter" installed, both showing VPN support. If these are not already present, you can add

Figure 8-3. Windows ME Network Configuration screen.

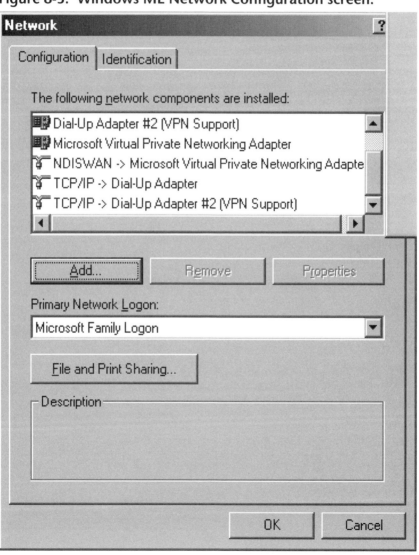

them by clicking on the "Add" button under the configuration tab and selecting the additional network component types (i.e., "Clients" and "Protocols") that you wish to install (see Figure 8-4). You will then be prompted to reboot your machine.

After your machine reboots, the installation of VPN client support on your home computer or laptop will be complete.

Making the VPN Connection

Now that all the necessary software is in place, let's go through the steps on how to make the VPN connection to another VPN-enabled computer across the Internet using the industry standard PPTP. In this example, we will use Windows ME for illustration purposes. Other Microsoft operating systems follow a similar type of VPN setup. In order to create a VPN connection across the Internet, you must first have an ISP connection (e.g., AOL, MSN, Juno) already established. Then you should follow these steps:

1. Access your computer's "Dial-Up Networking" options (see Figure 8-5).

Figure 8-4. Windows ME Select Network Component Type screen.

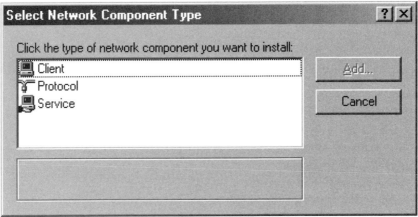

Figure 8-5. Windows ME My Computer screen.

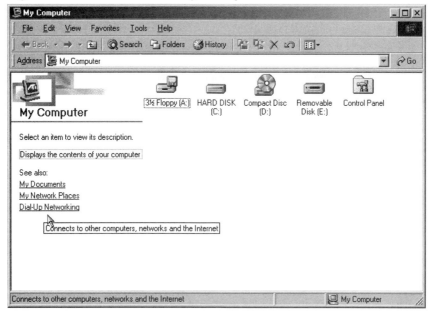

2. Double click on the "Make New Connection" icon (see Figure 8-6).

3. Type in the name of the computer with which you wish to establish a VPN connection. (This is for user reference only and can be any name you wish. This approach is used primarily to make it easier for you to find your VPN connections.)

4. In the "Select a Device" drop-down menu, make sure "Microsoft VPN Adapter" is selected (see Figure 8-7).

5. Follow the prompt to enter the "Host Name" or "IP Address" of the computer for which you are establishing a VPN connection (see Figure 8-8). In our example, this would be the IP address of the company network server or, if a router is employed as a firewall, the router's IP address.

6. Click the "Finish" button, and a new connection icon will appear that looks a bit different from ordinary dial-up connection icons (see Figure 8-9).

Internet Security Made Easy

Figure 8-6. Windows ME Dial-Up Networking screen.

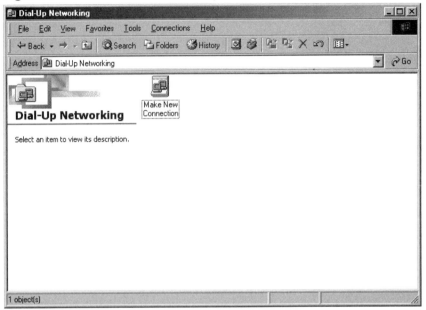

Now that we've established a VPN-enabled dial-up connection to your company's network, let's go through the steps for establishing this connection over the Internet. They are as follows:

1. Click "Start," point to "Settings," click "Control Panel," and then double click on "Dial-Up Networking." If you don't see this item, click "View All Control Panel Options," and then double click the "Dial-Up Networking" option.

2. Double click the connection to your ISP and establish a connection to the Internet. (You can skip this step if you use an ISP such as AOL or Juno, which use proprietary software that you must use to connect to Internet. In this case, you would establish your Internet connection as usual, then open up the "Dial-Up Networking" option and proceed to the next step.)

3. After you have successfully logged on to your Internet account, double click the VPN connection you wish to use. Type in your

Figure 8-7. Windows ME Make New Connection screen (initial dialog box).

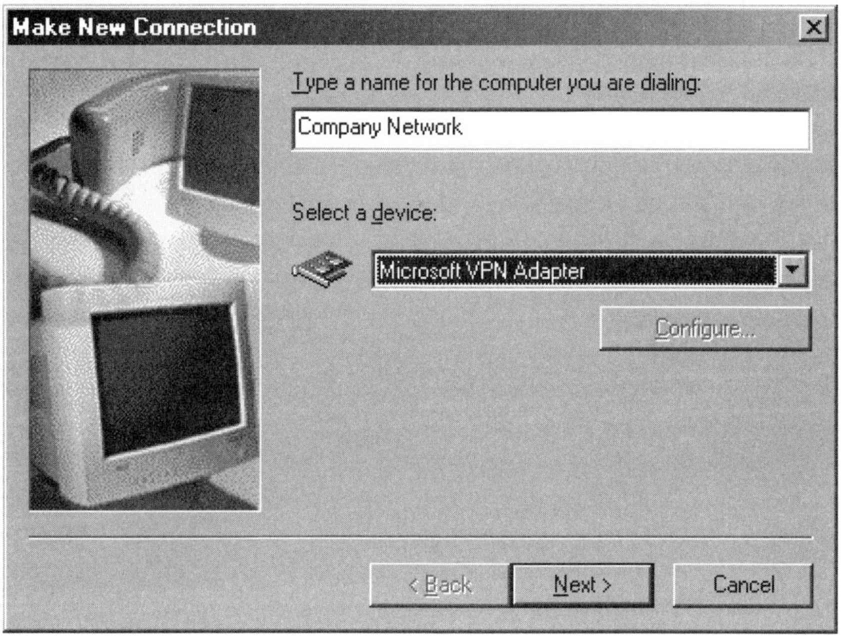

name and password; then click "Connect." Since a TCP/IP connection using PPP has already been established, when you click on the icon for the VPN connection, it will (in our example) connect to our company network, then establish a secure "tunneled" connection (in our example) to our company network.

Hackers and VPNs

Now that we've extolled all the virtues of a VPN, let's look at the danger of using such a method in remote connectivity. Many hackers use VPN connections to infiltrate company networks. Even though the data packets between VPN servers and clients are encapsulated and encrypted, hackers can easily trace these links. Instead of attempting to attack and penetrate the company network, the hacker targets the VPN client. Since some VPN clients fail to adequately protect their computers, it is easy for a hacker to break in and steal password and

Figure 8-8. Windows ME Make New Connection screen (dialog box requesting last name or IP address).

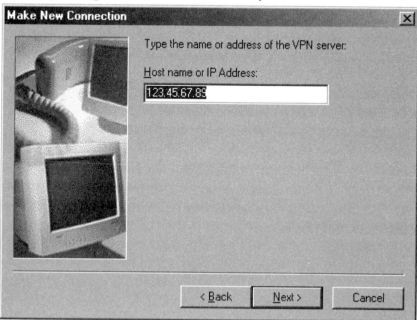

other logon information from them, thus giving the hacker access to your company's network. To help protect home telecommuters from incurring this type of attack, third-party software programs are available for added safety and security. Among the third party software products available to help make your VPN connection more secure are these:

- *ICEpac Security Suite* by NetworkICE Corporation (http://www. networkice.com) secures home or remote dial-up and VPN users, preventing hackers from pilfering logon identification information and accessing your network. This security software suite contains five different products that, according to the manufacturer, provide both remote connectivity and a high level of Internet security.

- *WinRoute Pro* by Tiny Software, Inc. (http://www.tinysoftware. com) is an ISCA(TruSecure)-certified software product that

Figure 8-9. Windows ME Dial-Up Networking screen.

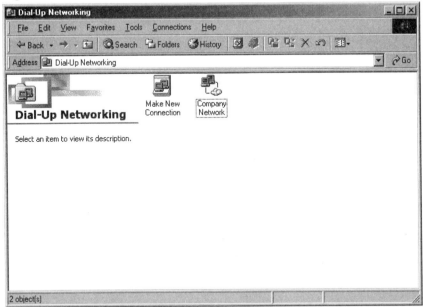

boasts full firewall capabilities, advanced NAT capabilities, port mapping, and, of course, VPN security support. It allows businesses to create their own secure WAN utilizing PPTP across the Internet.

- *PowerVPN* by Symantec Corporation (http://www.symantec.com) is an ICSA-certified firewall and Proxy-secured VPN server. The PowerVPN Server uses a proxy scanning technology to monitor and control all traffic passing through its VPN tunnels.

These are only a few of the many products available for VPN implementation and security. Because of the dynamic nature of Internet security, readers are encouraged to visit the manufacturers' Web sites for additional features and details on these products.

Summary

With increased use of the Internet for telecommuting, secure remote access is vital especially when there are data security and integrity issues. The critical components needed to secure remote access are as follows:

✓ PPP is the most widely used technology for connecting networks over standard serial (telephone) lines. It is more robust and flexible than its predecessor, SLIP and allows for authentication and identification across a network link.

✓ PPTP is a WAN that allows users to securely access a remote network across the Internet. Using the process known as tunneling, this protocol is often used in VPNs to provide data encapsulation and encryption.

✓ IPSec is used in the protection of IP communications. Like PPTP, IPSec provides encryption and authentication but it also includes additional security features not found in PPTP.

✓ L2F is a proprietary protocol developed by Cisco Systems, and is similar to PPTP. Unlike PPTP, L2F can be used in non-TCP/IP networks like Novell's IPX/SPX networking protocols.

✓ L2TP is a versatile, cross platform tunneling protocol that is quickly gaining popularity as the standard tunneling protocol used in VPNs.

✓ PAP and CHAP are two of the most common means to authenticate a user using a dial-up Internet account. Of these two protocols, CHAP is the most secure and is preferred when using a dial-up serial connection.

✓ VPNs use the Internet to transport data but provide a "virtual" private connection using secure encrypted connections between communicating computers. While VPNs are extremely secure, hackers have been known to use these types of connections to infiltrate company networks by "riding" the tunnel into the network through an unsecured client computer.

What Do We Do? We've Been Hacked!

9

Unfortunately, most companies today operate with an attitude toward Internet security best called lax. All companies are aware of the possibility of attack and the debilitation an attack can leave behind. Obviously, companies that take a lax attitude toward Internet security are most susceptible to an invader. Regrettably, a trespassing intruder sometimes hits even those companies that do adopt some security policies. In this chapter I highlight some steps to take once you've found that a penetration has already occurred.

Make the Proper Notifications

All members of your company must be notified the moment a security breach is discovered. If employees are not immediately advised, the intruder may be able to obtain additional company information (whether sensitive or not) if the attack is still in progress. Your entire system remains vulnerable, as well. Failure to make immediate notification may cripple your ability to remain fully (or even partially) operational.

You must first notify your management personnel, as well as your security staff. Law enforcement authorities and any security organization with which you are associated must also be informed. Several associations and institutes are dedicated to investigating, researching, and examining various aspects of Internet security. Some additional associations have jurisdiction over some type of Internet-related crime; these include the Federal Bureau of Investigation (FBI); the Secret Service; the Bureau of Alcohol, Tobacco, and Firearms (BATF); the Federal Trade Commission (FTC); the Customs Service; and the Securities and Exchange Commission (SEC).

You should put in place a "notification chain" before any intruder attack occurs. This chain will help disseminate information regarding your attack. The chain determines the order in which people will be informed and by whom. For utmost security, each individual in the chain should carry with her the chain information (links) she will need in case an intrusion occurs so that it is available on the spot should she need to make contact with the next individual(s) on the chain.

The amount of information revealed during the chain exchanges depends upon who is being contacted. Those lower on the chain do not require the same amount and level of information as do those higher up.

When relaying information about the breach, members on the chain must establish secure communication connections. This is a wise practice even when an attack has not been detected. For obvious reasons, all correspondence via company e-mail should cease. In some instances, even company fax and telephone use should be suspect and therefore curtailed. Face-to-face meetings are a secure alternative.

In the wake of or during the course of an intrusion, your company will likely uncover information regarding your attacker through remnant files the attacker leaves behind. These files sometimes include your Internet Protocol (IP) information, as well as the IP information of other hosts similarly attacked. Information you detect may include systems used by the attacker to gain access *to* your company's systems. It might also contain information on systems accessed by the attacker *from* your system. You may discover what systems the intruder used to attack your system, and you may find out about outside systems that the intruder attacked _from your_ system.

As you learn the identities of others affected by the attack, you are obligated to advise them of the intrusion. Certain Internet service providers will need to be alerted, since they usually (unwittingly) have provided the "transport" for the attacker. You should maintain a list of those contacted by you or your company, along with the date(s) of contact and the details of any information shared.

Gather and Guard Information

Whenever a breach occurs, information about the computer(s) and the cause of the breach must be obtained and preserved for future reference. This information is critical. Security personnel will need it for a careful review. By examining these data, those responsible for network security can learn about and correct any security holes in the systems. If the party responsible for the breach happens to be an employee of your company, having log files and any other tangible evidence will help management to admonish or terminate the employment of the employee responsible for the breach. In the event that you need to report the person(s) responsible to the proper authorities, having accurate evidence will aid in the process of prosecuting those accountable.

All evidence must be handled in a particular way, or it may not be admissible in a court of law. The procedures used to obtain evidence and the means of storage vary. I suggest that you contact local law enforcement agencies for specific details in this regard. Even though laws and procedures vary, the basic principles for investigating and prosecuting Internet crimes are similar throughout much of the world.

Use the Proper Data Collection Procedures

Collect all data about all applicable log files from the affected computers. Include any written accounts made by your response staff and any other evidence, such as audio- or videotapes that you may have obtained in the collection process. All information should be placed and secured in a written log file that addresses the following:

- Who had access to the systems?

- Who was alerted?

- What measures were taken?

- What was the date and time of each security breach?

- What evidence was acquired?

Safeguard Information

To guarantee that all of the obtained evidence will be acceptable to the proper authorities, companies should follow specific procedures that are in compliance with local codes and laws. Companies should also follow these steps:

- Maintain a course of action for preserving the required evidence in case of a criminal prosecution.

- Record all actions performed by all involved participants.

- Examine copies of all the evidence so that the originals remain intact. Be sure not to alter or affect the original evidence in any way, because this may render it useless to authorities.

Contact the Proper Authorities

You will need to notify the appropriate authorities as soon as you learn of a breach in security. They can assist you in limiting your legal responsibility in connection with the attack. If you keep your computer system operational during the effort to collect additional information about an intruder, you may be liable if your system is used by hackers as a launchpad for future attacks on other computers.

Since laws vary according to jurisdictions and states, you will need to verify the legal requirements of the community in which you are located. This is especially important when collecting and preserving evidence relating to the attack. Once you've determined what the requirements are, you will need to implement the necessary procedures to ensure that your company meets those requirements. Appendix A lists general procedures, along with contact information on reporting Internet-related crimes.

Limit the Scope of the Attack

After all the interested parties have been notified of the attack on your system, you must then limit the scope of the damage. This strategy includes preventing additional information from being discharged, thereby preventing additional sabotage of your system.

If a company computer is not rendered completely inoperable by an intruder attack, the damage potential may nevertheless necessitate a shutdown. Your system cannot be hacked if it is not on. A shutdown buys you time to diagnose the attack more specifically. Remember that while your system will be unavailable to hackers, it will also be inaccessible to your loyal employees.

Sometimes the shutdown itself causes the irretrievable loss of data. This includes data related to the attacker. A savvy intruder will have erased incriminating files from your hard drive. Shutting down will also erase them from your computers' RAM.

When a total shutdown is ill advised, limiting an intruder's attack can also be achieved by severing the assaulted computer's connection with the local area network (LAN). The rest of your users will maintain their ability to connect with the local network. This is a preferred choice when you are certain that other systems have not been affected. If the security of the others is in question, however, the possibility remains that the intruder will continue his assault.

Sever the Connection

Another option is to disconnect your LAN from the Internet. This allows your employees to continue using their individual computers and also permits them to communicate with one another within the company networked computer system. Contact with systems outside the company network will be severed. The three major drawbacks to this alternative are these:

- The disconnection will result in loss of revenue. The severity of the loss will depend upon how much business is usually generated via the Internet connection and how long the system remains disconnected.

- It is possible that continued use of the system could create additional damage to the already crippled system.

- Continuing to use your system—even if you've altered or adjusted components—can also result in losing information about your attacker. If possible, all data needed to examine and diagnose the attack should be removed or gathered before you alter your system. As noted earlier, this information should be retained in the event that prosecution is pursued later.

Modify the Systems

Once hacked, your system must be altered to prevent a repeat occurrence. Other computers in your system, even if not yet affected by the attack, must be protected from an identical attack in the future. It is common for intruders to mark an area of your computer that they will later visit to regain entry. Hackers install "back doors" specifically so that they may use them at will to reenter your system. A famous Trojan horse program called Back Orifice uses this method to gain access via a seldom-used, therefore usually not examined, port (#31337).

Make alterations to your system only if you've been successful in determining exactly where you've been damaged. Knowing where you've been invaded will help you uncover how the intruder broke into your system. Recognizing the manner used by the attacker to enter will enable you to correct your vulnerabilities and prevent future invasions via the same access route.

Two important security alterations are the regular changing of user passwords (detailed later in this chapter and also covered in Chapter 3) and the habitual systematic installation of patches as soon as they become available. When these duties are neglected, they open the door for intruders. Additional modifications may be required. Other potential problems, along with their alterations, include:

- *Allowing unlimited users to access and enter your system.* You should allow only a limited number of employees to use your system. Rights of use can be granted on a hierarchical scale depending on an employee's rank in your organization. As mentioned previously, you can also limit the duration of access and control that sites may be accessed.

- *Retaining undiscovered software program codes on your system.* These sometimes carry out their malicious functions for an extended period without being detected. As their existence becomes known, these programs should be reinstalled as new or from trusted copies.

- *Harboring damaging files executed during start-up.* Since some Trojan horses and back doors are launched during the start-up portion (boot) of operation, you should examine your system to see if any are present and reinstall secure versions of boot time files once Trojan horses or back doors are detected.

- *Permitting deficient or lax operating methods.* If you already have in effect proper operating procedures, you must enforce them rigorously. An outline of proper operating procedures should be perfected if your company has not already developed one.

Reenter and Reinstall

When the area attacked cannot be specifically isolated, you may have to reenter all your user information and actively reinstall your operating system. Some companies go this route as a precautionary measure when they believe it is possible that not all hacker activity has been discovered or when they are not sure that they will be able to eradicate all of the intruder's vandalism.

When the decision has been made to reinstall, it is important that the operating system be installed directly from the manufacturer. An unaltered, reliable copy will also suffice.

Once you have reinstalled the operating system, you can then reinstall software programs, along with their current patches, as well. Continual testing of the systems during and after installation will uncover flaws and irregularities as they occur.

When the new operating system is in place, you must ensure that it is secure before you begin running it. A relatively easy way to add security is to change your user passwords for the new operating system. Hackers are known to use password-sniffing programs (designed to capture data packets in transit) to pilfer passwords. While employees may resist changing to new, unaccustomed passwords, the company must insist on and enforce this practice for heightened security. Internet intruders often form close associations and freely exchange information, including system addresses, system accessing information, and information about already debilitated and impaired systems, as well as the tools needed for launching attacks.

Use Log Files

Not all intruder effects are readily apparent. You must establish which files have been deleted, added to, or altered because of your attack.

Maintaining specific log details permits your company to assign individual compromised files to selected employees. Using your log, you must compare the system files after the attack with copies of the files made prior to the attack. Without these crosschecks or secure copies, you will need to inspect the log files manually. Network administrators will determine the assignation of files. The administrator should ensure that patches, repair options, and vendor solutions are available to those charged with file inspections.

Conduct Security Audits

Software programs are available to help your company manage the security inspection. See www.vigilante.com for one such company providing this type of product. As discussed in Chapter 5, numerous companies are available if you decide to outsource the task of auditing your Internet-enabled computers for vulnerabilities. Whether your company chooses to perform the audit in-house or with the use of outside experts, remember that certain items require careful consideration during the audit of an intruded system. Among the items to consider are the following:

- Install protection devices on vulnerable areas of your system. Establish where the devices are needed (on either new or additional sites). Devices already in place may require adjustments to make them more effective.

- Bring firewalls up to date with new versions, and patch them if patches are available.

- Bring intrusion detection software up to date, and patch it, as well. Establish whether your software should be adjusted. This includes detecting new attack signatures.

- Ascertain whether your notification procedures are effective in quickly alerting those in charge of network security.

Get Systems Back Online

Returning affected computers to normal operation permits your employees to once again have access to system resources. The most appropriate time to do this is after outside intruder access has been eliminated. This will help to prevent or limit any reoccurrence of the same or similar types of intrusions.

Use Only Trusted Backups

Utilize the most trusted and up-to-date backup to restore data. The restoration of data must be done meticulously, with a high level of assurance that the restored data were not affected by the attack. In any case, you need to have all users confirm that there have been no unexpected changes to their data and caution them about the danger of not performing these checks. Verify that all restored data that were located on affected computers were not influenced by the intruder's actions.

Reestablish LAN Connectivity

Reestablish the connection of the restored computer to the company's LAN. If your company LAN contained the affected computer and was therefore severed from the Internet, you can now reestablish the Internet connection to that LAN, allowing it once again to have Internet access.

Monitor Network Activity

Companies often can collect a good deal more information about a hacker or intruder when they return to the scene after the crime than they can directly gather following an intrusion. Following an attack, many companies implement improved security and monitoring procedures and equipment. By monitoring any failed login attempts or any attempts to access back door programs, companies may be able to "catch" the original intruder redhanded. Each such subsequent incident should be further evaluated.

Once intruders have infiltrated a computer system, word gets out, and the vulnerability of the system becomes known in the hacker population. Because of this, compromised systems become major targets for subsequent attacks.

Summary

Despite the publicity generated by hackers and viruses, many people and organizations are negligent when it comes to adequately securing their Internet-enabled computers and networks. When a computer or network has been compromised, the following steps should be followed:

    ✓ Initially, all members of the company should be notified as soon as a breach is discovered to allow them to take immediate action and to prevent further damage. Management, security and law enforcement should also be notified.

✓ After a breach, all information gathered must be preserved for future reference. By examining collected data, security personnel can learn about and correct any holes that are found.

✓ After a breach has occurred, the system must be altered to prevent a repeat occurrence. Two examples of system alterations are the changing of passwords (this actually should be done periodically under normal circumstances, as well) and the regular installation of all available software patches.

✓ System administrators and those in charge of security should analyze log files before and after an attack.

✓ Security audits should be done both physically and by using software specifically developed for the task. While some companies conduct audits in-house, many companies prefer to outsource this onerous task.

✓ Getting systems online and returning computers to normal operation will permit employees to have system access and become productive once again.

✓ Only the most trusted and up-to-date backups should be used to restore data. It is important to verify that any restored data was not influenced by outside actions.

Cybercrime

10

As the number of Internet users worldwide continues to grow, so too will the accounts of cyber-related criminal activity. As in the population of any growing metropolis, in the ever-expanding realm of cyberspace, there are those who operate within the boundaries of societal laws and morality and those who do not. Any crime committed with the use of a computer is generally considered a cybercrime. These include age-old crimes like theft, fraud, and forgery, which can be perpetrated without the use of a computer. New crimes such as cyberstalking, which can be committed only via computer, are also counted as cyber-crimes.

It is an unfortunate fact that Web sites are regularly attacked. Many who conduct e-business on the Internet are plundered by e-pirates, often without their knowledge. Even when victims are aware they've been preyed upon, they often do not report the crime. The global economy has felt the impact as the tentacles of the cybercrime monster spread over the World Wide Web.

The free-wheeling Internet has no direct police force dedicated to protecting unsuspecting victims from cybercrime. This anarchical, unregulated "Mad Max" environment strengthens the resolve of those who operate outside the law. Legal systems, both domestic and international, have not yet met the challenge of keeping up with the new era of crime on the Internet. Several well-known cases (including those of Dave LaMacchia , Kevin Mitnick, and Jake Baker, defendants in trials involving cybercrimes) point to the need for specific laws geared toward crimes perpetrated with the use of the Internet.

While there are several government agencies that can be called upon once an attack has occurred, Internet users must fend for themselves in order to achieve any real level of protection against violations via cybercrime. Remember that the Internet is a public network consisting of millions of interconnected users who exchange and share information (sometimes private), buying and selling products and services. Users do not know who's watching them or when and if a hacker may strike. The invasions that garner the most press and are universally feared are those perpetrated by miscreants who engineer network break-ins and criminally misuse credit card information (commit fraud).

Credit Card Fraud

Nearly anonymous thieves are making fraudulent online purchases every day with the use of credit cards. It is not unheard of for crooks to know more about a legitimate cardholder than does the credit card company.

Using someone's credit card fraudulently is considered a form of identity theft. Merchants lose millions of dollars doing business on the Internet with these criminals. When a valid credit card number is used fraudulently (whether the transaction occurs in person or in cyberspace), the rightful cardholder is usually not liable for more than $50. This is a leftover aspect of credit card purchasing procedures developed before the advent of Internet commerce, when merchant and buyer closed the deal in person; signing a credit card purchase agreement in person affords the buyer less anonymity than does an online purchase. The merchant's liability remains the same whether the purchase is made in person or via the Internet. The merchant is usually required to reimburse the card-issuing bank for fraudulent purchases (with additional service fees, to boot). Companies that lose money in this fashion are seeking to limit their losses by understanding how fraudulent credit card numbers are obtained and by using improved methods for verifying purchaser identities.

In some instances, the credit card numbers used by thieves are not numbers in existence for making purchases. Illegal, bootleg software programs are available that can produce effective, yet false credit card numbers. These numbers will likely be accepted if other purchaser information passes merchant inspection.

Whether the credit card numbers are software generated or pilfered from valid cardholders from online databases, merchants should be alert to the possibility of a fraudulent purchase when the order or request originates from a free or Web-based address. Orders that originate from e-mail-forwarding addresses should also be suspect. Most fraudulent orders come from such addresses, since they are virtually anonymous and impossible to trace.

Some businesses find that simply requesting a faxed photocopy of the credit card as well as the cardholder's signature deters criminal credit card use. Companies should request the customer's name, mailing address, and telephone number and then verify that these (1) actually exist and (2) are not false. The order should be suspect if the telephone number is not in service or is not operational. Merchants should also be suspicious of buyers who request that orders be shipped to post office boxes or to foreign countries.

Most of the time, of course, the people placing orders are honest, reliable cardholders. Protecting the information these customers send to your business is as important as verifying their identity. Encryption is a key element of secure transactions. As explained in Chapter 7, using secure socket layer encryption ensures that the information exchanged during your e-commerce transaction remains private. Using digital certificates (also explained in detail in Chapter 7) ensures the consumer that you are a valid business. Secure electronic transaction (SET), as described in Chapter 7, currently provides the ultimate in secure transactions. In its present state, however, SET requires too much input from the average consumer and is therefore of limited benefit in current e-commerce.

See Appendix B for more information on credit card fraud and identity theft.

Network Break-Ins

Experienced computer hackers can enter your system through computers that are physically distant from your network. Called "crackers," they use software programs to break in and plant viruses and worms, install back doors and Trojan horses, and steal valuable (and also invaluable) information.

Social Engineering

Some hackers dupe or mislead a company employee in order to break into the organization's network. By misrepresenting themselves as repairmen or technicians who need a password in order to get started or by acting as a colleague who's forgotten his password, hackers often easily get the information they're after. Hackers call this manipulation social engineering.

A break-in does not always result in the perpetration of other criminal acts. Nevertheless, the practice itself is illegal. Break-ins are not always discovered, and enforcement of the law remains difficult.

Defacing Web Pages

Once hackers have gained access to a Web page, they are free to change all or parts of its content at will. Defacing Web pages can range from mischievous pranks to alterations that result in major damage. The *New York Times* and the CIA are just two of the many organizations that have been targeted in this manner.

Password Sniffing

Sniffing is a popular form of attack among crackers. Like spoofing (explained later), password sniffing is often the first part of a more elaborate Internet crime. Crackers use programs to obtain the passwords and names of Internet users as they access their network or the Internet. These programs, called password sniffers, keep lists of each user and her password. Crackers can then gain access to confidential and private areas by masquerading as the legitimate user. Once admitted into the system, the trespasser is free to meander at will.

Spoofing

As the name implies, spoofing is the technique by which a cybercriminal electronically alters his computer to masquerade as a different computer (the victim). This is accomplished by modifying the packet headers so that it appears they're coming from a trusted port. Spoofing is used to enter a restricted system to which the victim computer has access. It is often the first part of more elaborate Internet crimes. Software tools such as WinRoute Professional by Tiny Software, Inc. (www.tinysoftware.com), which provide packet filtering to block incoming spoofing packet attacks, are available.

E-Mail Bombs

Internet e-mail bombs are cybercrimes that are the result of sending massive amounts of e-mail messages to a mail server or servers. They are considered a form of cyberstalking (other cyberstalking practices are explained later in this chapter). The servers are "bombarded" with mail. The vast number of duplicate e-mails is intended to overwhelm servers that lack the capacity to handle so many messages at once. Servers characteristically crash or freeze as a result of the onslaught. A reboot usually corrects the problem. The problem, therefore, sounds easy enough to fix. The downtime before the reboot or other corrective measure is taken may be lengthy, however, if adequate staff are not available to quickly tackle the problem. As a result, although they are not directly damaging, e-mail bombs can overwhelm the recipient's personal account on the server and have the potential to shut down entire systems, making the server unavailable to its other users, as well. If companies use the server to conduct e-commerce, they will suffer serious financial losses if clients and customers cannot contact them.

E-mail bombers are usually young men in their late teens who enjoy causing Internet mischief. E-mail bombing takes no special training or computer-hacking ability. Any run-of-the-mill computer user can send them.

Chain Bombs

Less common and more complicated than ordinary e-mail bombs are chain bombs. With chain bombs, massive numbers of e-mails are sent to the first link (mail server) on a chain program (script) created by the bomber. If the first server is overwhelmed during the onslaught and shuts down, the remaining messages are automatically directed to the second server on the chain. The bombing continues to all servers included on the script. If a server successfully handles the e-mail, the bomb is then delivered in its entirety to the next address on the chain. In this way, either a percentage or the entire bomb is always delivered to attack multiple servers.

Like regular e-mail bombs, chain bombs cripple servers by causing a total denial or delay of mail service. Those in charge of the mail server must separate the bomber's e-mail messages from the permitted, trustworthy messages. While culling the messages is time-consuming, it must be done in order to clear the malicious messages from the system. If the mail server is restarted without clearing these messages, the bombing will begin again with the next server on the chain.

Error Message Bombs

This type of bombs exploits the error message feedback system of the bomb recipient's mail server. The server is fooled into believing its legitimate user has sent an undeliverable e-mail message. The bomber achieves this by composing a message that he knows is undeliverable. The bomber removes his own return address from the message and replaces it with the (return) address of the victim. Once the message is sent and deemed undeliverable, the victim's mail server generates an error message and sends it to the victim. In the case of an error message bomb, massive amounts of error messages are returned to the victim. The unsuspecting victim, who has sent no such messages, may find his e-mail box disabled by the flood of error messages and his mail server incapacitated, as well.

Logic and Time Bombs

Logic and time bombs can wreak as much havoc as Trojan horses. Both logic and time bombs can be written months or even years before they are activated. Both of these bomb types remain hidden, idle, and inactive until they are triggered by the appearance or disappearance of a certain type of data. Logic bombs can be set off, for example, if the name of a particular new client is added to a customer list or if an employee's name is removed from the company's benefits program. Time bombs, on the other hand, are activated when a certain date or time registers on the computer host's calendar or clock. The infamous Michelangelo virus, for example, was imbedded in a time bomb, which was set to become active on March 6, Michelangelo's birthday. Once detonated, these bombs can generate a variety of damage from mere nuisances to the corruption of data.

Cyberstalking

Stalkers on the Internet are those who use computers to threaten their victims. A broad term, cyberstalking includes falsifying e-mail source addresses and sending unwanted files, messages, and threats. Making inappropriate comments and requests in chat rooms (i.e., not following the rules of netiquette) and posting a victim's private information (address, e-mail address, telephone number, and even photographs) on the Internet are considered cyberstalking.

Victims of cyberstalkers are usually inexperienced computer beginners. They sometimes unwittingly encourage a stalker by responding to negative messages. Evading stalkers is best achieved by leaving online conversations when they take an improper turn and by not providing personal information to strangers on the Internet.

Identity Theft

Identity theft is the criminal use of someone else's identity. Illegal in any form, identity theft becomes a cybercrime when a computer is used to commit the theft. Traditional crimes such as tampering with bank accounts are now being perpetrated via the Internet. Typical crimes taking place in cyberspace include appropriating funds from victims' bank accounts, obtaining credit under fraudulent pretenses, and accessing victims' credit cards and bank cards. Some thieves even have accounts with telephone companies and other utilities to obtain or steal services paid for by an unsuspecting third-party victim.

Thieves do not always steal identities with the intent of financial gain. Identity theft can be used to tarnish a victim's financial standing; a spiteful or disgruntled cybercriminal, for example, may decide to file for bankruptcy while posing as the victim.

Internet Piracy

Internet piracy is the act of using the Internet to illegally copy or distribute pirated materials. The Internet is also used to sell, buy, and advertise pirated software. Copying software is relatively easy to do and has become so commonplace that it is estimated that billions of dollars are lost as a result.

Trading pirated software on the Internet is a cybercrime. Hundreds of thousands of sites are dedicated to selling pirated software as authentic at ridiculously low (and sometimes steep) prices. Sometimes the pirated software reproductions operate as well as the originals, but the pirated versions usually cost a great deal less. Sometimes, instead of receiving bogus software programs, consumers receive nothing at all. With dealers easily setting up professional-looking sites (and just as easily closing up shop) on the Internet, dissatisfied consumers have little recourse. The consumer isn't the only one losing money in these schemes. Legitimate software publishers are losing enormous amounts of money due to loss of sales.

Software pirates often pose as liquidators who are offering discounted software in a collaborative effort with the publisher. They often try to fool consumers into believing they're legitimately selling discontinued or liquidated software from bankrupt companies. Online auction sites are notorious for selling bootleg and pirated software to unsuspecting buyers over the Internet.

Consumers can gain a slight measure of assurance by obtaining and keeping details about the merchant and sale (address, telephone number, order numbers, order confirmation messages, and company return policies). Another way to investigate the merchant is to call the software publisher directly. It can advise consumers as to whether the site is that of an authorized dealer (if it maintains such relationships) and can inform consumers of the usual selling price of the software. As with dealings anywhere, if it sounds too good to be true, it usually is. Let the buyer beware!

Cyberfraud

Cyberfraud is another broad term that encompasses both new schemes seen only on the Internet and scams that were seen in market-places in days of yore. The Internet has created almost boundless op-portunities for legitimate businesses and consumers and, of course, for ever-present criminals, as well. Internet frauds have an easy time broadcasting their swindles to unsuspecting victims. Although the magazine, newspaper, radio, and television media screen the advertis-ing that they put out, the Internet offers no such safety net.

For small investments of time and money, scammers reach thou-sands of people by creating Web sites, appearing on online auctions, engaging in online chats, and sending out large numbers of advertis-ing e-mail messages. Consumers in the know are skeptical and wary of the claims made in such venues. No filter, router, software program, or firewall can take the place of good common sense when it comes to protecting oneself from frauds on the Internet.

Included in cyberfraud are pyramid investment schemes, fraudu-lent contests and sweepstakes, Internet telephone scams, "off-shore" scams, unrealistic travel offers, stock-trading scams, and bogus work-at-home and other business opportunities. We next examine a few.

Pyramid Schemes
In this classic get-rich-quick scheme, participants are promised large sums of money for bringing in new recruits who pay to join the organi-zation. Since the potential is there to recruit thousands over the In-ternet, these schemes flourish there. The Internet affords anonymity and the ability to quickly "close up shop" once the pyramid caves in.

Long on promises but short on details, pyramid schemes are presented as games, chain letters, mail order companies, investment firms, and buying clubs. (Internet users should remain alert, because these "opportunities" often arrive as e-mail messages.) In reality, no goods are usually sold. The promoters (a few scammers) reside at the top of the pyramid and recruit others to get money into the program. The cost of entering the pyramid is steep. Containing elements of a lottery, these schemes are considered illegal and in violation of the Postal Lottery Statute.

Sometimes pyramid schemes are thinly disguised in e-mail messages offering memberships in "free merchandise clubs." After paying a membership fee, the consumer is offered free goods for bringing in new participants. Like other pyramid schemes, these cons eventually collapse.

The actual retail selling of legitimate products is obviously not illegal. Recruiting large numbers of additional distributors for profit in the manner of pyramid schemes *is* illegal.

Internet Telephone and Cable Scams

One of the most notorious Internet telephone scams used a Trojan horse program to bilk unsuspecting Internet users out of hundreds of thousands of dollars (exact figures are not known, since such crimes are often underreported). Two Long Island Internet service providers (ISPs) were prosecuted for this crime. While visiting one of the several sites involved, a visitor would be offered free viewing of pornographic pictures. To display the pictures, viewers needed to download a Windows 95 software viewer (not an untoward request, since downloads are made from the Internet by surfers all the time). While the downloaded program placated the viewer with a pornographic photo, behind the scenes another (malevolent) program was at work. The second program muted the viewer's modem (so that it could not be heard making its telltale clicking and screeching sounds); disconnected the user from his ISP; and dialed a phone number in Moldova, a former Soviet republic. A computer in Moldova answered the call and reconnected the user with the site he was visiting. As long as the viewer had his computer on, while surfing other sites, and even when the computer was offline, the international phone call continued (at a cost of about $2 per minute). The call finally terminated only when the modem or computer was actually turned off.

This telephone-rerouting scam is estimated to have resulted in the billing of nearly one million calling time minutes. To help prevent you from falling victim to such crimes, it is wise to use one of the better-known established ISPs.

Cable service is sometimes included in Internet scams. E-mail messages arrive that offer inexpensive do-it-yourself assembly kits for cable signal descramblers. The scammers promise that the consumer will be able to receive cable television broadcasts without paying subscriber charges. Unfortunately (or fortunately!), the descrambler will not do the job it was touted to do (and not because the assembly instructions weren't followed correctly). Suffice it to say that theft of cable broadcasts is illegal.

Internet Investment Scams

Investment frauds that were once perpetrated in person or by mail and telephone are now also being carried out on the Internet in a variety of settings. Chat forums offer a relaxed and anonymous atmosphere, while extravagant Web pages often exude a veneer of wealth and indulgence. Newsletters and bulletin boards can impart a feeling of relevance to a company and its stock. These Internet investment-pushing sites are often created and maintained with little cost and work. Legitimate company sites and their logos and trademarks have been spoofed, fooling misguided victims into investing with confidence.

Online investment scammers find many of their victims by sending spam to hundreds of thousands of Internet users. Although most users are not lured in by the spam, if enough of them (even just a fraction of a percentage) fall prey, the scammers have succeeded.

Unlike spammed messages, online investment newsletters have the benefit of being viewed by people who have chosen to display them. While legitimate newsletters provide valuable data about companies for investors, disreputable investment newsletters act more like free (sometimes) advertising. In some cases, newsletters are produced by writers who are paid to praise a company and to advocate the purchase of the company's stock. By falsifying information, they promote stocks with little or no value. Writing for investment newsletters for pay is not illegal per se. However, these writers are supposed to divulge by whom and how much they've been paid. These writers are well compensated if investors buy into their exaggerations and lies and invest in the company stock. Online investment newsletter readers are cautioned to stick to reputable newsletters that publish unbiased and, if possible, independently researched company and stock descriptions.

Bulletin boards are another venue for online investment fraud. On these boards, users can read the reviews and opinions of other investors. Again, while most postings are probably legitimate, the bulletin board's anonymity makes for easy misuse. Companies and their stocks can be hyped and so-called confidential information about the company's new acquisitions, new technologies, or new inventions is disclosed and shared (with thousands of other visitors!). Bogus press releases inform visitors about the company's supposed impending new product lines and other false information. Fake upbeat reviews from supposedly satisfied stockholders add to the charade. It may seem that lots of different people are posting great reviews of a stock, but those reviews may actually come from just one (very interested) promoter.

In "offshore" investing schemes, online investors are encouraged to join with others in forming an offshore bank or financial institution that will produce large, risk-free, and, more important, tax-free rates of return. Their Web sites usually do not provide an easily verified company identity with address and telephone number. Investors should avoid Web sites that do not allow users to print or save a record to confirm the deal. In these schemes, initial investors are rewarded with money invested by later entrants; satisfied that their "bank" is a success, they invest yet more money and in earnest convince others to join, too. Investors should approach offers to invest outside the country, whether internationally or offshore, with caution and diligence, because U.S. law enforcement is limited in its ability to prosecute foreign scams.

Certain small public companies are not required to register with the Securities and Exchange Commission (SEC). Successful online investing with companies that do not file regular reports with the SEC requires serious commitment in terms of research. Consider this quotation from the SEC Web site, www.sec.gov: "The difference between investing in companies that register with the SEC and those that don't is like the difference between driving on a clear sunny day and driving at night without your headlights." All potential investors should take these steps before committing funds:

- Verify claims made by the company or by the company's promoters (e.g., by checking out their new products, looking into new contracts).

- Contact other people or organizations that the company claims to have done business with to prove that the company is indeed operational.

- If possible, investigate those in charge of the company to be sure they haven't been involved in or convicted of illegal activities.

- Examine the company's financial statements.

With any form of investing, if the promised return seems inconceivable in relation to the requested investment, the possibility of investment fraud should be considered. Please refer to Appendix C for a prepared statement from the Federal Trade Commission on Internet fraud.

Work-at-Home Scams

Like their traditional counterparts, Internet work-at-home scams offer remuneration for easy or little work. Instead, these "opportunities" frequently result in little or no earnings! Claiming that no experience is necessary, in some cases the scams require the victim to spend large sums of money to purchase supplies and then to produce a product that will be paid for by a company. After victims have invested their time and money, the company declines the product, stating that it does not fulfill their requirements.

Envelope-stuffing scams are different in that they ask the victim to recruit others (much like in a pyramid scheme). After an initial small monetary outlay, victims are surprised to receive instructions on how to place (or send) envelope-stuffing (e-mail) advertisements of their own, advertisements like the one they answered. If victims want to earn any money with this "opportunity," they will have to continue the scam and cheat unsuspecting, like-minded respondents.

Before the Internet, the victim/perpetrator did in fact stuff envelopes—with the instructions for ad placing, that is!

Online Service Offers

When they tell consumers they'll receive, perhaps, 500 free surfing hours for signing up with them, many ISPs are being deliberately deceitful. The providers neglect to mention that those 500 hours must be used within thirty days. Consumers can find this information only if they've read the fine print in the service agreement. Since this practice is not illegal and not fraudulent, even some popular, well-known ISPs have been guilty of this deception.

While 500 hours sounds like many days' or weeks' worth of surfing, it amounts to more than sixteen and a half hours per day during a thirty-day period. Yes, more than sixteen hours for one day is plenty, but obviously this level of service does not fulfill the needs of most consumers. If they take full advantage of their free hours, consumers are left with just over seven hours per day to go to work or school, never mind eating and sleeping! Maybe the premise is that they'll be so thrilled by their service that they won't require much else in their lives.

In the unlikely event that consumers exceed the 500 free hours during the thirty-day trial membership period, they are sometimes charged a monthly membership fee. Once the consumer has signed on for a free trial period, many companies automatically start charging their monthly membership fee after thirty days. It is the consumer's responsibility to take action to cancel the free membership before the thirty-day trial period ends.

In the case of some lesser-known ISPs, short-term free trials are actually just a means for cyberscammers to get your credit card information.

Before consumers decide to become members, they should make sure that their dial-up connection will be established using a local telephone number. The more choices offered by the server provider, the more likely it is that a local number will be available.

Travel Offers

Sometimes scams arrive in the guise of unsolicited e-mail messages congratulating Internet users on winning a trip. While these vacations are not free, their cost is low enough that they should be suspect. Consumers should remain aware that unsolicited e-mails are usually a part of commercial mass mailings and that statements indicating the recipient was "specifically chosen" are bogus.

Vague descriptions of hotel lodgings, conveniences, and services can deceive consumers into paying for the "luxury vacation." The beachfront views may be on the shores of an uninviting river or lake, not the ocean. Faced with these shabby surroundings upon arrival, some consumers feel obligated to pay (sometimes handsomely) for better accommodations. The vacation scammers can further rip off consumers by charging additional fees for travel with certain numbers of guests or with children or by tacking on added charges for travel during certain time periods. Consumers are best served by arranging their travel plans and accommodations using reputable airline carriers, cruise ships, hotel chains, or travel agencies.

Industrial Espionage

When corporations engage in cyberspying on other corporations, it is difficult to determine and prosecute those who are guilty. In fact, unless illegal methods are used to gain the intelligence, the spying in and of itself may be perfectly legal, if not totally ethical. Generally, information is regarded as public if an organization has not made reasonable attempts to keep it secret. Competitive intelligence can develop into industrial espionage. Not only are businesses spying on the corporate competition, but so too are the governments of nations. From a political standpoint, a nation's reward for industrial espionage can come in the form of superiority over another country in a particular industry. The information gathered may help it achieve a higher level of national security; in addition, nations can sell such information to yet other nations for profit.

Unlike ordinary hackers, who operate independently at home or in small groups, paid industrial cyberspies have the backing and support of large organizations and unlimited supplies of state-of-the-art equipment. The Internet has made it easier for spies to infiltrate the information files of networked corporations from both inside and outside their network boundaries. Industrial cyberspies can penetrate these networks from remote locations anywhere in the world. They need be present only in a virtual (electronic) sense.

An added incentive for engaging in industrial economic espionage via the Internet is that often organizations do not even know their systems have been breached. Cyberspies are experts at covering their tracks. Even when corporations are aware they've been the victims of an intrusion, they're often unable to tally how much, if any, revenue was lost in the aftermath. In some instances, disks or computer parts are stolen and the crime is described as a burglary, with those reporting it oblivious to the fact that, more important, valuable information was stolen.

While hackers play a large role in cyberspying, industrial espionage succeeds well with the use of a company's employees. Whether current or temporary employees, partners or subcontractors, the people already in an organization usually have the easiest time accessing privileged (and therefore valuable) information.

While some employees (acting as agents) knowingly and willingly sell confidential corporate information, others unwittingly allow this information to escape. As mentioned earlier in this chapter, cyberspies have been known to enter offices posing as computer technicians who need a password in order to get to work repairing or upgrading an office computer. They've masqueraded as colleagues from another department who've forgotten their password. Many cyberspies have obtained passwords or other information by simply requesting it from an employee over the telephone.

For obvious reasons, former employees, especially disgruntled former employees, pose a great threat, because they sometimes actively seek to leak or make public organizational information in an effort to retaliate or obtain revenge. In some instances, former employees take information with them that will win them superior employment opportunities with competing corporations or that will be useful in starting their own organizations in the same industry.

Cybercrime Synopsis

With the number of cybercrime criminals ever on the increase, users of the Internet must be vigilant at all times. Failure to take precautionary and proactive measures raises the continued risk of being trespassed or surveilled.

Abusers of the Internet have proved to be a varied bunch with motives ranging from greed to need; some believe in their own innocence, while others evince a feeling of justification. Some hackers are convinced that if a computer system *can* be infiltrated, then it *deserves* to be infiltrated (or, "I hacked it because it was there"). Others suppose that if they haven't stolen from unwitting users or damaged their systems, their hacking is a benign diversion. Another justification is that they're actually providing a learning lesson in that they point out to organizations or individuals that they're vulnerable. Gee, thanks!

Regardless of motivation, as long as there is an Internet, there will be hackers. For every sophisticated counteractive device developed by those in the security industry, there is a new, equally sophisticated hacker looming in the shadows. Alert and studied watchfulness will go a long way in protecting the business and home user from the depredations of unwanted cyberintruders.

The Future of the Internet: IPv6 and WAP

As the science of Internet security develops, the new protocol known as IPv6 will be one of the most important influences. While this may be a bold statement, numerous Internet engineers concur. The Internet requires the more refined aspects of IPv6 to make up for the various shortcomings of IPv4, the current version of Internet Protocol.

IPv6 ensures with a high margin of certainty that data packets have originated with the host declared in the source address of the Internet Protocol (IP) packet and have not been tampered with or altered in transit. IPv6 provides data confidentiality using a special feature called header extension that allows end-to-end encryption to occur directly at the network layer of the Transmission Control Protocol (TCP)/IP protocol model. IPv6 uses a new IP packet structure wherein individual packets have authentication and confidentiality capabilities built directly in.

The Driving Force of IPv6

Because of the rapid growth of the Internet in recent years, IPv6 was developed as a means of overcoming the limitations in IPv4 that were becoming evident. While IPv6 is not a panacea for all the shortcomings of the Internet, it does address many of the problems that hinder the rapid expansion of the Internet today and in the future. Numerous organizations have adopted a "laissez-faire" attitude toward the change-over to IPv6. Their approach is, "why bother changing over if we already have sufficient IP addresses allocated to us?"

One good reason for change is that IPv6 is not simply IPv4 with a few bells and whistles attached. IPv6 is a completely new and secure way of using IP in the future. Its developers have seen the sometimes-failed expectations of the Internet and have come to its rescue with a protocol that will be able to handle almost unlimited address space and also be able to handle the dramatically increased global IP traffic of the future.

Another advantage of IPv6 is the use of secure routing protocols. Routing protocols are procedures used by routers to communicate or "talk" to one another for purposes of network maintenance. Routers maintain constant contact with one another across the Internet in order to determine the most efficient path for routing IP data packets (known as path determination). This process is insecure under IPv4, since it lacks encryption. IPv6 allows this procedure to occur in an encrypted format.

The Internet of the future will boast increased use of instantaneous transactions as intranets, extranets, and the Internet all blend into one homogeneous data transport system. The Internet of the future will carry vast amounts of information that will certainly include media-rich, bandwidth-intensive audio and video data.

IPv6 also attempts to get a handle on one of the currently biggest administrative dilemmas: how to properly configure the network. Many organizations today use a static addressing scheme in which lots of the computers or nodes of a network have a "fixed" address assigned to them. IPv6 effectively deals with how addresses are assigned and helps to automate and simplify the process.

Fear of Change to IPv6

Some people fear that the switchover from IPv4 to IPv6 will be instantaneous. They envision a chaotic switchover that will result in several months of frustration. In reality, this won't be the case, because the two very different systems can easily "speak" each other's language. Interoperability was a big issue in the development of IPv6 because its creators were well aware of the firmly entrenched IPv4 network currently in use by millions on the Internet. In order for networks that currently use IPv6 to be able to transfer data to other IPv6 networks, they must use the largely IPv4-based Internet. IPv6 capabilities allow this to occur over the IPv4 network.

The Goal: A New System

In the early 1990s, the Internet Architecture Board (IAB) began to investigate the rapid expansion of the Internet and the obvious shortage of Internet addresses. In Chapter 1 we discussed the fact that IPv4 has only a limited number of IP addresses available for public and private use. Because it uses a 32-bit dotted decimal number system, there are a limited number of numerical combinations available for issue to organizations and to the public. Since these IP addresses were rapidly becoming depleted, a new scheme was needed to increase the number of addresses available to organizations while still keeping within an IP infrastructure. Though the IAB anticipated that the number of people and groups using the Internet would increase dramatically, it never anticipated the other types of IP-enabled devices that have popped up in recent years. Web-enabled cell phones and Internet household appliances are just two of the devices that have exacerbated the problems associated with IP addressing. Cars of the future will also be Internet enabled, which will inevitably lead to an even greater increase in the number of IP addresses required. Additional IP-enabled devices are sure to appear in the near future, and these will consume the remaining supply of IPv4 addresses.

Enter the Internet Engineering Steering Group

Because of the anticipated increase in the number of IP addresses in use, the Internet Engineering Steering Group (IESG) assigned a group of engineers the monumental task of developing and defining the next generation of Internet protocols. Those engineers, along with others, studied the limitations of IPv4 and the enhancements to the TCP often used along with IP for Internet data transmission. After a few years of consideration, Requests for Comments (RFC) 1752 was issued in 1994. (As explained in Chapter 1, RFCs are official documents regarding Internet-related technologies.) Following RFC 1752, other RFCs (see Table 11-1) were issued to help finalize the IPv6 blueprint. In April 1994, RFC 1933 helped to address the all-important issue of the changeover to the IPv6 addressing system.

A Little More About IPv4

Having served the public for the better part of twenty-five years, IPv4, the workhorse of the Internet, is starting to show signs of age. As the use of the Internet continues to increase, the limitations of IPv4 become more apparent. Its lack of built-in security requires that users obtain separate, third-party software (encryption) products (e.g., public key encryption) to achieve protection and privacy. While large business organizations may enforce security, the average public Internet user does not bother to acquire additional protection. IPv6 incorporates the added security of encryption as a built-in component, obviating the need for users to make this modification. While IPv4's 32-bit address range allows for a potential four billion hosts, the way that IPv4 is structured greatly reduces the possible number of hosts. Class A addresses, those that allow for millions of hosts, are already taken. Nearly all Class B and C addresses are also taken. Keep in mind that, for every domain name system (DNS) name on the Internet (e.g., www.mydomain.com), there is a corresponding 32-bit numerical IP address associated with it. Once the numerical addresses run out, there is no way to assign IP addresses to new domain names. As a result, domain names with corresponding numerical IPv4 addresses associated with them also begin to suffer.

Domains like .com, .org., .net, or .gov are almost depleted. Consequently, you may have noticed new domain extensions beginning to appear. Domains like .tv or .fm (television or radio) are emerging like weeds. All these new top-level domains will require associated corre-

(text continues on page 180)

Table 11-1. Requests for commands for IPv6.

RFC1809
Using the Flow Label Field in IPv6. C. Partridge. June 1995. (Status: INFORMATIONAL)

RFC1881
IPv6 Address Allocation Management. IAB & IESG. December 1995. (Status: INFORMATIONAL)

RFC1887
An Architecture for IPv6 Unicast Address Allocation. Y. Rekhter, T. Li, Editors. December 1995. (Status: INFORMATIONAL)

RFC1924
A Compact Representation of IPv6 Addresses. R. Elz. April 1996. (Status: INFORMATIONAL)

RFC1933
Transition Mechanisms for IPv6 Hosts and Routers. R. Gilligan, E. Nordmark. April 1996. (Status: PROPOSED STANDARD)

RFC2080
RIPng for IPv6. G. Malkin, R. Minnear. January 1997. (Status: PROPOSED STANDARD)

RFC2081
RIPng Protocol Applicability Statement. G. Malkin. January 1997. (Status: INFORMATIONAL)

RFC2133
Basic Socket Interface Extensions for IPv6. R. Gilligan, S. Thomson, J. Bound, W. Stevens. April 1997. (Status: INFORMATIONAL)

RFC2147
TCP and UDP Over IPv6 Jumbograms. D. Borman. May 1997. (Status: PROPOSED STANDARD)

RFC2185
Routing Aspects of IPv6 Transition. R. Callon, D. Haskin. September 1997. (Status: INFORMATIONAL)

RFC2292
Advanced Sockets API for IPv6. W. Stevens, M. Thomas. February 1998. (Status: INFORMATIONAL)

RFC2374
An IPv6 Aggregatable Global Unicast Address Format. R. Hinden, M. O'Dell, S. Deering. July 1998. (Obsoletes RFC2073) (Status: PROPOSED STANDARD)

(continues)

Table 11-1. (Continued).

RFC2375
> IPv6 Multicast Address Assignments. R. Hinden, S. Deering. July 1998. (Status: INFORMATIONAL)

RFC2428
> FTP Extensions for IPv6 and NATs. M. Allman, S. Ostermann, C. Metz. September 1998. (Status: PROPOSED STANDARD)

RFC2460
> Internet Protocol, Version 6 (IPv6) Specification. S. Deering, R. Hinden. December 1998. (Obsoletes RFC1883) (Status: DRAFT STANDARD) (in French)

RFC2461
> Neighbor Discovery for IP Version 6 (IPv6). T. Narten, E. Nordmark, W. Simpson. December 1998. (Obsoletes RFC1970) (Status: DRAFT STANDARD)

RFC2462
> IPv6 Stateless Address Autoconfiguration. S. Thomson, T. Narten. December 1998. (Obsoletes RFC1971) (Status: DRAFT STANDARD)

RFC2463
> Internet Control Message Protocol (ICMPv6) for the Internet Protocol Version 6 (IPv6) Specification. A. Conta, S. Deering. December 1998. (Obsoletes RFC1885) (Status: DRAFT STANDARD)

RFC2464
> Transmission of IPv6 Packets Over Ethernet Networks. M. Crawford. December 1998. (Obsoletes RFC1972) (Status: PROPOSED STANDARD)

RFC2465
> Management Information Base for IP Version 6: Textual Conventions and General Group. D. Haskin, S. Onishi. December 1998. (Status: PROPOSED STANDARD)

RFC2466
> Management Information Base for IP Version 6: ICMPv6 Group. D. Haskin, S. Onishi. December 1998. (Status: PROPOSED STANDARD)

RFC2467

Transmission of IPv6 Packets Over FDDI Networks. M. Crawford. December 1998. (Obsoletes RFC2019) (Status: PROPOSED STANDARD)

RFC2470

Transmission of IPv6 Packets Over Token Ring Networks. M. Crawford, T. Narten, S. Thomas. December 1998. (Status: PROPOSED STANDARD)

RFC2471

IPv6 Testing Address Allocation. R. Hinden, R. Fink, J. Postel (deceased). December 1998. (Obsoletes RFC1897) (Status: EXPERIMENTAL)

RFC2472

IP Version 6 Over PPP. D. Haskin, E. Allen. December 1998. (Obsoletes RFC2023) (Status: PROPOSED STANDARD)

RFC2473

Generic Packet Tunneling in IPv6 Specification. December 1998. (Format: TXT = 77,956 bytes) (Status: PROPOSED STANDARD)

RFC2474

Definition of the Differentiated Services Field (DS Field) in the IPv4 and IPv6 Headers. K. Nichols, S. Blake, F. Baker, D. Black. December 1998. (Obsoletes RFC1455, RFC1349) (Status: PROPOSED STANDARD)

RFC2491

IPv6 Over Non-Broadcast Multiple Access (NBMA) Networks. G. Armitage, P. Schulter, M. Jork, G. Harter. January 1999. (Status: PROPOSED STANDARD)

RFC2492

IPv6 Over ATM Networks. G. Armitage, P. Schulter, M. Jork. January 1999. (Status: PROPOSED STANDARD)

RFC2497

Transmission of IPv6 Packets Over ARCnet Networks. I. Souvatzis. January 1999. (See Also: RFC1201) (Status: PROPOSED STANDARD) sponding IP addresses. As address spaces expand to a 128-bit scheme, users will have an apparently infinite amount of available address spaces for Internet use. With the proliferation of IP-enabled devices, this increase couldn't arrive at a better time.

More Space for All

Initially, it might appear that it's unnecessary to have such a vast number of IP addresses. Having more address space available on the Internet will reduce congestion. With less congestion, it will be easier to route data packets, which will reduce the number of lost packets, making it harder for anyone other than the intended recipient to receive those packets and thereby improving privacy and security on the Web. Remember, IPv6 will allow nearly every electronic device currently in use, plus any future devices yet to be invented, the option of having a built-in IP address for Internet use.

Another important issue relating to the overallotment of address spaces is the simplification of routing functions. It may appear that more addresses mean more complicated routing functions. While this may superficially be true, more address space actually does not cost more in terms of resource usage. Engineers can create a multilevel hierarchical means of IP address distribution. This multilevel approach will allow routers to operate faster because the overhead required and the amount of space needed to hold the routing tables will be decreased. As all the major router manufacturers know, anything that can lessen the burden of path determination and packet switching (routing functions) will be a boon to the Internet. Finally, while the transition from IPv4 to IPv6 should go smoothly and with relatively few glitches, having underestimated the growth of the Internet in the past, we don't want to have to endure this again in the future—certainly not for a long while.

A Different Addressing Scheme

In Chapter 1 we discussed the IPv4 addressing scheme. IPv4 uses a 32-bit dotted decimal number such as 123.45.67.89 to represent a node on an IP network. Each of the number groups (e.g., the 123) represents an octet, or 8-bit number. It therefore follows that four of these 8-bit octets make up a 32-bit address (8 × 4 = 32). This numbering convention has been used and accepted since the development of IPv4. It doesn't look so bad when it's a 32-bit number. Now imagine a 128-bit dotted decimal number. It would look like something like this: 123.45.67.89.10.11.12.13.14.15.16.17.18.19.20.21. Quite a large and unruly figure. Network administrators might end up with the onerous task of trying to keep track of this type of address for all their workstations and servers.

Mercifully, the engineers behind IPv6 have decided that the days of dotted decimal numbers are over. Since all dotted decimal numbers are converted to a computer's native tongue (binary code) before the computer can use them, changing the addressing scheme would affect only the human component of manipulating these numbers.

IPv6 simplifies the scheme used for IP addressing. The engineers behind IPv6 decided to use a hexadecimal system of numbering for their IP addresses. Now, without trying to give you a lesson on binary or hexadecimal numbering, accept that a hexadecimal numbering system is a base 16 numbering system. It uses the numbers 1–10, and then, instead of the numbers 11–16, it uses the letters A through F. Ten numbers plus six letters gives you a base 16 numbering system. For those who are interested in this sort of thing, Windows comes with a built-in calculator that can convert from binary or decimal numbers to hexadecimal ones. Using hexadecimal addressing, a very long 128-bit dotted decimal number would read: FFEE:A357:BE8A:B638:8F56:B00F:9555:87E0. This is still a large number (8 groups), but it's smaller than its dotted decimal (16 group) cousin. Instead of dots, colons separate each 16-bit grouping. There are other shortcuts available in a hexadecimal system that allow for the consolidation of a group of zeros. For example, 0000 can be represented as :: (double colons), and a number such as 0055 becomes just 55.

New IP Headers

One of the biggest deficiencies of IPv4 was that the headers used in its implementation were complex in nature. Headers are found at the beginning of data packets and contain the information that computers and routers need to deliver them to their proper destination. As discussed earlier, the IPv6 headers contain extensions that allow for the mandatory use of authentication and data confidentiality through encryption. IPv4 used ten fields in its header plus the two (32-bit) address fields (source and destination). If these were to grow at the same exponential rate as the numerical address, the header would become overwhelmingly large and complex. Under IPv6, there are two larger 128-bit addresses (source and destination) but only six fields in its header. Overall, the entire IPv6 address header size comes in at only twice that of the IPv4 address, even though the two address fields used in the header are four times larger than those used under IPv4. In other words, IPv6 is "relatively" smaller and yet more efficient.

Autoconfiguration

The architects behind IPv6 decided from the start to design the new system to be as easy to implement as possible. Their goal for IPv6 was to allow a host to ascertain all the necessary information and parameters needed to allow it to successfully connect to the Internet. Computer users familiar with IPv4 are familiar with a similar process, known as Dynamic Host Configuration Protocol (DHCP). With DHCP, the address for the host is dynamically assigned by another device (such as a router or a server) on the network. Under IPv6, the host should be able to create a unique IP address and find the IP address of a router even if that router or server is not located on the same local network. Autoconfiguration will be a boon to the variety of Internet-enabled appliances that will soon populate our homes.

The Big Shift

One significant shift that will occur in Internet traffic of the future is an enormous increase in media-rich data, including data such as high-bandwidth audio and video data. While IPv4 can adequately handle this type of content, IPv6 will contain new features that will allow it to more effectively handle traffic of this nature. IPv6 will allow Internet traffic to be routed according to priority, so that the most important data will be delivered first. This will be achieved by enabling the system to recognize an assigned value in the data packet header. The packet will be then routed as determined by its assigned importance level. The various applications being used (e.g., an e-mail program) will define what priority the information packet should have and then adjust the header accordingly.

IPv6—More Secure Than IPv4

One of the biggest complaints about the Internet is its lack of security at its most basic level. IPv6 was designed with security in mind right from its humble beginnings. The encapsulated security payload (ESP) and the authentication header (AH) are the means to provide security in Internet protocol. The use of these two mechanisms provides authentication, integrity, and confidential security services under IP. Both ESP and AH are defined for use in IPv6 and IPv4. The main distinction is that the use of these security mechanisms is optional for IPv4 but mandatory for IPv6.

IP security design is defined as a fundamental part of IPv6. Thus, every vendor who claims to offer IPv6-compliant implementation must support both AP and ESP. The AH confirms that the originator stated is indeed the true sender of an IP packet (message). The AH ensures that the data have not been tampered with or altered en route to their final destination. While the AH does provide authentication of the entire contents of an IP packet, it does not authenticate the entire header itself. While this demonstrates a lapse in security, it is not usually significant, because the "payload" portion of the packet (the message) is most often what requires the greatest security. Using AH in this manner is known as transport mode.

AH can also be supplied in what is known as tunnel mode. Tunnel mode creates a brand-new IP header that "wraps around" or encompasses the original IP packet, including the IP transport mode header. Under tunnel mode, AH authenticates the entire IP packet, including headers, which means the receiving computer can determine whether any portion of the packet has been altered in transit. The advantage of using tunnel mode is that it entirely protects the encapsulated IP packet.

The ESP is part of the Internet protocol security architecture known as IPSec. ESP's main purpose is to support privacy and integrity of the IP data packet. Like AH, ESP may operate in either transport or tunnel mode and often operates in conjunction with AH because, unlike AH, which provides only authentication and integrity, ESP encrypts the contents of the message, providing added confidentiality.

Support for the AH and ESP does not mean that these services must be used, but it does mean that they must be available for use, if needed. When security is provided at the basic Internet level, it becomes a standard service that all applications can call upon and use. Applications can request that the operating system set up a security relationship before making a TCP or User Datagram Protocol (UDP) connection.

Although the use of encryption and authentication adds to IP processing costs and increases the time it takes for two IP nodes to communicate, the protection provided by these security services is worth the price.

Internet Household Appliances

We are about to see the dawn of a completely new era on the Internet. The time is rapidly approaching when numerous devices (e.g., household appliances, automobiles, and personal communication systems) will become extensions of the Internet. We've already seen the addition of Web-enabled cell phones. Other devices are sure to follow. These devices might take the form of Internet-enabled microwave ovens with small liquid crystal display (LCD) screens, which will allow users to send and receive e-mail or look up recipes at a favorite culinary Web site. Other devices might include alarm clocks that will not only wake us up but also provide us with real-time news feeds and current events. Heating and cooling systems controlled from remote locations could serve to help cut energy costs. The growing popularity of Internet-controlled household appliances will, however, increase the risk that hackers will sabotage not only one's computer but one's entire home.

For the consumer, this will mean that the Internet will become an integral part of daily life. In much the same way that television changed family entertainment, Internet appliances will affect the way we live and communicate. By permitting several different household devices to communicate with one another, the Internet will reduce the time it takes to perform many of the tasks that currently occupy much of our time. In the end, household Internet appliances and devices will be limited only by the imagination of their inventors. The imaginations of those with malicious intent will be fueled, as well. As new technologies develop, new means of thwarting their saboteurs will surely follow.

The Providers

Service providers, device manufacturers, and those who build and handle everything from machinery and appliances to automobiles and consumer goods have essential roles to play in the establishment of this new era of the Internet. They will be both the facilitators and the benefactors. With the increased need for Internet security, these manufacturers and organizations will be forced to help pave the transition from IPv4 to the more secure IPv6.

In the past few years, numerous noteworthy changes have materialized, pointing to the growing momentum for the new-era Internet. A universal, available way to conduct global relations and business has developed. New developments in computer technology have allowed computers and communication devices to become smaller, more powerful, and less expensive. New developments in computer networking have improved the ability of businesses and users to communicate and conduct business with one another, mostly through their networked PCs. Companies of all sizes are starting to wonder what effect the new-era Internet will have on other types of IP-enabled communication devices. These devices can come in the form of Pocket PCs, Palm Pilots, or even the Web-enabled cell phones that are becoming so popular.

Other Internet-Enabled Devices

In the very near future, even automobiles and security monitoring systems will all be linked to the Internet in one way or another. Inexpensive Internet devices that allow users to surf the Web and send/receive e-mail will become more popular. These types of devices usually cost less than the typical PC and are smaller and easier to use. Their small size and ease of use will make them more attractive to anyone with limited space or those fearful of trying new technology. Because of the rapid expansion of the Internet into personal devices, security will always be a major concern. Internet appliances and intelligent devices will provide new, extended services that PCs do not by serving a specific and distinct function. This will not eliminate the need for personal computers, which provide such a vast array of functions. What Internet appliances will do is create a shift away from the PC as a Web-surfing tool and offer an alternative means of personal and business communication.

The more devices that use IP, the greater the number of available targets for hackers to attack. This reality will inevitably lead to more increased concerns about security. New protocols such as IPv6 will help to make Internet security a basic component of these new devices.

Future Trends

Current trends suggest that there will be a large increase in the number of state-of-the-art devices being internetworked over the next few years. Companies are determined to form strong bonds with their customers and are especially attracted to those consumers who embrace new technology. A strong connection with those consumers ensures that they will continue doing business as both the company and the consumer adapt to emergent technology. In this new era, Internet devices of all types will work together to automatically complete tasks with minimal human intervention. This network of interconnected devices will result in considerable gains in productivity and will have a dramatic effect on the way e-commerce is conducted.

The Internet Will Be Willing and Ready

Much of the necessary network infrastructure and networking technologies have already been developed and put into place. Participants in the new era of the Internet will be able to inexpensively take advantage of this already-existing internetworking infrastructure. Fiberoptic cables and faster routers and switches, using new technologies currently under development, will enable communications to move across the Internet at speeds far greater than they travel today. The world will truly have become a smaller place.

Wireless Handheld Devices

The number of wireless handheld devices is growing at an astonishing rate. It's no wonder; with the advent of Wireless Access Protocol (WAP) standards, that more and more vendors are beginning to produce practical wireless devices. Web-enabled cell phones, Palm Pilots (and their clones), and pocket personal computers all allow for mobile, wireless Web content. We are on the cusp of a wireless revolution as more and more vendors begin to produce handheld devices capable of accessing the Internet. Wireless devices are becoming popular with people in all sorts of business because the equipment offers convenience coupled with mobility. Almost anything you can now do on your desktop computer you will be able to accomplish with a wireless device. The underlying protocol that allows all of these wireless devices to communicate with each other and with the Internet is known as WAP.

Wireless Access Protocol

WAP is the de facto standard for providing wireless Internet communications across a wide platform of devices. WAP is an open standard that allows mobile wireless users to interact with information in a wide variety of formats. WAP devices can be anything from cell phones and pagers to personal digital assistants. WAP can be used by virtually any operating system and is designed to work with a wide variety of wireless networks.

One of the nice features of WAP is that it allows interoperability of multiple vendors' products. WAP is a broad and scaleable protocol that uses a client server approach. Users access their Web content directly from a WAP gateway residing at their Internet service provider (ISP). The services and applications that many of these wireless devices utilize actually reside in the Web servers that deliver the wireless Web content and not in the devices themselves. As a result, WAP-enabled wireless devices do not generally need a great amount of computing power or resources to adequately perform their functions.

WAP's Humble Beginnings

The WAP specification initiative began in June 1997, and the WAP Forum was founded in December 1997. The WAP Forum drafted a global wireless protocol specification for all wireless networks. This universal specification puts all players on the same page. WAP enables manufacturers, network operators, content providers, and application developers to offer compatible products and secure services on all devices and networks. This results in greater universal access to information.

WAP Forum

The WAP Forum is the industry association that is responsible for developing and fostering the growth of the WAP, an open, global standard that allows mobile users of wireless hand-held devices to securely access and interact with Internet/intranet/extranet content, applications, and services. The WAP Forum comprises more than 600 members, representing 99 percent of the handsets sold worldwide and more than 300 million global subscribers. Members include worldwide handset manufacturers, carriers, infrastructure providers, software developers, and other wireless solution providers. For more information about the WAP Forum, including a current listing of its members, visit www. wapforum.org.

The forum came about when several wireless phone manufacturers (Motorola, Phone.com [now known as openwave.com], Ericsson, and

Nokia) united to form the WAP Forum. Others in the wireless industry soon joined the effort in linking wireless users to the Internet. The leader in this group is Phone.com, which produces UP.Link, the most popular of the WAP gateways.

The members of the WAP Forum bring with them more than 300 million subscribers. They all work to offer solutions to some of the common problems within the wireless industry. Goals of the WAP Forum include the following:

- Providing digital cell phones and other wireless devices with the most sophisticated information services and Internet content available

- Establishing a worldwide wireless protocol specification that will enable diverse wireless systems to interoperate

- Encouraging the development of applications and materials that span a variety of wireless networks and equipment

- Supporting and broadening the scope of current standards and technology

- Acting as the specifications body driving mobile Internet-specific technologies across all relevant industry segments

- Developing mobile Internet specifications

- Collaborating with related standardization activities to advance the mobile Internet experience

How WAP Works

The natural differences between wired and wireless networks established the need for WAP. Current wireless networks (unlike wired networks) have restrictions that limit their ability to operate successfully using the TCP/IP stack. TCP/IP is inadequate when used with the limited bandwidth and high-latency times of wireless networks, together with the restrictive processing and display capabilities of wireless equipment. WAP emerged after attempts were made to provide Internet service to wireless phone users. Procedures were needed that would overcome the shortcomings of cellular networks, and WAP was born.

WAP is a protocol for communications that supports various applications. It is a less complex protocol than TCP/IP. As such, it doesn't consume all of the lower bandwidth and tax the undersized processors of the wireless devices used for Internet connection.

By eliminating three-way Challenge Handshake Authentication Protocal (CHAP) of TCP/IP, WAP dramatically reduces overhead. Instead, the Wireless Transport Protocol (WTP) layer of the WAP uses a lower overhead request-response procedure employing the T/TCP (TCP for Transactions).

The five layers of the WAP stack (with brief descriptions) are:

Wireless Session Protocol (WSP): Provides WAP Application Layer with the interface required for two session services to be conducted.

Wireless Transaction Protocol (WTP): Provides lightweight, transaction-oriented protocol for limited-power mobile-client implementations suitable for operation over networks with limited bandwidth availability.

Wireless Transport Layer Security (WTLS): Based on secure socket layer (SSL) technology, WTP is optimized for use over the limited bandwidth communication channels often used in wireless communications. It also provides several additional security features including:

—Authentication and Data Integrity (achieved by ensuring that data are unchanged in transit).

—Privacy (by ensuring that the data transmitted are secure and free from prying eyes).

—Denial-of-Service (DoS) Protection (by protecting the upper layer protocols). This makes typical DoS attacks harder to achieve.

Wireless Datagram Protocol: Provides a connectionless, unreliable datagram server similar to the way UDP does in the TCP/IP model.

Wireless Application Environment (WAE): Offers the software platform environment for the application software to utilize. WAE is built into the self-styled microbrowser program, working much like normal WWW browsers that interpret hypertext markup language (HTML) and JavaScript. WAE consists of wireless markup language (WML), WMLScript, and Wireless Telephony Application.

Wireless device users access their Web content directly from the WAP gateways located at their ISP. The WAP gateway provides several functions that enable the wireless Internet model to become a true working model. Among these are the following:

- Completing the WAP stack

- Converting markup languages

- Providing wireless access control

- Translating protocols

- Caching Internet data

- Providing domain name resolution services (DNS)

- Providing security for wireless transmission

It is evident that the WAP gateway provides most of the tools necessary for accomplishing wireless transmission of Internet data. Since most wireless devices have relatively small LCD screens, a Web page that was originally designed to be displayed on your PC's monitor is not displayed properly on a wireless Internet device. As a result, the HTML code that makes up much of a Web page must be converted and somewhat truncated (made smaller) to fit on the small screen of a wireless device. Since most wireless Internet devices use the WML to display Web pages in their "miniature" Web browsers and the Internet uses mostly HTML, the WAP gateway must also convert Internet data from HTML format to the WML format so that the Web page is displayed properly on the wireless device.

WAP Security

With the proliferation of wireless devices, the issue of security has become the top concern of wireless users. Many of the types of technologies that help protect us on wired connections to the Internet can help protect us in the "unwired" world. Unlike their tethered counterparts, however, wireless devices have additional security concerns. How can users be assured that sensitive data will remain confidential while being transmitted across open airwaves?

Many of the manufacturers of wireless devices (e.g., Ericsson and Nokia) understand the public concern regarding this pressing issue. As a result, many of the larger wireless manufacturers have developed several security protocols to ensure the safety of data transmitted via wireless networks. In October 1999, for example, Ericcson and Sonera SmartTrust jointly developed a digital signature technology for use on WAP-enabled cell phones in order to increase security. SmartTrust is a leader in security solutions for the mobile or wireless Internet. Several wireless security products are available on its Web site, www.smart trust.com.

One of the few factors with the potential to limit the rapid expansion of wireless technology is the public's uneasiness over the ability of wireless devices to provide adequate security. With the development of powerful, proven security protocols, users can feel sure that the data they transmit over the wireless Internet are as secure as those sent over its wired counterpart.

The "Safety Net" Protocols

WAP security is normally implemented using two protocols. These two protocols, working hand-in-hand, help to provide secure transmission of data to users of WAP-enabled devices. The two leading security protocols and their functions are as follows:

Secure Hypertext Transport Protocol. The WAP gateway connects to Internet Web servers using a secure connection the same way that your desktop Web browser makes a secure Hypertext Transfer Protocol connection. To achieve the highest level of security, the WAP gateway must exist on the same local network as the Web server. A good example of this type of setup is a company that wishes to allow outside salespeople to access its company intranet via their WAP-enabled phones.

WTLS. The WAP gateway encrypts all Web data before they are sent over the wireless network. The mobile phone can then decrypt the content and display the information to the user. WTLS incorporates security features that are based upon the established TLS protocol standard. These include data integrity checks, authentication, and privacy on the client side of the WAP gateway. WTLS provides a secure network connection session between a WAP device and a WAP gateway.

The Hole in WAP

Any communications between WAP-enabled wireless devices and WAP servers are secured by an integrated encryption technology called WTLS. As soon as the Internet connection is established, it is usually protected by the SSL protocol (the Internet standard for the encryption of data sent between two computers). There is, however, one drawback in the application of this procedure. When Internet data are transferred from the WTLS protocol to the SSL protocol, they are done in an unencrypted format, briefly leaving data exposed to hackers. Some security experts have expressed concern over this security hole. Openwave.com (a merger of the former Phone.com and Software.com) produces and sells solutions that eliminate the WAP security hole. More information about these products is available at the company's Web site, www. openwave.com.

The WAP Gateway Target

When WAP gateways of wireless Internet service providers are not strong enough to support secure Web transactions, they become a prime target of hackers. These hacker attacks can originate anywhere on the Internet. To fully shield their wireless clientele, businesses may wish to use third-party software programs for securing WAP servers.

New Technologies

The next-generation Internet will be a more secure, higher-bandwidth version of the current Internet. With the gradual switchover to IPv6 and the development of newer (and less expensive) broadband technologies, many devices will be reengineered and adapted for Internet use. Television, the gold standard of family entertainment for the past fifty years, will eventually give way to the expanded diversions of the Internet. The Internet of the future will deliver a broad spectrum of audio and visual entertainment, with computers and televisions blending into single devices. This Internet-enabled computer/TV will allow users to interact with information providers in real time, allowing for a more rich and dynamic experience.

Companies across the United States are helping to lay the foundation for this new Internet. Fiberoptic technology will play a large role in making it happen. Fiberoptic cables capable of carrying enormous amounts of data will be the roadways for the information superhighway. Using modulated lightwaves to provide digital connectivity, fiberoptic technology will be used for years to come. Many of the Internet's biggest players, such as Cisco, IBM, and Agilent Technologies, are developing special equipment (optical routers and high-speed switches) to handle the enormous bandwidth of the future. With all the advantages these growing technologies will provide, we can rest assured that Internet security will remain in the forefront and be a top priority as we proceed through the new millennium.

How to Report Internet-Related Crime

Internet-related crime, like any other crime, should be reported to appropriate law enforcement investigative authorities at the local, state, federal, or international levels, depending on the scope of the crime.

Citizens who are aware of federal crimes should report them to local offices of federal law enforcement. Some federal law enforcement agencies that investigate domestic crime on the Internet include the Federal Bureau of Investigation (FBI), the United States Secret Service, the United States Customs Service, the United States Postal Inspection Service, and the Bureau of Alcohol, Tobacco and Firearms (ATF). Each of these agencies has offices conveniently located in every state to which crimes may be reported. Contact information regarding these local offices may be found in local telephone directories. In general, victims may report federal crime to the local office of an appropriate law enforcement agency by telephoning and requesting the "Duty Complaint Agent."

Each law enforcement agency also has a headquarters (HQ) in Washington, D.C., which has agents who specialize in particular areas.

For example, the FBI and the U.S. Secret Service both have headquarters-based specialists in computer intrusion (i.e., computer hacker) cases. In fact, the FBI HQ hosts an interagency center, the National Infrastructure Protection Center (NIPC), which was created just to support investigations of computer intrusions. The NIPC Watch number for reporting computer crimes is 202-323-3205. The U.S. Secret Service's Electronic Crimes Branch may be reached at 202-435-5850. The FBI and the Customs Service also have specialists in intellectual property crimes (i.e., copyright, software, movie, or recording piracy, trademark counterfeiting). Customs has a nationwide tollfree hotline for reporting at 800-BE-ALERT, or 800-232-2538.

The FBI investigates violations of federal criminal law generally. Certain law enforcement agencies focus on particular kinds of crime. Other federal agencies with investigative authority are the Federal Trade Commission and the U.S. Securities and Exchange Commission.

To determine some of the federal investigative law enforcement agencies that may be appropriate for reporting certain kinds of crime, please refer to the following table:

Type of Crime	Appropriate Federal Investigative Law Enforcement Agencies
Computer intrusion (i.e., hacking)	FBI local office; NIPC (202-323-3205); U.S. Secret Service local office
Password trafficking	FBI local office; NIPC (202-323-3205); U.S. Secret Service local office
Copyright (software, movie, sound recording) piracy	FBI local office; if imported, U.S. Customs Service local office (800-BE-ALERT, or 800-232-2538)
Theft of trade secrets	FBI local office
Trademark counterfeiting	FBI local office; if imported, U.S. Customs Service local office (800-BE-ALERT, or 800-232-2538)
Counterfeiting of currency	U.S. Secret Service local office; FBI local office

Child pornography or exploitation	FBI local office; if imported, U.S. Customs Service local office (800-BE-ALERT, or 800-232-2538)
Child exploitation and Internet fraud matters that have a mail nexus	U.S. Postal Inspection local office
Internet fraud	The Internet Fraud Complaint Center; FBI local office; Federal Trade Commission; if securities fraud, Securities and Exchange Commission
Internet harassment	FBI local office
Internet bomb threats	FBI local office; ATF local office
Trafficking in explosive or incendiary devices or firearms over the Internet	FBI local office; ATF local office

The Internet Fraud Complaint Center

The Internet Fraud Complaint Center is a partnership between the FBI and the National White Collar Crime Center (NW3C). Their Web site provides a mechanism for victims of Internet fraud to report online fraud to the appropriate law enforcement and regulatory authorities.

Identity Theft: The Crime of the New Millennium

Sean B. Hoar,
Assistant United States Attorney,
District of Oregon

The Nature of the Problem

Identity theft has been referred to by some as the crime of the new millennium. It can be accomplished anonymously, easily, with a variety of means, and the impact upon the victim can be devastating. Identity theft is simply the theft of identity information such as a name, date of birth, Social Security number (SSN), or a credit card number. The mundane activities of a typical consumer during the course of a regular day may provide tremendous opportunities for an identity thief: purchasing gasoline, meals, clothes, or tickets to an athletic event; renting

This appendix is from *USA Bulletin,* March 2001. Reprinted with permission.

a car, a video, or home-improvement tools; purchasing gifts or trading stock on-line; receiving mail; or taking out the garbage or recycling. Any activity in which identity information is shared or made available to others creates an opportunity for identity theft.

It is estimated that identity theft has become the fastest-growing financial crime in America and perhaps the fastest-growing crime of any kind in our society.

Identity Theft: Is There Another You?: Joint Hearing Before the House Subcomms. on Telecommunications, Trade and Consumer Protection, and on Finance and Hazardous Materials, of the Comm. on Commerce, 106th Cong. 16 (1999) (testimony of Rep. John B. Shadegg). The illegal use of identity information has increased exponentially in recent years. In fiscal year 1999 alone, the Social Security Administration (SSA) Office of Inspector General (OIG) Fraud Hotline received approximately 62,000 allegations involving SSN misuse. The widespread use of SSNs as identifiers has reduced their security and increased the likelihood that they will be the object of identity theft. The expansion and popularity of the Internet to effect commercial transactions has increased the opportunities to commit crimes involving identity theft. The expansion and popularity of the Internet to post official information for the benefit of citizens and customers has also increased opportunities to obtain SSNs for illegal purposes.

On May 31, 1998, in support of the Identity Theft and Assumption Deterrence Act, the General Accounting Office (GAO) released a briefing report on issues relating to identity fraud entitled "Identity Fraud: Information on Prevalence, Cost, and Internet Impact Is Limited." The report found that methods used to obtain identity information ranged from basic street theft to sophisticated, organized crime schemes involving the use of computerized databases or the bribing of employees with access to personal information on customer or personnel records. The report also found the following: In 1995, 93 percent of arrests made by the U.S. Secret Service Financial Crimes Division involved identity theft. In 1996 and 1997, 94 percent of financial crimes arrests involved identity theft. The Secret Service stated that actual losses to individuals and financial institutions which the Secret Service had tracked involving identity fraud totaled $442 million in fiscal year 1995, $450 million in fiscal year 1996, and $745 million in fiscal year 1997. The SSA OIG stated that SSN misuse in connection with program fraud increased from 305 in fiscal year 1996 to 1,153 in fiscal year 1997. Postal Inspection investigations showed that identity fraud was perpetrated by organized crime syndicates, especially to support drug trafficking, and had a nationwide scope. Trans Union Corporation, one of the three major national credit bureaus, stated that two-thirds of its consumer inquiries to its fraud victim department involved identity fraud. Such inquiries had increased from an average of less than 3,000 a month in 1992 to over 43,000 a month in 1997. VISA U.S.A., Inc., and MasterCard International, Inc., both stated that overall fraud losses from their member banks were in the hundreds of millions of dollars annually. MasterCard stated that dollar losses relating to identity fraud represented about 96 percent of its member banks' overall fraud losses of $407 million in 1997.

Victims of identity theft often do not realize they have become victims until they attempt to obtain financing on a home or a vehicle. Only then, when the lender tells them that their credit history makes them ineligible for a loan, do they realize something is terribly wrong. When they review their credit report, they first become aware of credit cards for which they have never applied, bills long overdue, unfamiliar billing addresses, and inquiries from unfamiliar creditors. Even if they are able to identify the culprit, it may take months or years, tremendous emotional anguish, many lost financial opportunities, and large legal fees to clear up their credit history.

How Does Identity Theft Occur?

Identity theft occurs in many ways, ranging from careless sharing of personal information to intentional theft of purses, wallets, mail, or digital information. In public places, for example, thieves engage in "shoulder surfing," watching you from a nearby location as you punch in your telephone calling card number or credit card number or listening in on your conversation if you give your credit card number over the telephone. Inside your home, thieves may obtain information from your personal computer while you are on-line and they are anonymously sitting in the comfort of their own home. Outside your home, thieves steal your mail, garbage, or recycling. Outside medical facilities or businesses, thieves engage in "dumpster diving," going through garbage cans, large dumpsters, or recycling bins to obtain identity information, which includes credit or debit card receipts, bank statements, medical records like prescription labels, or other records that bear your name, address, or telephone number.

In a recent case in the District of Oregon, a ring of thieves obtained identity information by stealing mail, garbage, and recycling material, by breaking into cars, and by hacking into Web sites and personal computers. The thieves traded the stolen information for methamphetamine, cellular telephones, or other favors. Before they were arrested, they had gained access to an estimated 400 credit card accounts and had made an estimated $400,000 in purchases on those fraudulently obtained accounts. One aspect of the case involved the theft of preapproved credit card solicitations, activating the cards, and having them sent to drop boxes or third-party addresses. Another scam involved taking names, dates of birth, and SSNs from discarded medical, insurance, or tax information and obtaining credit cards at various sites on the Internet. The thieves found most credit card companies to be unwitting allies. One of the thieves boasted about successfully persuading a bank to grant a higher credit limit on a fraudulently obtained credit card account. Another aspect of the case involved the use of a software application to hack into commercial Web sites or personal computers and mirror keystrokes to capture credit card account information. Two of the offenders were prosecuted federally for conspiracy to commit computer fraud and mail theft under 18 U.S.C. §§ 1030(a)(4), 371 and 1708, and consented to the forfeiture of computer equipment obtained as a result of the fraud-related activity pursuant to 18 U.S.C. § 982(a)(2)(B). One defendant was sentenced to serve a forty-one-month term of imprisonment and pay $70,025.98 in restitution. *United States v. Steven Collis Massey*, CR 99-60116-01-AA (D.Or. 1999). The other defendant was sentenced to serve a fifteen-month term of imprisonment and pay $52,379.03 in restitution. *United States v. Kari Bahati Melton*, CR 99-60118-01-AA (D.Or. 1999).

How Can Identity Theft Be Investigated and Prosecuted?

The investigation of identity theft is labor intensive, and individual cases are usually considered to be too small for federal prosecution. Perpetrators usually victimize multiple victims in multiple jurisdictions. Victims often do not realize they have been victimized until weeks or months after the crime has been committed and can provide little assistance to law enforcement. In short, identity theft has become the fastest-growing financial crime in America and perhaps the fastest-growing crime of any kind in our society, because offenders are seldom held accountable. Consequently, it has become a priority for the Departments of Justice and Treasury and the Federal Trade Commission (FTC) to pursue effective means of prevention, investigation, and prosecution of identity theft offenses. Toward that end, workshops were recently held for the purpose of identifying the best practices to combat identity theft, including remediation, prevention, and law enforcement strategies. Workshop participants included prevention specialists, federal agency representatives, state and federal investigators, and state and federal prosecutors.

The experience of workshop participants is that law enforcement agencies at all levels, federal and nonfederal, must work together investigating identity theft. Multiagency task forces have proven successful in investigating and prosecuting identity theft. By utilizing task forces, member agencies pool scarce resources to investigate and prosecute identity theft offenses and provide prevention training. Workshop participants also indicated that outreach to private industry is necessary as a prevention strategy, and it facilitates the identification of offenders.

Identity theft cases involving large numbers of victims present unique challenges. One challenge is communication with victims. Communication is necessary to obtain fundamental investigative information, including loss and restitution information. In complex cases, it is imperative to devise a system for communication with the victims at the outset of the case. The AUSA should work with victim/witness units to identify the best communication system for the case. The AUSA should also work with the system administrator to develop a link from the district's Web site for on-line communication with victims. The link can provide access to a database into which victims can enter case-related information. The link can also be used to provide updates on the status of the case. Notification to the victims regarding their use of the Web site can be provided through a form letter accompanying an investigative survey, which must be completed, in any event, to obtain loss and restitution information.

1. Federal Criminal Laws

There are a number of federal laws applicable to identity theft, some of which may be used for prosecution of identity theft offenses and some of which exist to assist victims in repairing their credit history. The primary identity theft statute is 18 U.S.C. § 1028(a)(7) and was enacted on October 30, 1998, as part of the Identity Theft and Assumption Deterrence Act (Identity Theft Act). The Identity Theft Act was needed because 18 U.S.C. § 1028 previously addressed only the fraudulent creation, use, or transfer of identification *documents*, and not the theft or criminal use of the underlying personal *information*. The Identity Theft Act added § 1028(a)(7), which criminalizes fraud in connection with the unlawful theft and misuse of personal identifying information, regardless of whether the information appears or is used in documents. Section 1028(a)(7) provides that it is unlawful for anyone who:

> knowingly transfers or uses, without lawful authority, a means of identification of another person with the intent to commit, or to aid or abet, any unlawful activity that constitutes a violation of Federal law, or that constitutes a felony under any applicable State or local law.

The Identity Theft Act amended the penalty provisions of § 1028(b) by extending its coverage to offenses under the new § 1028(a)(7) and applying more stringent penalties for identity thefts involving property of value. Section 1028(b)(1)(D) provides for a term of imprisonment of not more than fifteen years when an individual commits an offense that involves the transfer or use of one or more means of identification if, as a result of the offense, anything of value aggregating $1,000 or more during any one year period is obtained. Otherwise, § 1028(b)(2)(B) provides for imprisonment of not more than three years. The Identity Theft Act added § 1028(f), which provides that attempts or conspiracies to violate § 1028 are subject to the same penalties as those prescribed for substantive offenses under § 1028.

The Identity Theft Act amended § 1028(b)(3) to provide that if the offense is committed to facilitate a drug trafficking crime or in connection with a crime of violence or is committed by a person previously convicted of identity theft, the individual is subject to a term of imprisonment of not more than twenty years. The Identity Theft Act also added § 1028(b)(5), which provides for the forfeiture of any personal property used or intended to be used to commit the offense.

Section 1028(d)(3) defines "means of identification," as used in § 1028(a)(7), to include "any name or number that may be used, alone or in conjunction with any other information, to identify a specific individual." It covers several specific examples, such as name, Social Security number, date of birth, government-issued driver's license and other numbers; unique biometric data, such as fingerprints, voice print, retina or iris image, or other physical representation; unique electronic identification number; and telecommunication identifying information or access device.

Section 1028(d)(1) modifies the definition of "document-making implement" to include computers and software specifically configured or primarily used for making identity documents. The Identity Theft Act is intended to cover a variety of individual identification information that may be developed in the future and utilized to commit identity theft crimes.

The Identity Theft Act also directed the U.S. Sentencing Commission to review and amend the Sentencing Guidelines to provide appropriate penalties for each offense under Section 1028. The Sentencing Commission responded to this directive by adding U.S.S.G. § 2F1.1(b)(5), which provides the following:

(5) If the offense involved:

(A) the possession or use of any device-making equipment;

—the production or trafficking of any unauthorized access device or counterfeit access device; or

—the unauthorized transfer or use of any means of identification unlawfully to produce or obtain any other means of identification; or (ii) the possession of [five] or more means of identification that unlawfully were produced from another means of identification or obtained by the use of another means of identification, increase by 2 levels. If the resulting offense level is less than level 12, increase to level 12.

These new guidelines take into consideration the fact that identity theft is a serious offense, whether or not certain monetary thresholds are met. For most fraud offenses, the loss would have to be more than $70,000.00 for the resulting offense level to be level 12. U.S.S.G. § 2F1.1(b)(1)(G). In providing for a base offense level of 12 for identity theft, the Sentencing Commission acknowledged that the economic harm from identity theft is difficult to quantify and that, whatever the identifiable loss, offenders should be held accountable. Identity theft offenses will usually merit a two-level increase because they often involve more than minimal planning or a scheme to defraud more than one victim. U.S.S.G. § 2F1.1(b)(2). Identity theft offenses may also provide for two- to four-level upward organizational role adjustments when multiple defendants are involved. U.S.S.G. § 3B1.1.

The Identity Theft Act also directed the FTC to establish a procedure to log in and acknowledge receipt of complaints from victims of identity theft, to provide educational materials to these victims, and to refer the complaints to appropriate entities. The FTC has responded to this directive by developing a Web site, great educational materials, a hotline for complaints, and a central database for information. The Web site can be found at www.consumer.gov/idtheft. The hotline is 1-877-ID THEFT. Identity theft complaints are entered into Consumer Sentinel, a secure, on-line database available to law enforcement. The FTC has become a primary referral point for victims of identity theft, and a tremendous resource for these victims and law enforcement.

2. Other Federal Offenses

Identity theft is often committed to facilitate other crimes, although it is frequently the primary goal of the offender. Schemes to commit identity theft may involve a number of other statutes, including identification fraud (18 U.S.C. § 1028(a)(1)–(6)), credit card fraud (18 U.S.C. § 1029), computer fraud (18 U.S.C. § 1030), mail fraud (18 U.S.C. § 1341), wire fraud (18 U.S.C. § 1343), financial institution fraud (18 U.S.C. § 1344), mail theft (18 U.S.C. § 1708), and immigration document fraud (18 U.S.C. § 1546). For example, computer fraud may be facilitated by the theft of identity information when stolen identity is used to fraudulently obtain credit on the Internet. Computer fraud may also be the primary vehicle to obtain identity information when the offender obtains unauthorized access to another computer or Web site to obtain such information. These acts might result in the offender being charged with both identity theft under 18 U.S.C. § 1028(a)(7) and computer fraud under 18 U.S.C. § 1030(a)(4). Regarding computer fraud, note that U.S.S.G. § 2F1.1(c)(1) provides a minimum guideline sentence, notwithstanding any other adjustment, of a six-month term of imprisonment if a defendant is convicted of computer fraud under 18 U.S.C. § 1030(a)(4).

Several examples of how identity theft schemes may involve other statutes may be helpful. These include the case of an offender who fraudulently obtains identity information by posing as an employer in correspondence with a credit bureau. This offender might appropriately be charged with both identity theft under 18 U.S.C. § 1028(a)(7) and mail fraud under 18 U.S.C. § 1341. An offender who steals mail, thereby obtaining identity information, might appropriately be charged with identity theft under 18 U.S.C. § 1028(a)(7) and mail theft under 18 U.S.C. § 1708. The offender who fraudulently poses as a telemarketer, thereby obtaining identity information, might appropriately be charged with both identity theft under 18 U.S.C. § 1028(a)(7) and wire fraud under 18 U.S.C. § 1343.

3. Recent Federal Cases

A number of cases have recently been prosecuted under 18 U.S.C. § 1028(a)(7) including the following.

In the Central District of California, a man was sentenced to a twenty-seven-month term of imprisonment for obtaining private bank account information about an insurance company's policyholders, while serving as a temporary employee of the company. Thereafter, he used that information to deposit over $764,000 in counterfeit bank drafts and withdraw funds from accounts of policyholders. *United States v. Anthony Jerome Johnson*, CR 99-926 (C.D.Ca. Jan. 31, 2000).

In the District of Delaware, one defendant was sentenced to a thirty-three-month term of imprisonment and $160,910.87 in restitution, and another defendant to a forty-one-month term of imprisonment and $126,298.79 in restitution for obtaining names and SSNs of high-ranking military officers from an Internet Web site and using them to apply on-line for credit cards and bank and corporate credit in the officers' names. *United States v. Lamar Christian*, CR 00-3-1 (D.Del. Aug. 9, 2000); *United States v. Ronald Nevison Stevens*, CR 00-3-2 (D.Del. Aug. 9, 2000).

In the District of Oregon, seven defendants have been sentenced to imprisonment for their roles in a heroin/methamphetamine trafficking organization, which included entering the United States illegally from Mexico and obtaining SSNs of other persons. The SSNs were then used to obtain temporary employment and identification documents in order to facilitate the distribution of heroin and methamphetamine. In obtaining employment, the defendants used false alien registration receipt cards, in addition to the fraudulently obtained SSNs, which provided employers enough documentation to complete employment verification forms. Some of the defendants also used the fraudulently obtained SSNs to obtain earned income credits on tax returns fraudulently filed with the Internal Revenue Service. Some relatives of narcotics traffickers were arrested in possession of false documents and were charged with possessing false alien registration receipt cards and with using the fraudulently obtained SSNs to obtain employment. A total of twenty-seven defendants have been convicted in the case to date, fifteen federally and twelve at the state level.

4. Federal Credit Laws

It is important for training purposes and to assist victims in repairing damage to their credit history that prosecutors have at least a cursory understanding of credit laws that impact identity theft. The Fair Credit Reporting Act establishes procedures and time frames for correcting mistakes on credit records and requires that your record be provided only for legitimate business, credit, or employment needs. 15 U.S.C. § 1681 *et seq.* The Truth in Lending Act limits liability for unauthorized credit card charges in most cases to $50.00. 15 U.S.C. § 1601 *et seq.* The Fair Credit Billing Act establishes procedures for resolving billing errors on credit card accounts *if* the unauthorized charge is reported within certain time frames. 15 U.S.C. § 1666. The Fair Debt Collection Practices Act prohibits debt collectors from using unfair or deceptive practices to collect overdue bills that your creditor has forwarded for collection. 15 U.S.C. § 1692. The Electronic Fund Transfer Act provides consumer protections for transactions using a debit card or electronic means to debit or credit an account. It also limits a consumer's liability for unauthorized electronic fund transfers if the unauthorized transfer is reported within certain time frames. 15 U.S.C. § 1693. If an ATM or debit card is reported lost or stolen within two business days of the loss or theft, the losses are limited to $50.00. If reported after two business days but within 60 days of the first statement showing an unauthorized transfer, the losses are limited to $500.00. Otherwise, losses may only be limited by the amount obtained. 15 U.S.C. § 1693(g)(a).

5. State Criminal Laws

Most states have laws prohibiting the theft of identity information. Where specific identity theft laws do not exist, the practices may be prohibited under other state laws or the states may be considering such legislation.

How Can Identity Theft Be Prevented?

While it is extremely difficult to prevent identity theft, the best approach is to be proactive and take steps to avoid becoming a victim. As prosecutors, it is important to learn how to prevent identity theft in order to provide training to law enforcement and private industry. We can also complement the assistance to victims provided by our victim/witness units. A thorough guide to preventing and responding to identity theft can be found in Mari Frank and Beth Givens, *Privacy Piracy! A Guide to Protecting Yourself from Identity Theft*, Office Depot (1999). Related information can be found at www.identitytheft.org. The FTC has also published a helpful guide entitled *FTC, ID Theft: When Bad Things Happen to Your Good Name* (August 2000). This and related information can be found at www.consumer.gov/idtheft. Also, the United States Postal Inspection Service has produced an excellent video about identity theft entitled *Identity Theft: The Game of the Name.*

1. *Share identity information only when necessary.* Be cautious about sharing personal information with anyone who does not have a legitimate need for the information. For instance, credit card numbers should never be provided to anyone over the telephone unless the consumer has initiated the call and is familiar with the entity with which he is doing business. Likewise, SSNs should not be provided to anyone other than employers or financial institutions who need the SSN for wage, interest, and tax reporting purposes. Businesses may legitimately inquire about a SSN if doing a credit check for purposes of financing a purchase. Some entities, however, may simply want the SSN for recordkeeping purposes. Businesses may choose to not provide a service or benefit without obtaining a person's SSN, but the choice as to whom a SSN is provided should be exercised with caution. In the event an entity, such as a hospital or a Department of Motor Vehicles (DMV), assigns a SSN as a patient or client identification number, the customer should request that an alternative number be assigned.

2. *Exercise caution when providing identity information in public.* "Shoulder surfers" regularly glean such information for their fraudulent use. Be especially cautious when entering account information at an Automatic Teller Machine (ATM) or when entering long-distance calling card information on a public telephone. Likewise, be cautious when orally providing this type of information on a public telephone. Also, do not put identity information, such as an address or license plate number, on a key ring or anything similar that can easily be ob-

served or lost. Identity information on such objects simply provides thieves easier means of finding and accessing homes and cars.

3. *Do not carry unnecessary identity information in a purse or wallet.* According to the FTC Identity Theft Clearinghouse, the primary means for thieves to obtain identity information is through the loss or theft of purses and wallets. To reduce the risk that identification information might be misappropriated, carry only the identity information necessary for use during the course of daily activities, such as a driver's license, one credit or debit card, an insurance card, and membership cards that are regularly required for use. There should be no need to carry a Social Security card, or anything containing a SSN. Likewise, there should be no need to carry a birth certificate or a passport. These items should be kept under lock and key in a safe or a safety deposit box. Credit or debit cards that are not regularly used should also be removed from a purse or wallet. The fewer pieces of identification carried in a purse or wallet, the easier it is to identify an individual piece that may have been lost or stolen, and the easier the task of notifying creditors and replacing such information should a purse or wallet be lost or stolen.

4. *Secure your mailbox.* According to the FTC, the second most successful means for thieves to obtain identity information is through stolen mail. Many thieves follow letter carriers at a discreet distance and steal mail immediately after it has been delivered to a residential mailbox. Do not place outgoing mail in residential mailboxes. Doing so, especially raising a red flag on a mailbox to notify the postal carrier of outgoing mail, is simply an invitation to steal. Deposit outgoing mail in locked post office collection boxes or at a local post office. If you prefer to have mail delivered to your residential address, install a mailbox which is secured by lock and key. Promptly remove mail after it has been delivered to your mailbox.

5. *Secure information on your personal computer.* Similar to telephonic inquiries, credit card numbers should not be provided to anyone on the Internet unless the consumer has initiated the contact and is familiar with the entity with which he is doing business. In addition

to cautiously choosing with whom identity information is shared, computer users should install a firewall on their personal computers to prevent unauthorized access to stored information. A personal firewall is designed to run on an individual personal computer and isolate it from the rest of the Internet, thereby preventing unauthorized access to the computer. The user sets the level of desired security, and the firewall inspects each packet of data to determine if it should be allowed to get to or from the individual machine, consistent with the level of security. A firewall is especially necessary for Digital Subscriber Line (DSL), cable modem, or other "always-on" connections. There are a number of quality firewall software applications that can be downloaded as freeware from sites on the Internet.

     6. ***Keep financial and medical records in a secure location.*** Thieves may be more interested in identity information from which they can access credit than in physical property. It is important, therefore, to keep all financial and medical records, and any other information containing identity information, in a secure location under lock and key.

     7. ***Shred nonessential material containing identity information.*** All nonessential documentary material containing any type of identity information should be shredded prior to being placed in garbage or recycling. The term "nonessential" should be interpreted as anything that an individual or business is not required by law or policy to retain. For individuals this includes credit or debit card receipts, canceled bank checks and statements, outdated insurance or financial information, and junk mail, especially preapproved credit applications and subscription solicitations. For businesses or medical facilities, this includes receipts of completed credit or debit card transactions, outdated client files, or prescription labels. The best shredding is done through a cross-cut shredder which cuts paper into small pieces, making it extremely difficult to reconstruct documents. Expired credit or debit cards should also be cut into several pieces before being discarded.

     8. ***"Sanitize" the contents of garbage and recycling.*** All nonessential documentary material containing any type of identity information should be shredded before being placed in garbage or recycling. While junk mail or old financial documents may appear to be innocuous, they can be a gold mine when obtained by an identity thief.

9. *Ensure that organizations shred identity information.* Many businesses, firms, and medical facilities are not sensitive to privacy issues arising from discarded material. Many of these entities regularly dispose of material containing customer identity information (e.g., customer orders, receipts, prescription labels) into garbage cans, dumpsters, or recycling bins without shredding the material. Tremendous damage can be done by these practices. Customers of businesses, clients of firms, and patients of medical facilities should insist that all data be shredded before being discarded and that all retained data be kept in secure storage.

10. *Remove your name from mailing lists.* Removing a name from a mailing list reduces the number of commercial entities having access to the identity information. It also reduces the amount of junk mail, including preapproved credit applications and subscription solicitations, thereby reducing the risk that the theft of such mail will compromise privacy. Many financial institutions, such as banks and credit card companies, and even state agencies, market identity information of customers unless a request is received, in writing, that such information is not to be shared. Customers of such businesses and agencies should submit such requests, notifying the entity in writing of their desire to opt out of any mailing lists and to not have identity information shared.

To opt out of the mailing lists of the three major credit bureaus (Equifax, Experian, and Trans Union), call 1-888-5OPT-OUT. To opt out of many national direct mail lists, write the Direct Marketing Association, DMA Preference Service, P.O. Box 9008, Farmingdale, NY 11735-9008. To opt out of many national direct e-mail lists, visit www.e-mps.org. To opt out of many national telemarketer lists, send your name, address, and telephone number to the Direct Marketing Association, DMA Telephone Preference Service, P.O. Box 9014, Farmingdale, NY 11735-9014.

11. *Carefully review financial statements.* Promptly review all bank and credit card statements for accuracy. Pay attention to billing cycles. A missing bill may mean a thief has taken over an account and changed the billing address to avoid detection. Report any irregularities to the bank or credit card company immediately.

12. *Periodically request copies of credit reports.* Credit reports are available for $8.00 from the three major credit bureaus (Equifax, Experian, and Trans Union). Credit bureaus must provide a free copy of the report if it is inaccurate due to fraud and it is requested in writing. The reports should be reviewed carefully to make sure no unauthorized accounts have been opened or unauthorized changes made to existing accounts.

To order a report from Equifax, visit www.equifax.com, call 1-800-685-1111, or write P.O. Box 740241, Atlanta, GA 30374-0241. To order a report from Experian, visit www.experian.com, call 1-888-EXPERIAN (397-3742), or write P.O. Box 949, Allen, TX 75013-0949. To order a report from Trans Union, visit www.tuc.com, call 800-916-8800, or write P.O. Box 1000, Chester, PA 19022.

What Steps Should Be Taken by a Victim of Identity Theft?

When someone realizes she has become a victim of identity theft, she should take the following steps while keeping a log of all conversations, including dates, names, and telephone numbers. The log should indicate any time spent and expenses incurred in the event restitution can be obtained in a civil or criminal judgment against the thief. All conversations should be confirmed in writing, with the correspondence sent by certified mail, return receipt requested. All correspondence should be kept in a secure location, under lock and key.

First, the victim should contact the fraud departments of each of the three major credit bureaus (Equifax, Experian, and Trans Union), inform the representative of the identity theft, and request that a "fraud alert" be placed on her file, as well as a statement asking that creditors call the victim before opening any new accounts. This can help prevent an identity thief from opening additional accounts in the victim's name. The victim should inquire about how long the fraud alert will remain on the file and what, if anything, must be done to extend the alert if necessary. Copies of credit reports from the credit bureaus should also be ordered. The reports should be reviewed carefully to identify unauthorized accounts or unauthorized changes to existing accounts. Also, if the reports indicate that any "inquiries" were made from companies that opened fraudulent accounts, a request should be made to remove the "inquiries" from the report. A request should also be made for the credit bureaus to notify those who have received a credit report in the last six months and alert them to the disputed and erroneous information. The victim should request a new copy of the reports after a few months, to verify that the requested changes have been made and to ensure no new fraudulent activity has occurred.

To report fraud to Equifax, visit www.equifax.com, call 1-800-525-6285, and write P.O. Box 740241, Atlanta, GA 30374-0241. To report fraud to Experian, visit www.experian.com, call 1-888-EXPERIAN, and write P.O. Box 949, Allen TX 75013-0949. To report fraud to Trans Union, visit www.tuc.com, call 1-800-680-7289, and write Fraud Victim Assistance Division, P.O. Box 6790, Fullerton, CA 92634.

Second, the victim should contact the security or fraud departments for any creditors of accounts in which fraudulent activity occurred. The telephone numbers for these creditors can be obtained from the credit bureaus. Creditors can include businesses, credit card companies, telephone companies and other utilities, and banks and other lenders. All conversations should be confirmed with written correspondence. It is particularly important to notify credit card companies in writing because it is required by the consumer protection laws set forth earlier. The victim should immediately close accounts that have been tampered with and open new ones with new Personal Identification Numbers (PINs) and passwords.

Third, the victim should file a report with a local police department or the police department where the identity theft occurred, if that can be determined. The victim should obtain a copy of the police report in the event creditors need proof of the crime. Even if the thief is not apprehended, a copy of the police report may assist the victim when dealing with creditors. The victim should also file a complaint with the FTC. The FTC should be contacted on its Identity Theft Hotline toll free at 1-877-ID THEFT (438-4338), TDD at 1-202-326-2502; by mail at FTC Identity Theft Clearinghouse, 600 Pennsylvania Avenue, N.W., Washington, DC 20580; or at www.consumer.gov/idtheft.

Fourth, certain situations may require additional action by the victim. For instance, if an identity thief has stolen mail, it should be reported to a local postal inspector. A phone number for the nearest postal inspection service office can be obtained from a local post office or the U.S. Postal Service web site at www.usps.com/postalinspectors. If financial information has been obtained, the financial entity (e.g., the bank, brokerage firm, credit union, or credit card company) should be contacted, the fraudulently affected accounts closed, and new accounts opened with new PINs and passwords, including affected ATM cards. Payment should be stopped on any stolen checks, and banks or credit unions should be asked to request the appropriate check verification service to notify retailers not to accept the checks. Three check verification companies that accept reports of check fraud directly from consumers are: Telecheck: 1-800-710-9898; International Check Services: 1-800-631-9656; and Equifax: 1-800-437-5120. If investments or securities may have been affected, brokers should be notified and the victim should file a complaint with the Securities and Exchange Commission (SEC). A complaint can be filed with the SEC at the SEC Enforcement Complaint Center, 450 5th Street, N.W., Washington, DC 20549-0202; at its web site: www.sec.gov; e-mail: enforcement @sec.gov; or by fax: (202) 942-9570.

If new phone service has fraudulently been established in a victim's name or billing for unauthorized service is made to an existing account, the victim should contact the service provider immediately to cancel the account and/or calling card and open new accounts with new PINs and passwords. If a victim has difficulty removing fraudulent charges from an account, a complaint should be filed with the Federal Communications Commission (FCC). A complaint can be filed with the FCC at the FCC Consumer Information Bureau, 445 12th Street, S.W., Room 5A863, Washington, DC 20554; at the FCC Enforcement Bureau web site: www.fcc.gov/eb; by e-mail: fccinfo@fcc.gov; or by tele-phone: 1-888-CALL FCC, or TTY 1-888-TELL FCC.

If someone is using a victim's SSN to apply for a job or to work, it should be reported to the Social Security Administration (SSA). The victim should first visit the SSA's web site at www.ssa.gov, read the Guidelines for Reporting Fraud, Waste, Abuse and Mismanagement, and then call the SSA Fraud Hotline at 1-800-269-0271, and file a re-port at SSA Fraud Hotline, P.O. Box 17768, Baltimore MD 21235, fax: 410-597-0118 or e-mail: oig.hotline@ssa.gov. The victim should also call the SSA at 1-800-772-1213 to verify the accuracy of earnings re-ported under the SSN and to request a copy of the victim's Social Security Personal Earnings and Benefit Estimate Statement. The State-ment should reveal earnings posted to the victim's SSN by the identity thief. If an SSN has been fraudulently used, the Internal Revenue Service (IRS) Taxpayer Advocates Office should be contacted. The fraudulent use of an SSN might result in what appears to be an under-reporting of a victim's taxable income and an attempt by the IRS to collect taxes on the underreported income. The IRS Taxpayer Advo-cates Office can be contacted at 1-877-777-4778 or www.treas.gov/irs/ci.

If someone has fraudulently obtained a driver's license or photo-graphic identification card in a victim's name through an office of a DMV, the local DMV should be contacted and a fraud alert should be placed in the license. Likewise, if someone has stolen any other identification document, the entity responsible for creating the docu-ment should be contacted and informed of the theft. If a passport has been lost or stolen, the United States State Department should be contacted at Passport Services, Correspondence Branch, 1111 19th Street, N.W., Suite 510, Washington, DC 20036, or www.travel.state.gov/passport_services. If someone has stolen a health insurance card, the theft should be reported to the insurer. Subsequent insurance statements should be reviewed for fraudulent billing.

If someone has fraudulently filed for bankruptcy in a victim's name, the U.S. Trustee should be contacted in the region where the bank-ruptcy was filed. A listing of the U.S. Trustees can be found at www.usdoj.gov/ust. A written complaint must be filed describing the situation and providing proof of the victim's identity. The U.S. Trustee, if appropriate, will make a referral to criminal law enforcement authorities. The victim should also file a complaint with the FBI in the city where the bankruptcy was filed.

In rare instances, an identity thief may create a criminal record under a victim's name by providing the identity when arrested. Victims of this type of problem should contact the FBI and initiate a request that the victim's name be cleared and retain an attorney to resolve the problem, as procedures for clearing one's name may vary by jurisdiction.

Conclusion

Identity theft was clearly identified as a serious crime two years ago when the Identity Theft Act was passed. Since that time great strides have been made to combat the problem, but much work remains to be done. Law enforcement agencies at all levels, federal and nonfederal, must work together to develop strategies for the investigation and prosecution of offenders. At the same time, the law enforcement community must work closely with private industry to develop effective education and prevention programs. The crime of the new millennium will not fade away soon, nor will passive efforts soften the devastating impact upon its victims. Yet with hard work, cooperation, and effective communication between law enforcement and the public, identity thieves will be held accountable in this new millennium.

About the Author

Sean B. Hoar has been an AUSA since 1991 and is the Computer and Telecommunications Coordinator (CTC) for the southern half of the District of Oregon. As such, he prosecuted the first case in the United States under the No Electronic Theft Act (NET Act) involving criminal copyright infringement on the Internet. He is primarily concerned with developing partnerships with local, state, and federal law enforcement agencies to prevent, investigate, and prosecute cyber crime. Previously he was involved primarily in the prosecution of organizational narcotics traffickers and received the Directors Award for his role in prosecuting a heroin trafficking organization based in Southeast Asia, which included a General in the Royal Thai Army who was a member of the Supreme Command of the Royal Thai Armed Forces.

FTC Statement on "Internet Fraud"

Prepared Statement of the Federal Trade Commission on "Internet Fraud" before the Committee on Finance United States Senate

Washington, D.C.,

April 5, 2001

Mr. Chairman, I am Hugh Stevenson, Associate Director of the Division of Planning and Information in the Federal Trade Commission's Bureau of Consumer Protection. I am pleased to be here today to testify about the FTC's efforts to combat fraud on the Internet.[1]

As one of the transforming events of our time, the advent of the Internet already has had a profound impact on the marketplace. The Internet has the potential to deliver goods and services more conveniently, faster, and at lower prices than traditional marketing methods. Moreover, at an ever increasing rate, it is stimulating the development of innovative products and services barely conceivable just a few years ago and enabling consumers to tap into rich sources of information that they can use to make better-informed purchasing decisions.

These developments promise enormous benefits to consumers and the economy. There is real danger, however, that these benefits may not be fully realized if consumers identify the Internet with fraud operators. Fraud on the Internet is an enormous concern for the Commission, and it has prompted a vigorous response using all the tools at the Commission's disposal, including law enforcement and education. The Commission appreciates the Subcommittee's interest in our Internet fraud program, and the Congress's support for funding both the development of our fraud database, Consumer Sentinel, and the creation of our toll-free consumer helpline. The Commission welcomes this opportunity to describe its Internet program and the challenges the agency is confronting.

I. Introduction and Background

A. The FTC and Its Law Enforcement Authority
The FTC is the federal government's primary consumer protection agency. While most federal agencies have jurisdiction over a specific market sector, the Commission's jurisdiction extends over nearly the entire economy, including business and consumer transactions on the Internet.[2]

Under the Federal Trade Commission Act,[3] the agency's mandate is to take action against "unfair or deceptive acts or practices" and to promote vigorous competition in the marketplace. The FTC Act authorizes the Commission to halt deception through civil actions filed by its own attorneys in federal district court, as well as through administrative cease-and-desist actions.[4] Typically, these civil actions seek preliminary and permanent injunctions to halt the targeted illegal activity, as well as redress for injured consumers. Where redress is impracticable, Commission actions generally seek disgorgement to the U.S. Treasury of defendants' ill-gotten gains. As discussed below, these tools have proven to be effective in fighting a broad array of fraudulent schemes on the Internet, in spite of the sheer size and reach of the Internet.

B. The Growth of Ecommerce and Internet Fraud
The growth of the Internet and ecommerce has been explosive. The number of American adults with Internet access grew from about 88

million in mid-2000 to more than 104 million at the end of the year.[5] Just this past holiday season, consumers spent an estimated $10.8 billion shopping on the Internet—a greater than 50 percent increase over the $7 billion they spent online during the same period in 1999.[6] Total ecommerce sales for 2000 were an estimated $25.8 billion, .8 percent of all sales.[7]

Unfortunately, but not surprisingly, the boom in ecommerce has opened up fertile ground for fraud. The Commission's experience is that fraud operators are always among the first to appreciate the potential of a new technology to exploit and deceive consumers. Long-distance telemarketing attracted con artists when it was introduced in the 1970s. They swarmed to pay-per-call technology when it became available in the late 1980s. Internet technology is the latest draw for opportunistic predators who specialize in fraud. The rapid rise in the number of consumer complaints related to online fraud and deception bears this out: in 1997, the Commission received fewer than 1,000 Internet fraud complaints through Consumer Sentinel; a year later, the number had increased eight-fold. In 2000, over 25,000 complaints—roughly 26 percent of all fraud complaints logged into Consumer Sentinel by various organizations that year—related to online fraud and deception. The need—and challenge—is to act quickly to stem this trend while the online marketplace is still young.

C. The FTC's Response to Protecting Consumers in the Online Marketplace

Stretching its available resources to combat the growing problem of Internet fraud and deception, the Commission has targeted a wide array of online consumer protection problems. This effort has produced significant results. Since 1994, the Commission has brought 170 Internet-related cases against over 573 defendants. It obtained injunctions stopping the illegal schemes and ordering more than $180 million in redress or disgorgement[8] and obtained orders freezing millions more in cases that are still in litigation. Its federal district court actions alone have stopped consumer injury from Internet schemes with estimated annual sales of over $250 million.[9]

II. Challenges Posed by Internet Fraud

The Commission faces a host of novel challenges in its efforts to combat fraud and deception online. Because it is both global in its reach and instantaneous, the Internet lends itself well not only to adaptations of traditional scams—such as pyramid schemes and false product claims—but also to new high-tech scams that were not possible before development of the Internet. In addition, the Internet enables con artists to cloak themselves in anonymity, which makes it necessary for law enforcement authorities to act much more quickly to stop newly emerging deceptive schemes before the perpetrators disappear. And because the Internet transcends national boundaries, law enforcement authorities must be more creative and cooperative to successfully combat online fraud. These novel challenges are discussed in greater detail below.

A. Combating Internet Fraud Requires New Methods of Collecting and Analyzing Information

The Commission is developing new methods of collecting and analyzing information about both the offline and online marketplace, drawing upon the power of new technology itself. A central part of this effort is Consumer Sentinel, a Web-based consumer fraud database and law enforcement investigative tool.[10] Consumer Sentinel receives Internet fraud complaints from the FTC's Consumer Response Center ("CRC"), which processes both telephone and mail inquiries and complaints.[11] For those consumers who prefer the online environment, an electronic complaint form at www.ftc.gov, first available in May of 1998, permits consumers to channel information about potential scams directly to the CRC and the fraud database.

Consumer Sentinel also benefits from the contributions of many public and private partners. It receives data from other public and private consumer organizations, including sixty-four local offices of the Better Business Bureaus across the nation, the National Consumers League's National Fraud Information Center, and Project Phonebusters in Canada. Additionally, a U.S. Postal Inspector has served for the past year as the program manager, and the U.S. Postal Inspection Service just signed an agreement to begin sharing consumer complaint data from its central fraud database with Consumer Sentinel.

The Commission provides secure access to this data over the Internet, free of charge, to over 300 U.S., Canadian, and Australian law enforcement organizations—including the Department of Justice, U.S. Attorneys' offices, the Federal Bureau of Investigation, the Securities and Exchange Commission, the Secret Service, the U.S. Postal Inspection Service, the Internal Revenue Service, the offices of all fifty state Attorneys General, local sheriffs and prosecutors, the Royal Canadian Mounted Police, and the Australian Competition and Consumer Commission. Consumer Sentinel is a dynamic online law enforcement tool to use against all types of fraud, especially online fraud.[12]

The central role that Consumer Sentinel plays in the Commission's law enforcement is exemplified by "Operation Top Ten Dot Cons," the Commission's latest broad "sweep" of fraudulent and deceptive Internet scams. In a yearlong law enforcement effort, the FTC and four other U.S. federal agencies,[13] consumer protection organizations from nine countries,[14] and twenty-three states[15] announced 251 law enforcement actions against online scammers. The FTC brought fifty-four of the cases.[16] The top ten scams, identified through analysis of complaint data in the Consumer Sentinel database, were:

Internet Auction Fraud

Internet Service Provider Scams

Internet Web Site Design/Promotions ("Web Cramming")[17]

Internet Information and Adult Services (unauthorized credit card charges)

Pyramid Scams

Business Opportunities and Work-at-Home Scams

Investment Schemes and Get-Rich-Quick Scams

Travel/Vacation Fraud

Telephone/Pay-Per-Call Solicitation Frauds (including modem dialers and videotext)[18]

Health Care Frauds

The Consumer Sentinel data enabled the FTC and the other enforcement agencies that joined us in this project both in the U.S. and abroad to identify not only the top ten types of scams but also the specific companies generating the highest levels of complaints about each of those types of scams. These companies became the targets for the law enforcement actions that comprised Operation Top Ten Dot Con. Finally, Consumer Sentinel data enabled the Commission and its partners to obtain and develop evidence against these targets from individual consumers whose complaints had been included in the database.

Consumer Sentinel first went online in late 1997. Since then, the Commission has upgraded the capacity of the Consumer Sentinel database and enhanced the agency's complaint-handling systems by creating and staffing a new tollfree consumer helpline at 1-877-FTC-HELP and adding several new functions to Consumer Sentinel. The first of these new functions, the "Top Violators" report function, allows a law enforcement officer to pull up the most common suspects and schemes by state, region, or subject area. The second new function, "Auto Query," enables an investigator to create an automatic search request. This automatic search can be set to run daily, weekly, or monthly, and if new complaints come in to Consumer Sentinel that match the search criteria, Consumer Sentinel will automatically alert the investigator via e-mail. Third, the "Alert" function enables law enforcers to communicate with each other and minimize duplication of their efforts, and a fourth new function performs a search of Commission court orders online. In 2000, Consumer Sentinel received over approximately 100,000 consumer complaints.[19] Currently, the database holds over 300,000 consumer complaints.[20]

The Commission's efforts to improve consumer complaint collection and analysis through the Consumer Response Center and Consumer Sentinel are complemented by a proactive program to uncover fraud and deception in broad sectors of the online marketplace through "Surf Days." Surf Days use new technology to detect and analyze emerging Internet problems. While Consumer Sentinel provides data on broad trends and the volume of complaints prompted by particular Internet schemes, Surf Days allow the Commission to take a "snapshot" of a market segment at any given time. The Commission also uses Surf Days to reach new entrepreneurs and alert those who unwittingly may be violating the law.

On a typical Surf Day, Commission staff and personnel from our law enforcement partners—often state attorneys general, sister federal agencies, or private organizations like the Better Business Bureau—widely "surf" the Internet for a specific type of claim or solicitation that is likely to violate the law. When a suspect site is identified, the page is downloaded and saved as potential evidence, and the operator of the site is sent an e-mail warning that explains the law and provides a link to educational information available at www.ftc.gov. Shortly thereafter, a law enforcement team revisits the previously warned sites to determine whether they have remedied their questionable claims or solicitations. The results vary, depending on the targeted practice of the particular Surf Day. In each of these efforts, between 20 to 70 percent of the Web site operators who received a warning come into compliance with the law, either by taking down their sites or modifying their claims or solicitations. Sites that continue to make unlawful claims are targeted for possible law enforcement action.

To date, the Commission has conducted 26 different Surf Days targeting problems ranging from "cure-all" health claims to fraudulent business opportunities and credit repair scams.[21]

More than 250 law enforcement agencies or consumer organizations around the world have joined the Commission in these activities; collectively, they have identified over 6,000 Internet sites making dubious claims. The law enforcement Surf Day has proven so effective that it is now widely used by other government agencies, consumer groups, and other private organizations.

B. Traditional Scams Use the Internet to Expand in Size and Scope

Out of the 170 cases brought by the Commission against Internet fraud and deception, over half have targeted old-fashioned scams that have been retooled for the new medium. For example, the Commission has brought twenty-eight actions against online credit repair schemes, twenty-five cases against deceptive business opportunities and work-at-home schemes, and eleven cases against pyramid schemes.

It is no surprise that the Internet versions of traditional frauds can be much larger in size and scope than their offline predecessors. A colorful, well-designed Web site imparts a sleek new veneer to an otherwise stale fraud; and the reach of the Internet allows an old-time con artist to think—and act—globally, as well.

Pyramid schemes are the most notable example of a fraud whose size and scope are magnified by the Internet.[22] By definition, these schemes require a steady supply of new recruits. The Internet provides an efficient way to reach countless new prospects around the world and to funnel funds more efficiently and quickly from the victims to the scammers at the top of the pyramid. As a result, the victims are more numerous, the fraud operator's financial "take" is much greater, and the defense is typically well funded and fierce when the FTC brings suit to stop a pyramid scheme operating online.

Despite the extensive resources required to pursue an online pyramid case, the Commission has asserted a strong enforcement presence, obtaining orders to pay more than $70 million in redress for victims[23] and pursuing millions more in ongoing litigation. In one case, *FTC v. Fortuna Alliance*, the Commission spent two years in litigation and negotiations and finally obtained a court order finding the defendants in contempt and a stipulated final order enjoining the defendants from further pyramid activities and requiring them to pay $5.5 million in refunds to over 15,000 victims in the United States and seventy foreign countries.[24] More recently, in *FTC v. Five Star Auto Club, Inc.*,[25] the Commission prevailed at trial against another pyramid scheme that lured online consumers to buy in by claiming that an annual fee and $100 monthly payments would give investors the opportunity to lease their "dream vehicle" for "free" while earning between $180 and $80,000 a month by recruiting others to join the scheme. The court issued a permanent injunction shutting down the scheme, barring for life the scheme's principals from any multilevel marketing business, and ordering them to pay $2.9 million in consumer redress.

C. Scams Are Increasingly High-Tech

Although most Internet fraud stems from traditional scams, the number of schemes uniquely and ingeniously exploiting new technology is multiplying. These are the most insidious schemes because they feed on the public's fascination with—and suspicion of—new technology. Their ultimate effect can only be to undermine consumer confidence in the online marketplace. To combat this type of high-tech fraud, the Commission has supported staff training and given its staff the tools to be effective cybersleuths.

Recognizing that most of its attorneys and investigators need to be Internet savvy, the Commission has hosted beginner and advanced Internet training seminars and held sessions on new technology, investigative techniques, and Internet case law. The Commission also makes this training available to personnel of other law enforcement agencies. In the past year, the Commission has presented Internet training seminars in seven U.S. cities and in Toronto, Canada, and Paris, France. In addition to FTC staff, these sessions trained approximately 800 individual participants from other law enforcement agencies. These participants represented twenty different countries, including the United States, twenty-six states, twenty-two federal agencies, and fourteen Canadian law enforcement agencies. Among those who have participated are representatives from the offices of state Attorneys General, the Department of Justice and U.S. Attorneys, the Securities and Exchange Commission, the FBI, and the Postal Inspection Service.

In addition to providing regular Internet training, the Commission also provides its staff with the tools they need to investigate high-tech fraud. The FTC's Internet Lab is an important example. With high-speed computers that are separate from the agency's network and loaded with the latest hardware and software, the Lab allows staff to investigate fraud and deception in a secure environment and to preserve evidence for litigation.

The Commission has used its training and tools to stop some of the most egregious and technically sophisticated schemes seen on the Internet. For example, the FTC's lawsuit against Verity International, Ltd.,[26] was prompted by the influx of hundreds of complaints in the last week of September 2000 through the CRC and logged in Consumer Sentinel. Investigation showed that high charges on consumers' phone lines were being initiated by "dialer" software downloaded from teaser adult Web sites. Many line subscribers had no idea why they received bills for these charges. Others discovered that a minor in their household—or another person who did not have the line sub-scriber's authorization—accessed the Web sites and downloaded the dialer software. The dialer program allowed users to access the "video-text" adult content without any means of verifying that the user was the line subscriber or was authorized by the line subscriber to incur charges on the line for such service. Once downloaded and executed, however, the program actually hijacked the consumer's computer modem by surreptitiously disconnecting the modem from the con-sumer's local Internet Service Provider, dialing a high-priced interna-tional long distance call to Madagascar, and reconnecting the consumer's modem to the Internet from some overseas location, opening at an adult Web site. The line subscriber—the consumer re-sponsible to pay phone charges on the telephone line—then began incurring charges on their phone lines for the remote connection to the Internet at the rate of $3.99 per minute. The court has ordered a preliminary injunction in this matter, and litigation continues.[27]

Earlier, in *FTC v. Carlos Pereira d/b/a atariz.com*,[28] the Commission attacked a worldwide, high-tech scheme that allegedly "pagejacked" consumers and then "mousetrapped" them at adult pornography sites. "Pagejacking" is making exact copies of someone else's Web page, including the imbedded text that informs search engines about the subject matter of the site. The defendants allegedly made unautho-rized copies of 25 million pages from other Web sites, including those of Paine Webber and the Harvard Law Review. The defendants made one change on each copied page that was hidden from view: they inserted a command to "redirect" any surfer coming to the site to another Web site that contained sexually explicit, adult-oriented mate-rial. Internet surfers searching for subjects as innocuous as "Oklahoma tornadoes" or "child car seats" would type those terms into a search engine and the search results would list a variety of related sites, includ-ing the bogus, copycat site of the defendants. Surfers assumed from the listings that the defendants' sites contained the information they were seeking and clicked on the listing. The "redirect" command im-bedded in the copycat site immediately rerouted the consumer to an adult site hosted by the defendants. Once there, defendants "mouse-trapped" consumers by incapacitating their Internet browser's "back" and "close" buttons, so that while they were trying to exit the defendants' site, they were sent to additional adult sites in an unavoidable, seemingly endless loop.

Using the new tools available in the Internet Lab, the Commission was able to capture and evaluate evidence of this "pagejacking" and "mousetrapping." In September 1999, the Commission filed suit in federal court and obtained a preliminary order stopping these activities and suspending the Internet domain names of the defendants. Since then, the Court has entered default judgments against two defendants and a stipulated permanent injunction against a third, barring them from future law violations. A fourth defendant, Carlos Pereira, has evaded law enforcement authorities in Portugal.

D. Online Scams Spread Quickly and Disappear Quickly

One hallmark of Internet fraud is the ability of perpetrators to cover their tracks and mask their locations and identities. Using anonymous e-mails, short-lived Web sites, and falsified domain name registrations, many fraud operators are able to strike quickly, victimize thousands of consumers in a short period of time, and disappear nearly without a trace.

To stop these swift and elusive con artists, law enforcement must move just as fast. The FTC's Internet Rapid Response Team was created for this very purpose. It draws heavily upon complaints collected by the FTC's Consumer Response Center and the Consumer Sentinel system. The team constantly reviews complaint data to spot emerging problems, conduct quick but thorough investigations, and prepare cases for filing in federal courts. Based on such data review, FTC staff had completed the investigation and was in court successfully arguing for an ex parte temporary restraining order and asset freeze in *FTC v. Verity International, Ltd.* within a little more than a week after the first complaints began coming in to the Consumer Response Center.

In another exemplary effort of the Rapid Response Team, *FTC v. Benoit*,[30] the Team quickly moved against defendants who allegedly used deceptive e-mails or "spam" to dupe consumers into placing expensive international audiotext calls.[31] The defendants allegedly sent thousands of consumers an e-mail stating that each recipient's "order" had been received and that his or her credit card would be billed $250 to $899. The e-mail instructed consumers to call a telephone number in the 767 area code if they had any questions. Most consumers did not realize that 767 was the area code for Dominica, West Indies. When consumers called the number expecting to reach a customer representative, they were connected to an audiotext entertainment service with sexual content and charged expensive international rates.

Even though a string of telephone carriers could not identify who operated the audiotext number in question, the Internet Rapid Response Team constructed a compelling case in about three weeks. The Commission quickly obtained a federal court order to stop the scheme and freeze any proceeds of the fraud still in the telephone billing system.

E. Effective Remedies Are More Difficult to Achieve in the Global Online Market

The globalization of the marketplace poses new and difficult challenges for consumer protection law enforcement. Anticipating this development, the Commission held public hearings in the fall of 1995 to explore business and consumer issues arising from technological innovation and increasing globalization. Over 200 company executives, business representatives, legal scholars, consumer advocates, and state and federal officials presented testimony, and the Commission published a two-volume report summarizing the testimony and the role of antitrust and consumer protection law in the changing marketplace. As reported in *Anticipating the 21st Century: Consumer Protection in the New High-Tech, Global Marketplace*, there was a broad consensus that meaningful consumer protection takes (1) coordinated law enforcement against fraud and deception; (2) private initiatives and public/private partnerships; and (3) consumer education through the combined efforts of government, business, and consumer groups.[32] These principles have guided FTC policy regarding the Internet ever since.

In addition to gathering information through hearings and workshops, the FTC has gained practical knowledge about the effects of globalization and ecommerce through its litigation. In this respect, the Commission has found that pursuing Internet fraud often involves a difficult and costly search for money that has been moved offshore. For example, in *FTC v. J.K. Publications*,[33] the Commission obtained an ex parte temporary restraining order, a preliminary injunction, and an asset freeze against defendants that allegedly made unauthorized charges of $19.95 per month on consumers' credit or debit cards for purported Internet services. Based upon evidence gathered by Commission staff, the defendants may have charged over 900,000 consumers a total of $45 million for unordered or unauthorized Internet services. According to the receiver appointed in this case, the defendants moved millions of dollars to the Cayman Islands, Liechtenstein, and Vanuatu in the South Pacific. The Commission continues to litigate this case, and the receiver continues to attempt to locate defendants' foreign assets and repatriate them to the United States.

In *FTC v. Fortuna Alliance*, one of the pyramid schemes described above, the Commission found that the defendants had transferred $2.8 million to Antigua, West Indies. With the assistance of the U.S. Department of Justice's Office of Foreign Litigation, the Commission obtained an order from an Antiguan court freezing those funds and a stipulated final judgment in U.S. court that required the defendants to repatriate that money for consumer redress. In the process, however, it cost $280,000 in fees alone to litigate the case in foreign court.[34]

In addition to fraud proceeds moving offshore quickly, fraudulent online operators may be beyond the reach of the Commission and U.S. courts, practically if not legally. There is now limited recognition of civil judgments from country to country. Even if the Commission were to bring an action and obtain a judgment against a foreign firm that has defrauded U.S. consumers, the judgment might be challenged in the firm's home country, and the ability to collect any consumer redress might be frustrated. In light of this possibility, U.S. law enforcement must look for more effective remedies available under U.S. law and must work more cooperatively with law enforcement officials in other countries. To that end, the FTC has executed cooperation memoranda with agencies in Canada, the United Kingdom, and Australia.[35]

The Commission's actions in *FTC v. Pereira* represent significant strides in the right direction. In that case, the Commission realized that the defendants' "pagejacking" and "mousetrapping" scheme had operated through Web sites registered with a U.S.-based company. Thus, in its request for a temporary restraining order and preliminary injunction, the Commission asked that the registrations for these Web sites be suspended, thereby effectively removing the defendants and their deceptive Web sites from the Internet, pending a full trial. At the same time, the Commission reached out to its international colleagues in Portugal and Australia. The Australian Competition and Consumer Commission (ACCC) proved especially helpful in providing information about the defendants and their business operations in Australia. The ACCC also began its own investigation, executed a number of search warrants, and began pursuing potential legal action against the defendants in that country.

III. Consumer and Business Education

Law enforcement alone cannot stop the tide of fraudulent activity on the Internet. Meaningful consumer protection depends on education, as well. Consumers must be given the tools they need to spot potentially fraudulent promotions, and businesses must be advised about how to comply with the law. The FTC's consumer and business education program uses the Internet to communicate antifraud and educational messages to reach vast numbers of people in creative and novel ways quickly, simply, and at low cost. As more consumers and businesses come online, use of the Internet to disseminate information will grow.

A. Fraud Prevention Information for Consumers

More than 200 of the consumer and business publications produced by the FTC's Bureau of Consumer Protection are available on the agency's Web site in both text and .pdf format. Indeed, the growth in the number of our publications viewed online between 1996 and 1999 (140,000 vs. 2.5 million) tells the story of the Internet's coming of age as a mainstream medium and highlights its importance to any large-scale dissemination effort. Those 2.5 million page views are in addition to the 6 million print publications the FTC distributes each year to organizations that disseminate them on the FTC's behalf.

B. Link Program

In addition to placing publications on its own Web site, the FTC actively encourages partners—government agencies, associations, organizations, and corporations with an interest in a particular subject—to link to its information from their sites and to place banner public service announcements provided by the FTC on their sites. Links from the banners allow visitors to click through to the FTC site quickly to get the information they're looking for exactly when they want it. Examples of the varied organizations that have helped drive traffic to the valuable consumer information on www.ftc.gov are Yahoo!, American Express, Circuit City, AARP, North American Securities Administrators Association, the Alliance for Investor Education, the Better Business Bureau, CBS, motleyfool.com, the U.S. Patent and Trademark Office, Shape Up America!, the National Institutes of Health, and the Arthritis Foundation.

C. "Teaser" Pages

Too often, warning information about frauds reaches consumers *after* they've been scammed. For the FTC, the challenge is reaching consumers *before* they fall victim to a fraudulent scheme. Knowing that many consumers use the Internet to shop for information, agency staff have developed teaser sites that mimic the characteristics that make a site fraudulent and then warn the reader about the fraud. Metatags embedded in the FTC teaser sites make them instantly accessible to consumers who are using major search engines and indexing services as they look for products, services, and business opportunities online. The teaser pages link back to the FTC's page, where consumers can find practical, plain English information. The agency has developed more than a dozen such teaser sites on topics ranging from fraudulent business opportunities and wealth-building scams to weight loss products, vacation deals, and investments.[36] Feedback from the public has been overwhelmingly positive: visitors express appreciation—not only for the information, but for the novel, hassle-free, and anonymous way it is offered.

D. Consumer.gov

Following its vision of the Internet as a powerful tool for consumer education and empowerment, the FTC organized a group of five small federal agencies in 1997 to develop and launch a Web site that would offer one-stop access to the incredible array of federal consumer information. On the theory that consumers may not know one federal agency from another, the information is arranged by topic area. Federal agencies have responded well to consumer.gov. The site now includes contributions from 170 federal agencies. Consumers also find it useful, with over 182,500 visits to the site recorded in the first half of FY 2001.

Visitors to consumer.gov find special initiatives, too: the President's Council on Y2K Conversion asked the FTC to establish a Y2K consumer information site; the Quality Interagency Coordination Task Force requested a special site on health care quality; and the U.S. Postal Inspection Service asked that consumer.gov house the site to support the kNOw Fraud initiative, an ongoing public-private campaign initiated with the sending of postcards about telemarketing fraud to 115 million American households in the fall of 1999.[37] The FTC continues to maintain the site.

E. Business Education for Online Marketers

As part of its mission, the FTC provides guidance to online marketers on how to assure that basic consumer protection principles apply online. Many of these entrepreneurs are small, start-up companies that are new to the Internet and to marketing in general and are unfamiliar with consumer protection laws. The Commission's publication, "Advertising and Marketing on the Internet: Rules of the Road," is designed to give practical, plain-English guidance to them.[38] The FTC also has used a variety of other approaches to get its messages out to the business community, from posting compliance guides, staff advisory letters, and banner public service announcements on the Web to speaking at industry and academic meetings and conferences, using the trade press to promote the availability of information on the agency site, and holding workshops on online issues and posting the transcripts. Most recently, on January 30 of this year, the Commission, in cooperation with the Electronic Retailing Association, presented "Etail Details" a case-driven Internet marketing seminar for Internet retailers, marketers, and suppliers on applying offline rules and regulations online. The seminar was designed to ensure e-tailers understand and comply with FTC rules regarding e-tailing.

IV. Conclusion

The Commission has been involved in policing the electronic marketplace for six years—before the World Wide Web was widely used by consumers and businesses. So far, we have kept pace with the unprecedented growth of the electronic marketplace by targeting our efforts, making innovative use of the technology, and leveraging our resources. We have done all this with limited resources, and without retreating from our important consumer protection work in traditional markets.

The Commission greatly appreciates the opportunity to describe its efforts to combat fraud on the Internet.

Notes

1. The views expressed in this statement represent the views of the Commission. My responses to any questions you may have are my own and are not necessarily those of the Commission or any Commissioner.
2. The FTC has limited or no jurisdiction over specified types of entities and activities. These include banks, savings associations, and federal credit unions; regulated common carriers; air carriers; non-retail sales of livestock and meat products under the Packers and Stockyards Act; certain activities of nonprofit corporations; and the business of insurance. See, e.g., 15 U.S.C. §§ 44, 45, 46 (FTC Act); 15 U.S.C. § 21 (Clayton Act); 7 U.S.C. § 227 (Packers and

Stockyards Act); 15 U.S.C. § 1011 et seq. (McCarran-Ferguson Act).

3. 15 U.S.C. § 45(a). The Commission also has responsibilities under more than forty-five additional statutes, e.g., the Fair Credit Reporting Act, 15 U.S.C. § 1681 et seq., which establishes important privacy protections for consumers' sensitive financial information; the Truth in Lending Act, 15 U.S.C. §§ 1601 et seq., which mandates disclosures of credit terms; and the Fair Credit Billing Act, 15 U.S.C. §§ 1666 et seq., which provides for the correction of billing errors on credit accounts. The Commission also enforces over thirty-five rules governing specific industries and practices, e.g., the Used Car Rule, 16 C.F.R. Part 455, which requires used car dealers to disclose warranty terms via a window sticker; the Franchise Rule, 16 C.F.R. Part 436, which requires the provision of information to prospective franchisees; and the Telemarketing Sales Rule, 16 C.F.R. Part 310, which defines and prohibits deceptive telemarketing practices and other abusive telemarketing practices.

4. 15 U.S.C. §§ 45(a) and 53(b).

5. Pew Internet and American Life Project, *More Online, Doing More* (reported at http://www.pewinternet.org/reports/toc.asp?Report =30) (stating that comparing figures gathered in tracking survey in May and June with figures gathered between Thanksgiving and Christmas, the number of American adults with Internet access grew from about 88 million to more than 104 million in the second half of 2000).

6. Jupiter Communications, Inc., *Online Holiday Sales Increased by 54 Percent This Holiday Season, Despite Dot Com Closures and Soft Offline Purchase* (Jan. 17, 2001) (estimating November and December 2000 online sales of $10.8 billion, compared to $7 billion for those months in 1998) (reported at www.jup.com/company/pressrelease.jsp?doc=pr010117). The Census Bureau of the Department of Commerce estimated that in the fourth quarter of 2000, not adjusted for seasonal, holiday, and trading-day differences, online retail sales were $8.686 billion, an increase of 67.1

percent from the fourth quarter of 1999 (reported at www.census.gov/mrts/www/current.html).

7. *Id.*

8. To date, the Commission has collected more than $55 million in redress for victims of Internet fraud and deception.

9. These figures are based on estimated annual fraudulent sales by defendants in the twelve months prior to filing the complaint. Fraudulent sales figures are based on, among other things, financial statements, company records, receiver reports, and deposition testimony of company officials.

10. See www.consumer.gov/sentinel.

11. The CRC now receives over 12,000 inquiries and complaints per week. They cover a broad spectrum—everything from complaints about get-rich-quick telemarketing scams and online auction fraud to questions about consumer rights under various credit statutes and requests for educational materials. Counselors record complaint data, provide information to assist consumers in resolving their complaints, and answer their inquiries.

12. In 1998, the Interagency Resources Management Conference Award recognized Consumer Sentinel as an exceptional initiative to improve government service.

13. U.S. agencies participating included the Commodity Futures Trading Commission, the Department of Justice, the Securities and Exchange Commission, and the United States Postal Inspection Service.

14. Participants in "Operation Top Ten Dot Cons" included consumer protection agencies from Australia, Canada, Finland, Germany, Ireland, New Zealand, Norway, the United Kingdom, and the United States.

15. Cases were brought by the Attorneys General of Arizona, Colorado, Florida, Illinois, Iowa, Indiana, Louisiana, Maryland, Massachusetts, Michigan, Missouri, Nevada, New Jersey, North Carolina, Ohio, Oregon, Pennsylvania, Tennessee, Texas, and Washington State. Consumer protection offices in West Virginia and Wisconsin also took action, as did the Louisiana Department of Justice, the Okla-

homa Department of Securities, and the Washington State Securities Division.

16. The SEC's contribution to this project consisted of seventy-seven cases.

17. "Web cramming" is a type of unauthorized billing scam. Web crammers call their victims—often small businesses—and offer a "free" Web page; then they start billing the victims, typically on their monthly telephone statements, without authorization. In many cases the small business victims are not even aware that they have a Web site or are paying for one.

18. Telephone/Pay-Per-Call Solicitation Frauds are schemes that exploit the telephone billing and collection system to charge consumers for telephone-based entertainment programs ("audiotext" in industry parlance) or other so-called enhanced services that are not telecommunications transmission but are often billed on consumers' telephone bills. Modem dialers and videotext schemes, like the operation attacked in *FTC v. Verity International*, No. 00 Civ. 7422(LAK) (S.D.N.Y. 2000), described *infra,* are ones that, unbeknownst to a consumer, cause his or her computer modem to disconnect from his or her usual Internet service provider, dial an expensive international telephone number, and reconnect to the Internet at a remote location overseas, charging the consumer as much as $5.00 or more per minute for as long as the consumer continues online.

19. Consumer Sentinel has also been upgraded and expanded to provide participants access to the Identity Theft Data Clearinghouse, the central repository for federal identity theft complaints.

20. The FTC recently has signed an agreement with the Department of Defense to collect consumer complains from men and women serving in the military through a project called "Soldier Sentinel."

21. The FTC has coordinated or cosponsored the following Surf Days, listed by date of their announcements: Pyramid Surf Day (December 1996), Credit Repair Surf (April 1997), Business Opportunity Surf Day (April 1997), Coupon Fraud Surf Day (August 1997), North American Health Claims Surf (October 1997), HUD Tracer Surf Day (November 1997), International Surf Day (October

1997), Kids Privacy Surf Day (December 1997), Junk E-mail Harvest (December 1997), Privacy Surf (March 1998), Textile and Wool Labeling Surf (August 1998), Y2K Surf (September 1998), International Health Claims Surf (November 1998), Investment Surf Day (December 1998), Jewelry Guides Surf (January 1999), Pyramid Surf Day II (March 1999), Green Guide Surf (April 1999), Coupon Fraud II Surf Day (June 1999), Jewelry Guides Surf II (January 2000), Scholarship Services Surf (January 2000), GetRichQuick.com Surf (March 2000), False or Unsubstantiated Lice Treatment Claims Surf (April 2000), Credit Repair Surf II (August 2000), Childrens' Online Privacy Protection Act Compliance Surf (August 2000), False Claims of Authenticity for American Indian Arts and Crafts Surf Day (October 2000), and TooLate.Com [Surf of Online Retailers' Compliance with the Mail or Telephone Order Merchandise Rule] (November 2000).

22. Pyramid operators typically promise enormous earnings or investment returns, not based on commissions for retail sales to consumers but based on commissions for recruiting new pyramid members. Recruitment commissions, of course, are premised on an endless supply of new members. Inevitably, when no more new recruits can be found, these schemes collapse, and a vast majority of participants lose the money they invested.

23. To date, the Commission has collected about $42.6 million in these cases.

24. *FTC v. Fortuna Alliance, L.L.C.*, No. C96-799M (W.D.Wash. 1996). See also *FTC v. JewelWay International, Inc.*, No. CV97-383 TUC JMR (D.Ariz. 1997) ($5 million in redress for approximately 150,000 investors); *FTC v. Nia Cano*, No. 97-7947-CAS-(AJWx) (C.D.Cal. 1997) (approximately $2 million in redress); *FTC v. FutureNet*, No. 98-1113GHK (AIJx) (C.D.Cal. 1998) ($1 million in consumer redress); *FTC v. Five Star Auto Club, Inc.*, 97 F. Supp. 2d 502 (S.D.N.Y. 2000) ($2.9 million in consumer redress); *FTC v. Equinox International Corp.*, No. CV-S-990969-JBR-RLH (D.Nev. 1999) (pyramid promoted through many devices, including some use of the Internet; $50 million in consumer redress).

25. *FTC v. Five Star Auto Club, Inc.*, 97 F. Supp. 2d 502 (S.D.N.Y. 2000).

26. *FTC v. Verity International, Ltd.,* No. 00 Civ. 7422 (LAK) (S.D.N.Y. 2000).
27. Other modem hijacking cases include *FTC v. Audiotex Connection, Inc.,* No. CV-97-0726 (DRH) (E.D.N.Y. 1997) (final stipulated injunction halting the unlawful practice and ordering that 27,000 victims receive full redress totaling $2.14 million*); FTC v. RJB Telcom, Inc.,* No. CV 00-2017 PHX SRB (D.Az. 2000); *FTC v. Ty Anderson,* No. C 00-1843P (W.D.Wash. 2000).
28. *FTC v. Carlos Pereira d/b/a atariz.com.*[29]
29. Civil Action No. 99-1367-A.
30. *FTC v. Benoit* (previously *FTC v. One or More Unknown Parties*), No. 3:99 CV 181 (W.D.N.C. 1999). In the course of the litigation, Commission attorneys were able to identify the operators of the scheme.
31. "Audiotext" services are telephone-based entertainment or information services.
32. See Bureau of Consumer Protection, Federal Trade Commission, *Anticipating the 21st Century: Consumer Protection in the New High-Tech, Global Marketplace,* iii (May 1996), and *Looking Ahead: Consumer Protection in the Global Electronic Marketplace* (September 2000).
33. *FTC v. J.K. Publications,* No. 99-000-44ABC (AJWx) (C.D.Cal. 1999).
34. In this case, the Department of Justice's Office of Foreign Litigation paid $50,000 up front, and the U.S. court ordered the defendants to pay the remaining $230,000 in fees. In other cases, the Commission may have to bear all or most of the cost of litigating in foreign court.
35. The Commission is increasingly cooperating with international colleagues in a number of venues. Among them is the International Marketing Supervision Network, a group of consumer protection agencies from the thirty countries that are members of the Organization for Economic Cooperation and Development.
36. The titles of the teaser sites are: Looking for Financial Freedom?; The Ultimate Prosperity Page; Nordicalite Weight Loss Product; A+ Fast Ca$$h for College; EZTravel: Be an Independent Agent; EZTravel: Certificate of Notification; EZToyz Investment Opportu-

nity; HUD Tracer Association; CreditMenders Credit Repair; Net-Opportunities: Internet Is a Gold Mine; National Business Trainers Seminars; VirilityPlus: Natural Alternative to Viagra; ArthritiCure: Be Pain-Free Forever.

37. The original consumer.gov team received the Hammer Award, presented by the Vice President to teams of federal employees who have made significant contributions to reinventing government.

38. There has been an astonishing growth in page views of this publication in the past year: from 33,448 views in FY 1999 to 110,473 in FY 2000.

Working with Victims of Computer Network Hacks

Richard P. Salgado
Trial Attorney
Computer Crime and Intellectual Property Section

In our ten years' experience in detecting, locating, and prosecuting network intruders (hackers), we have seen that, as with many offline crimes, robust law enforcement alone cannot solve the network intruder problem. To be effective, any overall strategy must include the owners and operators of the nation's computer networks. They are the first line of defense and have the responsibility to take reasonable

This appendix is from *USA Bulletin*, March 2001. Reprinted with permission.

measures to ensure that their systems are secure. They are also in the best position to detect intrusions and take the first critical steps to respond. At the most basic level, we rely on network operators to report to us when their systems are hacked. Intrusion victims, however, are often even more reluctant to call law enforcement than other business victims. This reluctance has been reflected in the surveys conducted jointly by the Computer Security Institute and the FBI. In the year 2000 survey, for example, only 25 percent of the respondents who experienced computer intrusions reported the incidents to law enforcement. To better understand why and to learn how we can promote reporting, the Department of Justice has undertaken a concerted effort to reach out to the operators of our nation's computer networks.

As part of this effort, the Department, through the Computer Crime and Intellectual Property Section, has participated with the Information Technology Association of America in several industry-government summits this past year. The first two summits (held in Palo Alto, California, and Herndon, Virginia, respectively) were national in scope. Several regional summits followed, with more in the planning. The discussions in the summits concentrated on how law enforcement and victims of computer intrusions could work better together. Although several larger themes common to all the summits became apparent, one theme of particular concern was that private victims of computer network intrusions are reluctant to report the crimes to law enforcement.

The reluctance of intrusion victims to report poses a significant problem to the development of networked computers generally, and the Internet in particular. Although, upon finding a hacker in his or her system, a system administrator may be content to close the intruder's account and fix the vulnerability (essentially kicking the hacker out and locking the door), this provides little true security. Not only is the hacker free to try the exploit on another company's network; the hacker may have left behind back doors through which he or she can return to the computer undetected. In addition, through the hacker community, others may learn of the exploit and, emboldened by the lack of any law enforcement response, join in compromising computer systems. It is folly to believe that any particular hacker is motivated by the desire to show off computing prowess with no real intent to damage, steal, or defraud. What may appear to be a simple hack with no real risk of damage can, in fact, be a part of a larger scheme to launch a very destructive attack against other highly sensitive machines. Intruders may compromise many systems, collecting them like baseball cards. Some hackers use the "stolen" computers to launch attacks against other computers, shutting down the next victim, taking information from the systems, and using the stolen data in extortion schemes or to engage in innumerable other types of illegal conduct. With each compromise, the security of our nation's networks diminishes. Without reporting by victims, law enforcement cannot provide an effective and appropriate response.

Myths and Misunderstandings

During the summits, some of the industry participants claimed a wide variety of reasons for the reluctance to report hacks. The perception on the part of some businesses is that there is little upside to reporting network intrusions. The perceived rationale for not reporting an intrusion includes the following:

- The victim company does not know which law enforcement entity to call. Surely, the victim reasons, the local or state police will not be able to comprehend the crime and the FBI and Secret Service would have no interest in my system.

- If the victim company does report the intrusion to an appropriate agency, law enforcement will not act. Instead, the fact of the intrusion will become public knowledge, irreparably shaking investor confidence and driving current and potential customers to competitors who elect not to report intrusions.

- If law enforcement does act on the report and conducts an investigation, law enforcement will not find the intruder. In the process, however, the company will lose control of the investigation. Law enforcement agents will seize critical data, and perhaps entire computers; damage equipment and files; compromise private information belonging to customers and vendors; and seriously jeopardize the normal operations of the company. Only competitors will benefit as customers flee and stock value drops.

- If law enforcement finds the intruder, the intruder likely will be a juvenile, reside in a foreign country, or both, and the prosecutor will decline or be unable to pursue the case.

- If the intruder is not a minor, the prosecutor will conclude that the amount of damage inflicted by the intruder is too small to justify prosecution.

- If law enforcement successfully prosecutes the intruder, the intruder will receive probation or at most insignificant jail time, only to use his or her hacker experience to find fame and a lucrative job in network security.

As formidable as the list of excuses may appear, these deterrents to reporting can be overcome by better-informed computer network owners and operators and skillful investigatory and prosecutorial practice. Further, the risk presented by failing to report intrusions is tremendous. For the foreseeable future, our nation's networks are only going to get more complex, more interconnected, and thus more vulnerable to intrusions. Networks are also going to be more important to our private lives, the nation's defense, and our world's economy. If there was a single clear mandate from the summits, it was that we must get the word out explaining why victims should report intrusions.

The Case for Reporting

Law enforcement needs to debunk the myths that have developed about the dangers of reporting intrusions and to sharpen our investigatory and prosecutorial practices. We also need to make an affirmative case for reporting to large network computer operators, focusing on the value to the company of reporting. In the course of the summits, it became clear that the message to operators and owners of computer networks is best delivered before a crises arises, when relationships can be built without the pressure of an ongoing investigation.

Debunking the Myths and Explaining the Basics

Perhaps the most basic piece of information to convey to victims concerns to whom the victim should report. Law enforcement agencies at all levels have developed some familiarity with computer crime investigations in the recent years, and, if they are not equipped to handle complex computer intrusion cases, they are at least able to promptly refer reports to agencies that are. We need to ensure that large computer network operators know the law enforcement agencies in their area that have the necessary forensic and prosecutorial expertise and resources. Victims also need to understand that law enforcement does view intrusions as important and will respond appropriately.

Publicity that may follow reporting was also a concern that pervaded the summits. As a rule, agents and prosecutors need to ensure that they handle business information with a great deal of discretion. Similarly, law enforcement has to be sensitive to victims' concerns arising from the seizure of data from internal corporate networks. Most of the industry participants in the summits thought that law enforcement investigators would remove the servers, proceed without any victim input; that it would disrupt the normal operations of the company for weeks at a time; and that law enforcement's involvement would mean that the company could not take steps to secure the system or conduct its own investigation. Contrary to this belief, many investigations actually require input from the victim's system operator for technical operations. Communication with potential victims prior to any investigation would likely go a long way to address these concerns. Similarly, during investigations, law enforcement can work with the victims to ensure that the investigation remains confidential.

Certainly every investigation poses its own unique challenges, and there is no way to predict, with certainty, how any particular investigation will proceed. We have seen, and undoubtedly will see again, instances where a victim wants to take measures that are in conflict with the investigative strategy. For example, where there is a series of intrusions into a victim's network, the victim may want to shut the intruder out of the system and patch the vulnerability. Law enforcement may prefer that the company leave the system open so that the hacker will not know he or she has been detected and the agents can monitor the hacker's activity and track the hacker's origins. If there is a cooperative and trusting relationship between law enforcement and the victim that predates the intrusion, the agents and the company are more likely to find a resolution that works for both. In this example, the agents and system operator may be able to configure the network such that it is secure against future exploits but appears to the hacker to remain open. Law enforcement can both protect the victim and pursue the intruder.

Many of the industry representatives expressed doubt about the ability of law enforcement to find the culprits. Certainly, tracking intruders is a very challenging task for a variety of reasons. Industry representatives readily acknowledged, however, that intruders will not be caught if the victim does not report. In any event, law enforcement has become much more sophisticated at tracking communications in recent years and even juvenile intruders are not immune from prosecution. Even if the juvenile is outside the United States, many foreign countries have been willing to prosecute.

Highlighting the Value of Reporting

There are also business reasons for companies to report intrusions cases. The two primary values to victims in calling law enforcement come from the deterrence that prosecution provides and potential restitution to the victim.

Specific deterrence is perhaps one of the most compelling reasons for a company to report an intrusion. When law enforcement catches and successfully prosecutes an intruder, that intruder is deterred from future assaults on the victim. This is a result that no technical fix to the network can duplicate with the same effectiveness. Intrusion victims may try to block out an intruder by fixing the exploited vulnerability, only to find that the intruder has built in a back door and is able to access the system at will. There have been instances in which a system operator, believing he or she is locking the intruder out for good, expends a great deal of time and effort to completely rebuild the network using backup media, only to find that the exploit was present in the backup and was simply reintroduced. Of course, a victim could initiate its own investigation to find the intruder. If successful, the victim may be able to initiate a civil suit for damages. In many (if not most) cases, however, the victim is at a substantial disadvantage relative to law enforcement in this effort. Law enforcement is able to obtain wiretap, pen/trap, and trace orders; enforceable data preservation requests; and other criminal process unavailable to a private party. Further, a monetary award is unlikely to serve as the same deterrent as a jail sentence or even probation. The general deterrence that criminal law enforcement provides also benefits victims and potential victims in the long run.

Restitution is also an attractive motive for victim reporting. Being a victim of intrusion is almost always an expensive proposition. A responsible victim must survey the system to determine whether any data was taken or damaged and, if so, must repair the damage. The victim must analyze the network to determine if there are any remaining holes in the system, check the integrity of the logs, identify the means by which the intruder accessed the system, and patch the vulnerability. The costs can be very high and can grow when the victim includes the loss of business and the lost productivity of the technical staff dedicated to the intrusion. The victim may be able to recoup some or all of the expenses through restitution.

Reporting a criminal computer intrusion to law enforcement may also help the victim recover under insurance policies for damage to its system or damage inflicted on a third party resulting from the intrusion. Director and Officer insurance policies, for example, may exclude coverage if, as a result of the victim's decision not to report the intrusion to law enforcement, the intruder inflicted additional damage to the victim system or attacked another's network using the victim's system. By reporting the intrusion in the first instance, however, the victim decreases the risk that the carrier could deny a claim made.

Similarly, where a victim's network is compromised and used to attack another system downstream, the victim may find itself a defendant in civil litigation brought by that downstream victim. If the victim has reported to law enforcement, it will be able to use the fact that it called in law enforcement as part of its defense of a claim, for example, that the victim did not take reasonable steps to prevent its network from being used as a platform to attack the plaintiff.

Making the Case and Selecting the Appropriate Audience

The summits illustrated that informal face-to-face meetings between law enforcement and representatives of potential intrusion victims are a valuable means to address concerns that the victims may have about reporting. Those industry representatives at the summits that had pre-existing relationships with law enforcement almost uniformly expressed an understanding of the need to report intrusions and a willingness to do so. Those most reluctant to report, it appeared from the summits, were representatives who had no such relationship. Discussions in the heat of an investigation are far less likely to be productive than frank and informal dialogue prior to an incident. Prosecutors and agents should take the time to reach out to the large computer operators in their jurisdictions and build such relationships.

It is imperative that the message is heard by those who make the decisions. Some information security (IS) managers, for example, are very protective of "their" systems and will take umbrage at intrusions. They may not be content with simply resecuring the system in the hope that the hacker will not return and will want the criminal arrested and prosecuted. They view law enforcement as a part of their security system; one of many resources that responsible network operators will use when the security of the network has been compromised. Other IS managers may be less receptive to reporting intrusions, even to their own superiors. The very fact of an intrusion, an IS manager may fear, suggests that he or she failed to properly secure the system. It has also become common for law enforcement to receive hacking reports from

IS managers but receive less than enthusiastic cooperation from the victim company once the fact of the hack is brought to the attention of the victim's higher-level management or general counsel. For the message to be effective, it must be heard by all the decision makers.

To get the word out, prosecutors and agents should take the time to reach out to the large computer operators in their jurisdictions. In addition to meeting with representatives of information technology companies such as Internet and telecommunications service providers, agents and prosecutors should look to other common targets of hacks including universities, e-commerce and Web-based retailers, and any organization that is reliant on large computer networks for operations. In addition, many jurisdictions are the home for information security associations, computer technology bar associations, and similar organizations. Those groups can provide law enforcement a solid forum in which to reach many network operators and counselors. The Computer Crime and Intellectual Property Section can help in this effort.

The perception that law enforcement and private computer network operators have separate and independent responsibilities in the battle against hackers is wrong. Although the network owners have the obligation to secure their systems, and law enforcement has an obligation to investigate and prosecute when appropriate, neither can function effectively without the other. Network operators need to view law enforcement as a necessary part of system protection, and law enforcement agencies need to be able to count on the cooperation of victims to fulfill their responsibilities.

About the Author

Richard P. Salgado is a trial attorney in the Computer Crime and Intellectual Property Section of the Criminal Division of the United States Department of Justice. In that role, he addresses a wide variety of complex legal and policy issues that arise in connection with new technologies. His responsibilities include training investigators and prosecutors on the legal and policy implications of emerging technologies and related criminal conduct. Mr. Salgado also prosecutes and provides advice on computer hacking and network attacks and other advanced technology crimes, including denial-of-service attacks, logic bombs, viruses and computer extortion, wiretaps, and other technology-driven privacy crimes. Mr. Salgado also participates in policy development relating to emerging technologies and in the Department's computer crime industry outreach efforts. Mr. Salgado has also served as lead negotiator on behalf of the Department in discussions with communications service providers to ensure that the ability of the Department to enforce the laws and protect national security is not hindered by foreign ownership of the providers or foreign-located facilities.

Internet Denial-of-Service Attacks Statement

Statement of Eric Holder, Deputy Attorney General of the
United States, Before the Subcommittee on Crime of the House
Committee on the Judiciary and the Subcommittee on
Criminal Oversight of the Senate Committee on the Judiciary
on Internet Denial-of-Service Attacks and the Federal Response,
February 29, 2000

Mr. Chairmen and other Members of the Subcommittees, I want to thank you for this opportunity to testify on the recent Internet "denial-of-service" attacks and the federal response to these incidents, with a particular focus on the challenges facing the Department of Justice in its fight against cybercrime. Both Subcommittees have been very helpful in providing the Department with the resources and tools we need to keep pace with the ever-changing demands of law enforcement and public safety, particularly the new challenge of cybercrime. At a time where new technologies abound and our society becomes increasingly reliant on computer networks and thus vulnerable to cybercrime, we look forward to working again with you to ensure that law enforcement, in cooperation with the private sector, can play an appropriate and critical role in protecting the well-being of Americans.

Comments on the Recent Attacks

I would be happy to address your questions on the recent attacks, to the extent I can do so without compromising our investigation. At this point, I would simply say that we are taking the attacks very seriously and that we will do everything in our power to identify those responsible and bring them to justice. In addition to the malicious disruption of legitimate commerce, so-called denial-of-service attacks involve the unlawful intrusion into an unknown number of computers, which are in turn used to launch attacks on the eventual target computer, in this case the computers of Yahoo, eBay, and others. Thus, the number of victims in these types of cases can be substantial, and the collective loss and cost to respond to these attacks can run into the tens of millions of dollars—or more.

Overview of Investigative Efforts and Coordination

Computer crime investigators in a number of FBI field offices and investigators from other agencies are investigating these attacks. They are coordinating information with the National Infrastructure Protection Center (NIPC) of the FBI. The agents are also working closely with our network of specially trained computer crime prosecutors who are available twenty-four hours a day, seven days a week, to provide legal advice and obtain whatever court orders are necessary. Attorneys from the Criminal Division's Computer Crime and Intellectual Property Section (CCIPS) are coordinating with the Assistant United States Attorneys in the field. We are also obtaining information from victim companies and security experts, who, like many in the Internet community, condemn these recent attacks. We are also working closely with our counterparts in other nations. I am proud of the efforts being made in this case, including the assistance we are receiving from a number of federal agencies.

The Emergence of Cybercrime

It is worth remembering that just ten years ago, the Internet was largely unknown and unavailable to the average person. There was no e-commerce, no eBay, no Amazon.com, very little dot-anything. At that time, the Internet was a collection of military, academic, and research networks serving a small community of trusted users. Many of us were just learning about pagers and cell phones, VCRs, and videocams.

That world is history. The far-reaching, ever-expanding, and ever more rapid advances in computer and software technology over the last ten years have combined with the explosive growth of the Internet to change the world forever. For the most part, the Internet and other technologies are providing wonderful benefits to our society—from providing new, high-wage jobs to our economy, to expanding educational opportunities, to improving health care, and in countless other ways.

Unfortunately, these wonderful technologies also provide new opportunities for criminals. Online crime is rapidly increasing. We are seeing more "pure" computer crimes, that is, crimes where the computer is used as a weapon to attack other computers, as we saw in the distributed denial-of-service attacks I just spoke about, and in the spread of malicious code, like viruses. Our vulnerability to this type of crime is astonishingly high—it was only this past December that a defendant admitted, when he pled guilty in federal and state court, to creating and releasing the Melissa virus, that he caused over 80 million dollars in damage. These crimes also include computer intrusions designed to obtain information of the most sensitive sort—such as credit cards, companies' trade secrets, or individuals' private information.

These crimes not only affect our financial well-being and our privacy; they also threaten our nation's critical infrastructure. Our banking system, the stock market, the electricity and water supply, telecommunications networks, and critical government services, such as emergency and national defense services, all rely on computer networks. For a real-world terrorist to blow up a dam, he would need tons of explosives, a delivery system, and a surreptitious means of evading armed security guards. For a cyberterrorist, the same devastating result could be achieved by hacking into the control network and commanding the computer to open the floodgates.

We are also seeing a migration of "traditional" crimes—including threats, child pornography, fraud, gambling, and extortion—from the physical to the online world. When these crimes are carried out online, perpetrators often find that they can reach more victims quickly and quite easily, turning what were once "local" scams into crimes that cross interstate and international borders. Computers and computer networks provide a cheap and powerful means of communications, and criminals take advantage of this just like everyone else. In addition, sophisticated criminals can readily use the easy anonymity that the Internet provides to hide their crimes.

Challenges of Cybercrime

The Internet and computers have brought tremendous benefits to our society, including greater freedom of expression and economic growth. But we must also recognize that as a result of our society's increasing reliance on technology, investigators and prosecutors at all levels—international, federal, state, and local—are encountering unique challenges. These challenges generally can be divided into three categories:

1. *Technical challenges* that hinder law enforcement's ability to find and prosecute criminals operating online

2. *Legal challenges* resulting from laws and legal tools needed to investigate cybercrime lagging behind technological, structural, and social changes

3. *Resource challenges* to ensure we have satisfied critical investigative and prosecutorial needs at all levels of government

Before I discuss each of these challenges, let me say that we recognize that we in government will not be able to solve all of these problems. In fact, we believe the private sector should take the lead in protecting private computer networks, through more vigilant security efforts, information sharing, and, where appropriate, cooperation with government agencies. The private sector has the resources, the technical ability, and the trained personnel to ensure that, as technology continues to develop and change rapidly, the Internet is a safer place for all of us. Thus, the private sector can and should take the lead on improving security practices and the development of a more secure Internet infrastructure.

Our society will also need the assistance of the everyday user in making sure that safeguards are taken and practices are followed. The best infrastructure and most secure means of electronic commerce will be ineffective if the users of the technology, that is, all of us, don't follow the basic "rules of the road."

However, even assuming that users and companies do everything they can to provide a safe, secure, and vibrant Internet, there will be instances where the practices and safeguards fail. Criminals rob banks even though banks use numerous security measures. In such cases, law enforcement must be prepared and equipped to investigate and prosecute cybercriminals in order to stop their criminal activity, to punish them, and to deter others who might follow the same path. This is the reason that it is so important that we work together to address the challenges I am about to discuss.

Technical Challenges

When a hacker disrupts air traffic control at a local airport, when a child pornographer sends computer files, when a cyberstalker sends a threatening e-mail to a public school or a local church, or when credit card numbers are stolen from a company engaged in e-commerce, investigators must locate the source of the communication. Everything on the Internet is communications, from an e-mail to an electronic heist. Finding an electronic criminal means that law enforcement must determine who is responsible for sending an electronic threat or initiating an electronic robbery. To accomplish this, law enforcement must in nearly every case trace the "electronic trail" leading from the victim back to the perpetrator.

Tracking a criminal online is not necessarily an impossible task, as demonstrated last year when federal and state law enforcement agencies were able to track down the creator of the Melissa virus and the individual who created a false Bloomberg News Service Web site in order to drive up the stock price of PairGain, a telecommunications company in California. In both cases, technology enabled us to find the individuals who were engaging in criminal activity.

Unfortunately, despite our successes in the Melissa and PairGain cases, we still face significant challenges as online criminals become more sophisticated, often wearing the equivalent of Internet electronic gloves to hide their fingerprints and their identity.

It doesn't take a master hacker to disappear on a network. Ironically, while the public is justifiably worried about protecting the legitimate electronic privacy of individuals who use networks, a criminal using tools and other information easily available over the Internet can operate in almost perfect anonymity. By weaving his or her communications through a series of anonymous remailers; by creating a few forged e-mail headers with powerful, point-and-click tools readily downloadable from many hacker Web sites; or by using a "free-trial" account or two, a hacker, online pornographer, or Web-based fraud artist can effectively hide the trail of his or her communications.

As we consider the challenge created by anonymity, we must also recognize that there are legitimate reasons to allow anonymity in communications networks. A whistleblower, a resistance fighter in Kosovo, a battered woman's support group—all of these individuals may understandably wish to use the Internet and other new technologies to communicate with others without revealing their identities.

In addition to problems related to the anonymous nature of the Internet, we are being challenged to investigate and prosecute criminals in an international arena. The Internet is a global medium that does not recognize physical and jurisdictional boundaries. A criminal no longer needs to be at the actual scene of the crime to prey on his or her victims. As a result, a computer server running a Web page designed to defraud U.S. senior citizens might be located in Europe or Asia. A child pornographer may distribute photographs or videos via e-mail, sending the e-mails through the communications networks of several countries before they reach their intended recipients. With more than 190 Internet-connected countries in the world, the coordination challenges facing law enforcement are tremendous. And any delay in an investigation is critical, as a criminal's trail might, in certain circumstances, end as soon as he or she disconnects from the Internet.

Likewise, evidence of a crime can be stored at a remote location, either for the purpose of concealing the crime from law enforcement and others or simply because of the design of the network. In certain circumstances, the fact that the evidence is stored and held by a third party, such as an Internet service provider, might be helpful to law enforcement agencies, who might be able to use lawful process to get that information. However, storing information remotely can also create a challenge to law enforcement, which cannot ignore the real-world limits of local, state, and national sovereignty and jurisdiction. Obtaining information from foreign countries, especially on an expedited basis, can be a daunting task, especially when a country may be in a different time zone, use a different language, have different legal rules, and may not have trained experts available. Consequently, even as the Internet and other new technologies have given us new abilities to find criminals remotely, our abilities can be hindered if we cannot obtain the necessary legal cooperation from our counterparts in other countries.

The vast majority of Internet companies are good corporate citizens and are interested in the safety of our citizens. In fact, several companies have been engaged in discussions with law enforcement regarding our concerns. Despite these efforts, we have learned that we cannot take for granted the nature of any Internet service provider's services, its recordkeeping practices, and its ability or willingness to cooperate with us. We have encountered a handful of companies involved in criminal activity. In addition, even those companies that are not involved in criminal activities might not be able to assist us because of business reasons or privacy concerns that have resulted in them not keeping the records that are necessary to investigate a particular crime.

Moreover, users connect to the Internet from anywhere in the world over old-fashioned telephone lines, wireless phones, cable modems, and satellite systems. Each of these telecommunications systems has its own protocols for addressing and routing traffic, which means that tracking all the way back to the criminal at his or her computer will require agents to be fluent in each technical language. Gathering this evidence from so many kinds of providers is a very different proposition from the days when we simply obtained an order for a telephone company to trace a threatening call.

Legal Challenges

Deterring and punishing computer criminals requires a legal structure that will support detection and successful prosecution of offenders. Yet the laws defining computer offenses, and the legal tools needed to investigate criminals using the Internet, can lag behind technological and social changes, creating legal challenges to law enforcement agencies.

Some of the legal challenges we encounter can easily be corrected through legislative action. For example, the Computer Fraud and Abuse Act, 18 U.S.C. § 1030, arguably does not reach a computer hacker who causes a large amount of damage to a network of computers if no individual computer sustains over $5,000 worth of damage. The Department of Justice has encountered several instances in which intruders have gained unauthorized access to protected computers (whether publicly or privately owned) used in the provision of "critical infrastructure" systems and services—such as those that hospitals use to store sensitive information and to treat patients, and those that the military uses to defend the nation—but where proof of damage in excess of $5,000 has not been readily available.

The laws under which we are able to identify the origin and destination of telephone calls and computer messages also need to be reviewed. For example, under current law we may have to obtain court orders in multiple jurisdictions to trace a single communication. Obtaining court orders in multiple jurisdictions does not advance any reasonable privacy safeguard, yet it can be a substantial impediment to a fast-paced investigation. As the Attorney General testified recently, it might be extremely helpful, for instance, to provide nationwide effect for trap and trace orders.

Another concern focuses on the problem of online threats and serious harassment—that is, cyberstalking. Current federal law does not address those situations where a cyberstalker uses unwitting third parties to bombard a victim with messages, transmits personal data about a person—such as the route by which the victim's children walk to school—in order to place such person or his family in fear of injury, or sends an e-mail or other communications under someone else's name with the intent to abuse, harass, or threaten that person. We believe federal law may need to be amended to address this gap.

These aren't hypothetical changes that we are proposing to address. Just ask the California woman who was awakened six times in the middle of the night to find men knocking on her door offering to rape her. She discovered that a man whom she had told she was not romantically interested in had posted personal advertisements on a variety of Internet services pretending to be her. Each posting, which contained her home address and telephone number, claimed that she fantasized about being raped. We need to ensure that laws against harassment clearly prohibit such horrific actions, particularly since access to the Internet means immediate access to a wide audience.

Resource Challenges

In addition to technical and legal challenges, we face significant resource challenges. Simply stated, we need an adequate number of prosecutors and agents—at the federal, state, and local level—trained with the necessary skills and properly equipped to effectively fight all types of cybercrime.

While Congress has been very supportive of the Department's cybercrime efforts, we need additional resources to ensure we are adequately equipped to continue our battle against cybercriminals. The President has requested $37 million in new money in FY 2001 to expand our staffing, training, and technological capabilities to continue the fight against computer crime. Together, these enhancements will increase the Department's 2001 funding base for computer crime to $138 million, 28 percent more than in 2000.

Last, the Department of Justice would like to work with Congress to develop a comprehensive, five-year plan—with FY 2001 as our baseline—to prevent cybercrime and, when it does occur, to locate, identify, apprehend, and bring to justice those responsible for these types of crimes. On February 16, the Attorney General testified before Congress regarding a proposed ten-point plan to identify the key areas we need to develop for our cybercrime capability. The key points of this plan she touched upon include:

- Developing a round-the-clock network of federal, state, and local law enforcement officials with expertise in, and responsibility for, investigating and prosecuting cybercrime.

- Developing and sharing expertise—personnel and equipment—among federal, state, and local law enforcement agencies.

- Dramatically increasing our computer forensic capabilities, which are so essential in computer crime investigations—both hacking cases and cases where computers are used to facilitate other crimes, including drug trafficking, terrorism, and child pornography.

- Reviewing whether we have adequate legal tools to locate, identify, and prosecute cybercriminals. In particular, we may need new and more robust procedural tools to allow state authorities to more easily gather evidence located outside their jurisdictions. We also need to explore whether we have adequate tools at the federal level to effectively investigate cybercrime.

Because of the borderless nature of the Internet, we need to develop effective partnerships with other nations to encourage them to enact laws that adequately address cybercrime and to provide assistance in cybercrime investigations. A balanced international strategy for combating cybercrime should be at the top of our national security agenda.

We need to work in partnership with industry to address cybercrime and security. This should not be a top-down approach through excessive government regulation or mandates. Rather, we need a true partnership, where we can discuss challenges and develop effective solutions that do not pose a threat to individual privacy.

And we need to teach our young people about the responsible use of the Internet. The Department of Justice and the Information Technology Association of America have already taken steps to do so through the development of the Cybercitizen Partnership, but more needs to be done.

Efforts Against Cybercrime

Despite the technical, legal, and resource challenges, the Department has made strides in our fight against cybercrime. We have and will continue to develop extensive investigatory and prosecutorial programs to counter cybercrime. Let me take a few moments to detail some of our efforts to date.

On the investigatory side, we have the FBI's National Infrastructure Protection Center (NIPC) and specialized squads located in sixteen field offices.

On the prosecutorial side, we have trained attorneys, both in headquarters and in the field, who are experts in the legal, technological, and practical challenges involved in investigating and prosecuting cybercrime. The cornerstone of our prosecutor cybercrime program is the Computer Crime and Intellectual Property Section. CCIPS, which currently has eighteen attorneys, was founded in 1991 as the Computer Crime Unit and was elevated to Section status in 1996. CCIPS works closely on computer crime cases with Assistant United States Attorneys known as "Computer and Telecommunications Coordinators" (CTCs) in U.S. Attorneys' Offices around the country. Each CTC is given special training and equipment and serves as the district's expert in computer crime cases. As a result of these programs, the number of cases and prosecutions by the Department is growing at a tremendous rate. For example, in 1998, U.S. Attorneys' Offices filed eighty-five computer crime cases against 116 defendants. This represents a 29 percent increase in the number of cases filed and a 51 percent increase in the number of defendants, compared to the previous year. During that same period of time, a total of sixty-two cases against seventy-two defendants were terminated, with 78 percent of those defendants being convicted.

At the same time, our prosecutors are working with numerous other federal, state, and local investigators and prosecutors, providing assistance in any case involving computers and other high technology, such as computer searches and seizure. In sum, the Department and, in particular, its investigators and prosecutors take seriously our responsibility to protect the nation's computers and the Internet from computer crime.

In addition to the Department's efforts, other agencies, including Customs, the Secret Service, the Securities and Exchange Commission, and the U.S. Postal's Inspectors General, have played a role in the investigation and prosecution of computer crimes.

Conclusion

On behalf of the Department, I want to thank Congress for all the support it has given to our efforts to combat cybercrimes. Advancements in technology indicate that our efforts are only just beginning. We look forward to working with Congress and the private sector to ensure that we have a robust and effective long-term plan for combating cybercrime, protecting our nation's infrastructure, and ensuring that the Internet reaches its full potential for expanding communications, facilitating commerce, and bringing countless other benefits to our society.

Glossary: Hacker Vernacular

Throughout this book there are numerous references to the varied words and phrases that make up computer security-related jargon. What follows is a list of several of the most common security terms, along with a brief explanation of each. Chapter 10 delves more specifically into some of the terms on this list.

Ankle Biter Synonymous with Script-Kiddies, these are the neophytes of the hacker world (hence the reference to their undeveloped, diminutive stature). While they do aspire and attempt to be hackers, their limited knowledge and experience make them less of a threat.

Back Door A security hole unintentionally left by programmers or system administrators that can allow a hacker unauthorized access to a computer system. In some instances, back doors are deliberately included by system administrators or programmers so that the system can be more easily accessed by certain personnel (e.g., service technicians).

Breach   The successful defeat of security measures, resulting in the infiltration of a computer system.

Buffer Overflow   As the name implies, a buffer overflow occurs when too many data are placed into a computer's buffer, exceeding the buffer's capacity and triggering an overflow. (A buffer is a specially selected area of computer memory or disk space [holding tank] reserved for temporarily storing data.)

Bug   A flaw in a computer program that can cause it to malfunction.

Compromise   A computer system intrusion during which the unauthorized disclosure, alteration, or destruction of sensitive data may have occurred.

Crack   A popular hacking tool used to decode encrypted passwords. System administrators often use Crack to determine whether weak passwords are being used by novice users. This detection helps to enhance the security of their computer systems.

Cracker   An individual who uses a password-cracking tool to infiltrate a computer or network.

Data-Driven Attack   An attack that is hidden in seemingly harmless data. This type of attack can be hard to combat since it may have the ability to bypass a firewall.

Denial-of-Service Attack   Attack aimed at preventing a computer or system from carrying out its intended function.

Firewall   A hardware device or software program that implements a boundary between two or more networks.

Hacker   A malevolent or curious individual who tries to discover information by breaking into computers or networks and then snooping around.

Hacking   Illicit attempts to outwit or bypass the security mechanisms of a computer system or network.

Host   A single computer or device connected to a network.

IP Spoofing   An attack in which a computer user attempts to illegitimately masquerade as another by using its IP address.

Mail Bomb   Massive amounts of e-mail sent to a single computer system or person with the intent to crash the recipient's system.

Packet Sniffer   A device or program that examines data traveling between various computers on a network.

Phracker   An individual who combines phone phreaking with computer hacking.

Phreaker   An individual who uses his or her understanding of telephone system networks to manipulate them and to make calls at the expense of others.

Phreaking   The "science" of manipulating and cracking the telephone system network.

Piggy Back   Unauthorized access to a computer system by the use of a legitimate user's connection.

Protocol   An established and agreed-upon method of communication used by computers.

Replicator   Any program that acts to reproduce and make copies of itself.

Samurai   Also known as an ethical hacker, a Samurai is a hacker who hires out (outsources himself or herself) to provide authorized cracking services to people or organizations with legitimate reasons for needing such services. A Samurai can be likened to a locksmith. While your neighbor could not legally hire one to enter your home, as the legitimate owner you are permitted to enter with the locksmith's help if you've lost or forgotten your key.

Smurfing   A type of denial-of-service attack in which a hacker spoofs or fakes the source address of a PING request to a special broadcast address of a network. This causes all the computers on that network to simultaneously respond to the unsuspecting victim, flooding that victim with responses to a PING request he or she never actually made.

Sniffer   Program or device used to capture data packets traveling across a network, it is often used by hackers and crackers to obtain user IDs and passwords.

Spoofing   The act of pretending to be, mimicking, or masquerading as someone else on the Internet.

Index

About the Author

Douglas Schweitzer is a Cisco Certified Network Associate (CCNA), a Certified Internet Webmaster associate (CIW-A), and holds A+, Network+, and i-Net+ certifications from the Computing Technology Industry Association (CompTIA). He also maintains several Internet-related certifications from Brainbench (an online certification authority). Douglas earned a B.S. degree in business management from the State University of New York. He has an ardent interest in the field of Internet security, and his experience and activity in the field have helped many PC users with a wide range of information technology concerns. Douglas has appeared as a guest speaker on *Your Internet Show*, a cable television show airing daily in the tristate area, and is being considered for future segments. He is vice president of a New York actuarial consulting firm and is also responsible for corporatewide network design and security.